AF594665

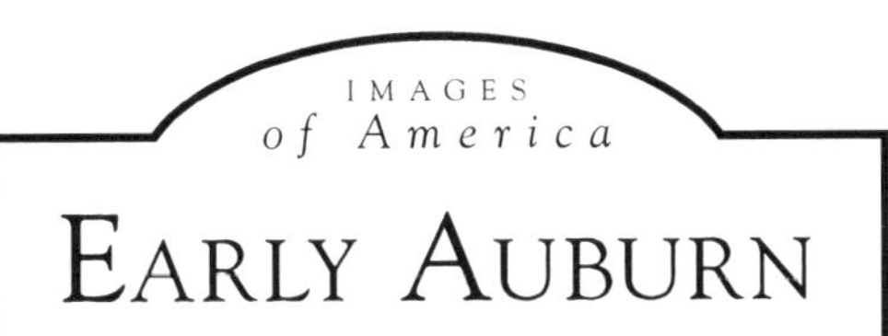
IMAGES
of America
EARLY AUBURN

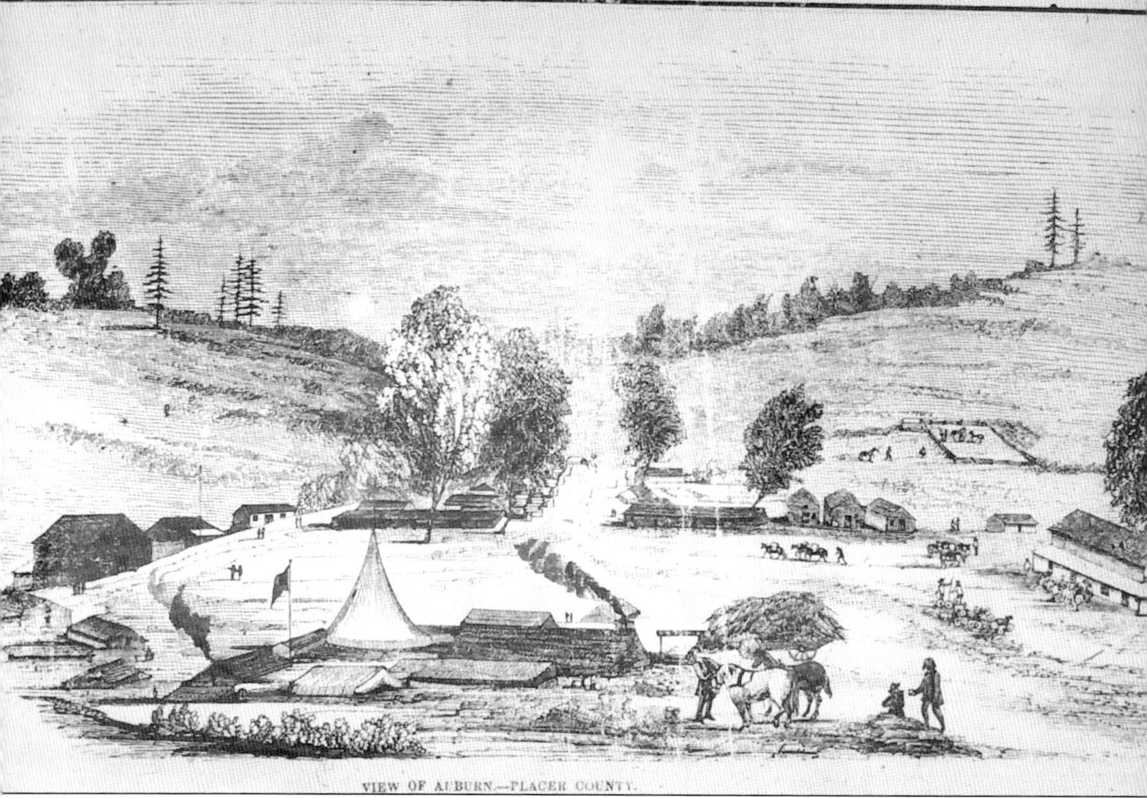

First Auburn Image. Created in 1851 by Thomas Armstrong, this is the first known image of Auburn. There are men digging for gold in the foreground. In the early 1850s, newspaper reports from the *Sacramento Transcript* tell of the streets in Auburn being dug up right to the storefronts' entrances. The tent behind the flagpole is one of the "round tents" that were used for gambling houses, stores, and even a courtroom. (Placer County Museum.)

On the Cover. Though few of the gold seekers who came to Auburn were successful, some did strike it rich. Jacob Hart Neff was one of the most successful men in the mining business over a period of several years. He purchased this fountain, which provides drinking water for people, horses, and dogs, from the J.L. Mott Iron Works and presented it to the city of Auburn in 1908. It still stands on the grounds of the historic Placer County Courthouse. (Author's collection, Art Sommers.)

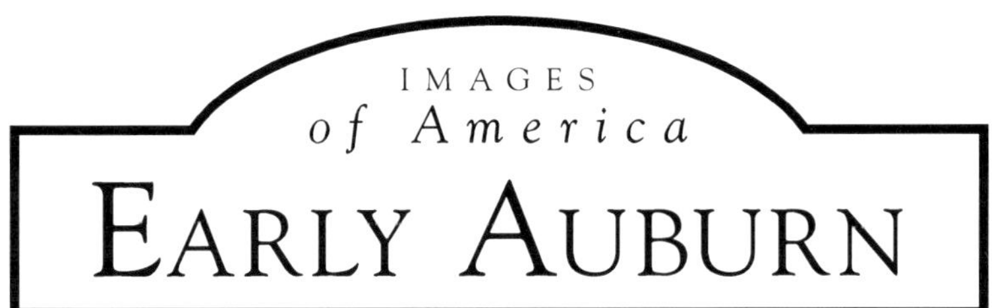

Art Sommers, John Knox,
and April McDonald-Loomis

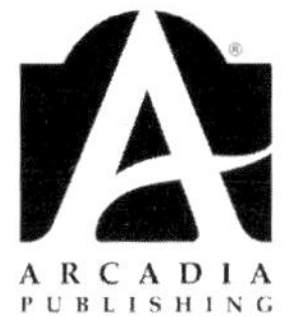

ISBN 978-1-4671-3276-3

Published by Arcadia Publishing
Charleston, South Carolina

Printed in the United States of America

Library of Congress Control Number: 2014945493

For all general information, please contact Arcadia Publishing:
Telephone 843-853-2070
Fax 843-853-0044
E-mail sales@arcadiapublishing.com
For customer service and orders:
Toll-Free 1-888-313-2665

Visit us on the Internet at www.arcadiapublishing.com

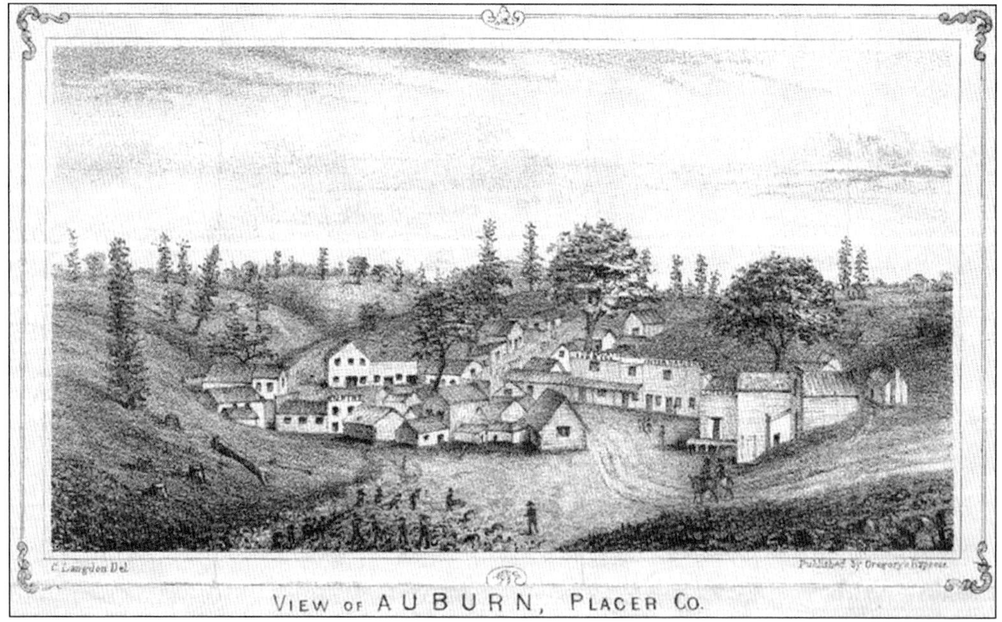

THE GROWTH OF AUBURN. The town developed at the junction of several ravines and up the slopes of adjoining hillsides, as shown in this early lithograph from the mid-1850s. One miner wrote home, describing Auburn as follows: "It is a wonderful healthy climate—the streets are uncertain in their angles—never laid out—just grew from circumstance." In 1852, another reported, "By the enterprise of its citizens, it became a flourishing and not unsightly town." (PCM.)

Contents

ACKNOWLEDGMENTS

The authors would like to thank the three reviewers of our draft: Carmel Barry-Schweyer, Carol Cramer, and Michael Loomis. Each one gave us valuable insights and new ideas. Debbie Poulsen and Rodi Lee at the Placer County Archives are always stalwart supporters. Many of the photographs we used are from the collection of author Arthur Sommers (AJS), a collector who loves to share his treasures. A large number of the photographs used come from the collection at the Placer County Archives, part of the Placer County Museum system (PCM). Additional image sources include the California State Library (CSL), the Library of Congress (LOC), and the Smithsonian Institution (SI). Other photographs come from the Shasta Historical Society (SHS), the California Supreme Court (CSC), Thompson & West's *History of Placer County from* 1882 (TW), the Alaska State Library (ASL), and Wells Fargo Company (WFC). Several individuals were generous with photographs from their personal collections as well; we thank Cathy Stevenson (CS), Barbara Leak (BL), Donna Howell (DH), Gene Dahlberg (GD), Jeannette Duff (JD), Dawn Bleyle (DB), Patrice Foehner Stevens (PFS), April Moore (AM), John Knox (JK), the Hancock family (HF), and the Weber family (WF). These images help tell the story of Auburn from pre–Gold Rush times to the early 1900s.

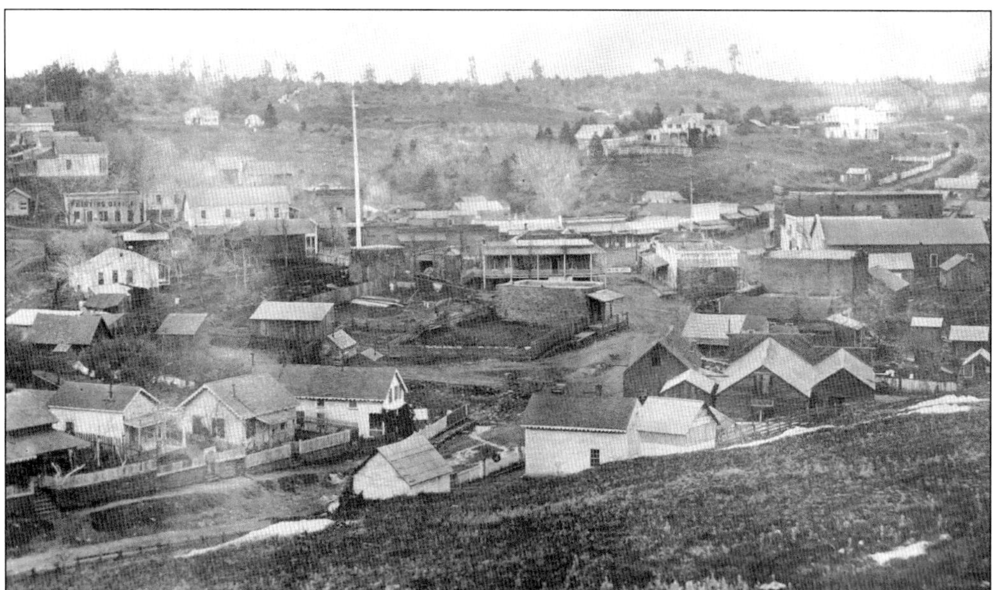

AUBURN, C. 1870. In this image, the mining camp of Auburn has grown to a sizeable town with a railroad, churches, hotels, schools, and a thriving business community. While many disappointed miners ended their great adventure and returned home, some, like John Kinkade, decided to stay. In an 1852 letter to his brother in Ohio, Kinkade explained why he was staying, writing, "for I am falling more in love with California every day." (AJS.)

INTRODUCTION

The gold camp of Auburn was much like the other early mining camps of Newtown (near present-day Lincoln) and Elizabethtown (near Iowa Hill). All were founded on an initial gold strike that immediately attracted miners, merchants, saloonkeepers, and gamblers. Elizabethtown was settled in the fall of 1850 but was deserted by 1854. Newtown was founded in 1855, and within a few years, it too had been abandoned. What made Auburn different? Why did it survive? As with the other two towns, the "easy" placer gold was soon played out, and most of the miners moved on to the next "big strike" location. Auburn, however, maintained its population and grew to be the most substantial town in the county because of its location and selection as the county seat.

In May 1848, Claude Chana was the first to find gold in the Auburn area, about a quarter mile south of Old Town on the Auburn Ravine, then quickly moved on. Nicholaus Allgeir, with several Indian workers, arrived next, but his party also did not stay long. Joe Woods and Tuck Warner came on the scene in late 1848 and found the extensive gold deposits at Rich Flat, near today's Railhead Park. Gold was also found in Old Town in what was called "the plaza," where several ravines converged.

By the time Hiram Hawkins arrived in July 1849, only a few miners remained in Auburn—two Chileans on Rich Ravine, a short distance from the American Hotel (Shanghai/Auburn Alehouse), and one miner on Auburn Ravine. Most fortune seekers had left the camp and headed for the rich strikes along the North and Middle Forks of the American River.

The winter of 1849 was the turning point in Auburn's history—its moment between slipping into obscurity and being listed in Gudde's *Mining Camps of California* or becoming a permanent settlement. Many miners in the river canyons scrabbled to build more substantial cabins in the winter of 1849–1850, but most fled to the nearest settlement—Auburn. An anonymous letter in the November 25, 1849, *Placer Times* stated, "This sudden visitation of the liquid element has entirely checked operations and taken miners all aback; and there being so few of the necessaries of life within their reach, it is thought there will be a general rush for this place [Auburn] and San Francisco very soon."

Merchants and hotelkeepers were quick to react to the influx of miners seeking shelter from the inclement weather. Several large public hotels were constructed, and according to historian Leonard Davis, "They were built of logs and roofed with shakes . . . within each was a great fireplace, a bar, gambling tables, a kitchen and a boarding house."

The miners were essentially stranded in Auburn during the severe winter of 1849–1850, when the rains came in deluges and the roads to Sacramento became virtually impassable. The aforementioned anonymous letter also noted, "The roads are altogether impassable for teams and for packing, it requires all the vigilance of the driver to keep the animals on their feet. To get up and down the high hills . . . it is altogether impossible for four legged animals to 'propel' at all."

One element that helped secure Auburn's future was its location on the road out of Sacramento that connected with those to the gold camps. San Francisco was the main port for incoming supplies, and from there, steamboats brought the goods as far as Sacramento and Stockton and as far upriver as Marysville. William Gwynn, Hudson House, and Walkup & Wyman, the early merchants in Auburn, began running freight wagons to Sacramento City. The round trip usually took three days, which Davis described as "one day in going down light and two days in coming back loaded."

The route from Sutter's Fort—and later, from the Embarcadero in Sacramento City—was the main trail into Auburn and then to the remote camps in the hills or on the riverbanks. In the earliest days, Auburn was found to be the farthest that a freight wagon could travel. Arriving at Auburn, supplies headed to the distant camps were loaded onto men's backs or onto pack mules for the journey over steep, rocky, narrow trails. Freight charges for the trip were $10 per 100 pounds in good weather, but they skyrocketed to $30–$40 in bad weather. John C. Boggs, later sheriff of the county, recalled that a barrel of sauerkraut that he paid $10 for in Sacramento City sold for $150 in Auburn that winter.

Mexican muleteers were among the first to take advantage of the lack of roads and the need for transporting every type of provision desired by the miners. Miners required food, liquor, clothing, bedding, tools, medicine, and hardware. Every conceivable item had to be brought in, and pack trains were vital for sheer survival. Mexican mules were considered far superior to those arriving from the eastern states, due to their strength, toughness, and endurance. The average train consisted of 40–50 mules with two muleteers. Packing the mules was a painstaking job, sometimes taking hours. Balancing the load was critical, as an unbalanced load could lead to the mule and cargo crashing down into steep canyons.

Within a few years, the network of trails developed into roads. The terminus of wagon freight moved farther into the county. Auburn maintained its preeminence as a transportation center with the convergence of roads centered in town near present-day Central Square. The first was the main road from Sacramento that ran through Auburn to Illinoistown (Colfax), approximately the route of present-day Auburn-Folsom Road to Auburn, then following the route of Interstate 80 to Colfax. The second road branched off the Sacramento-Auburn route to Grass Valley and Nevada City; the third extended westward to Ophir, Virginiatown, and Marysville; the fourth led to the camps on the Foresthill divide; and the fifth connected with the roads into El Dorado County.

The early roads followed the paths set by foot travel and the mule trains. Building roads was difficult and expensive. Tremendous obstacles were encountered in transforming treacherous, threadlike pack trails into passable roads, and the process required vast amounts of capital and labor. The lack of governmental infrastructure to fund road construction led to the rise of privately funded road building, resulting in toll roads as the backbone of commerce in the foothills.

In 1859, the *Placer Herald* estimated that nearly 200 tons of freight passed through Auburn daily. In July of that year, it reported, "As indicative of the immensity of the freight business through this place, we will state, that on Thursday morning twenty-eight loaded wagons, averaging four tons of freight each, passed through town on their way to the mountains, within less than two hours time."

The gold seeker, after "making his pile," was interested in mainly two things: getting news from home and safely transporting the precious gold he had obtained. The early express companies fulfilled both these needs. Post offices were few in number, and the mail, slow and irregular. Sam Holladay, the camp's first alcalde, recalled walking from Auburn to Sacramento and then taking a boat to San Francisco, searching for any mail from home.

Among the first express companies in Auburn were Gregory's Express and Hunter & Company. They were followed by Adams & Company and, eventually, Wells Fargo & Company. The express companies provided many services for the miners; they could not only send and receive mail on a regular basis but also transport gold with full insurance coverage. Auburn became the "express center for Placer County." On November 12, 1853, the *Placer Herald* reported, "The Express men of our town are now reaping a golden harvest. Thousands of dollars worth of dust are bought every week. Upon the rivers, especially, they make heavy purchases every few days."

John Q. Jackson, a 23-year-old Auburn agent for Wells Fargo & Company, wrote home in 1854 to describe his position: "What I have to do is quite confining, staying in my office till 10 at night, buying [gold] dust, forwarding & receiving packages of every kind, from and to everywhere, filling out drafts for the Eastern Mails in all sorts of sums, from $50 to $1000."

In 1854, Jackson forwarded over 750 pounds of gold to San Francisco in one month. He shipped 150 pounds at a time, explaining that it was "about as much as one likes to shoulder to and from the stages."

In addition to the express companies, stagecoach lines were established very early in Auburn, and it became "the chief distribution point for the mines." William Gwynn, a merchant, established a line as early as June 1850. His stage ran three times a week from Sacramento City to Auburn.

Another factor that influenced the growth of Auburn was its designation as the Sutter County seat in 1850. In an election thought to be influenced by ballot stuffing, Auburn emerged as the county seat over Ophir, Nicholaus, or Miner's Hotel. A contemporary newspaperman R.J. Steele wrote, "The favorable location of Auburn, its preponderance of population and the inexhaustible powers of voting possessed by its citizens and partisans decided the contest in its favor by a majority considerably exceeding the entire population."

Auburn remained the county seat for the newly formed Placer County in 1851. The amount of activity that centered in the courts and the recording offices was astounding. A citizen of the county came to Auburn to file a deed, claim a homestead, or file a mining claim. Brands for animals were recorded; married women could record and declare personal property or the right to become a sole trader; and business licenses, liquor licenses, and gambling licenses were applied for at the county offices. All kinds of statistics were collected and recorded at the county seat as well.

The courts for the county drew large numbers of citizens. A typical court of sessions trial in May 1859 summoned jurors from all over the county. Men came from Foresthill, Brushy Canon, Yankee Jim's, Iowa Hill, Illinoistown, and Todd's Valley.

An additional element in the growth of Auburn was its reputation for tolerance and safety. Auburn, like all the gold camps in the mother lode, was a place of massive cultural and ethnic diversity. One early miner wrote home that he had dinner at a French restaurant "run by a mulatto from Louisiana, who rented the building from a Jew, the meal was cooked by a Chinese cook, the drinks served by an Irish barman and the meal by an Australian waiter, Mexican women washed the linens, a Dutchman provided the meat, an Italian provided the vegetables and a Frenchman baked the bread." While Auburn may not have had this exact mix of cultures, the California miner certainly conveyed the wide-ranging backgrounds of people in the early gold camps. The place names in the area also show the diversity of locations the men had left to come west: Iowa Hill, Michigan Bluff, Yankee Jim's, Dutch Flat, Illinoistown, Spanish Flat, and Wisconsin Hill.

In many of the camps and villages, minorities were barely tolerated, but in Auburn, an air of tolerance seemed to exist. The local Native Americans, despite having their way of life disappear, did not themselves disappear. When anti-Chinese sentiment was running high throughout all of California in the 1870s, the Chinese in the communities of Roseville and Rocklin were run out of town in 1877, literally fleeing for their lives, while Auburn's Chinese population remained relatively undisturbed.

Many of the gold camps were violent places, but the village of Auburn also exhibited a different behavior in this regard, with few of the duels or lynchings that characterized other early settlements.

Auburn, although stripped of its surface gold within months, managed to hang on and avoid the boom-and-bust cycle of so many other gold camps in Northern California due to its location and its position as the county seat.

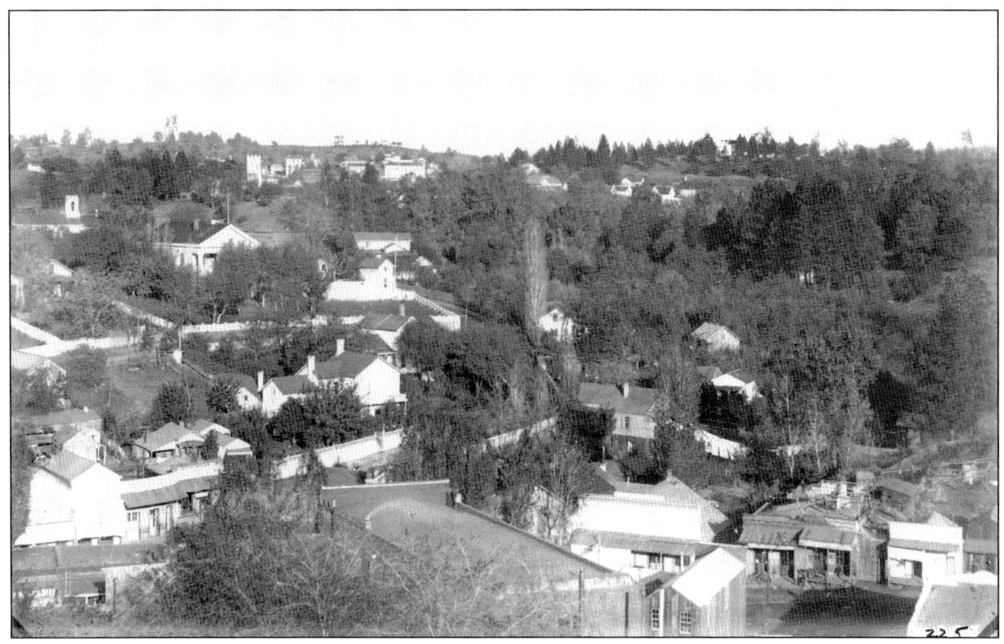

AUBURN, C. 1890. Looking down from Snowden's Hill, this photograph illustrates Auburn's eastward expansion. Acting as a boundary marker between old and new, the tower of St. Teresa's Catholic Church is visible in the upper left, above the old courthouse with its columns. In the center foreground is the roof of the American Hotel. To the left is the round corner location of the Union Saloon, and on the right is a portion of Sacramento Street. (PCM.)

FOREIGN MINER'S LICENSE.

No. 1470

Act approved March 30th, 1853.

Placer County, April 1st 1853.

This Certifies That Joseph Lee,

has this 1st day of April paid the Sheriff of

Placer County, FOUR DOLLARS, which entitles him to

labor in the Mines of this State for One Month from date.

Winslow S. Pierce Comptroller.
per Snyder

Jno. Shannon
Dep. Sheriff.

To be renewed upon expiration of Term.

FOREIGN MINER'S TAX. Joseph Lee, an Englishman, was subject to the foreign miner's tax in Placer County. First imposed in 1850, this tax was aimed at Latino miners. It was repealed in 1851, then reinstated in 1852, this time mostly directed at Chinese miners. The county treasurer's reports show that, in 1852 and 1856, this tax was the highest revenue producer for the entire county. (PCM.)

One

The Nisenan

Native Americans have lived in the Auburn area for thousands of years. The people here called themselves Nisenan, meaning "from among us" or "of our side." They were divided roughly by region as Valley Nisenan and Hill Nisenan. Overall, they were part of a larger grouping based on common culture and (generally) common language, called Maidu.

The lifestyle of these people was hard but not overly harsh. The climate was moderate, and the natural resources were seasonally abundant. The hill people generally would travel east and west with seasonal climate changes, their movement ranging from the crest of the Sierra Nevada to the eastern edge of the Sacramento Valley, following the drainage of the American River. They used group cooperation and a partnership of skills for food gathering and hunting, and they had a profound sense of community, with shared spiritual beliefs and traditions.

The Hill Nisenan were mostly spared the effects of early European contact, while the valley people had their numbers cut by one-third to one-half from malaria brought by the Hudson Bay trappers in 1833 and, later, from smallpox brought by the miners in 1853.

The "Eureka" moment of the gold discovery by James Marshall at Sutter's sawmill sounded the death knell for the pastoral lifestyle of the Hill Nisenan.

The hoards of gold seekers came into the foothills like locusts, destroying most everything that the Nisenan valued. Game was hunted to near extinction by hungry miners, the rivers that once held abundant runs of salmon were filled with silt and gravel from mining, and the oak trees that produced the all-important staple, the acorn, were cut down and used to heat miner's cabins, fire cookstoves, and fuel locomotives.

The Hill Nisenan were a resilient and viable people. As late as 1872, ethnographer Stephen Powers was able to collect significant information about the culture, religion, and way of life from the band led by Capt. Tom Lewis of Auburn. Pushed to the very edge of society and surviving by working for whites in agriculture, mining, logging, and ranching, the Auburn Hill Nisenan survived and today are a federally recognized group reaping the gains from a large and thriving casino enterprise.

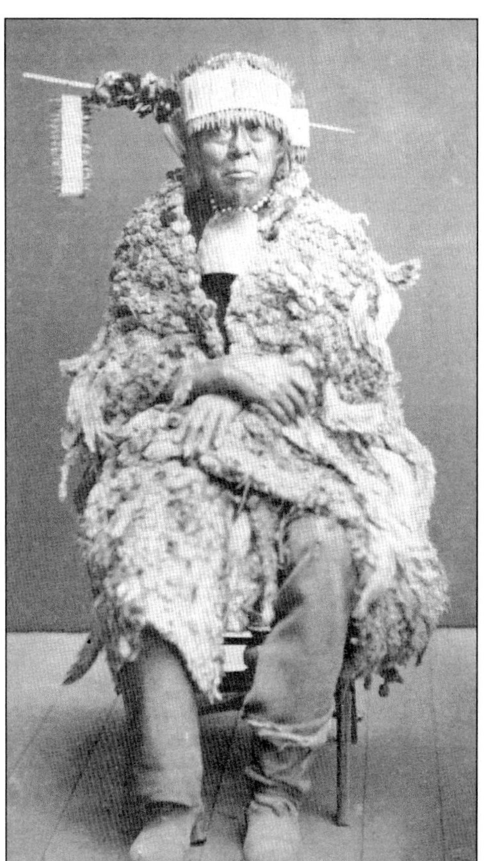

Capt. Tom Lewis. Captain Tom was the headman, or *huk*, of the local Nisenan. The flicker quill pendant he is wearing is indicative of his position. His band of Hill Nisenan was studied and photographed by Alexander Chase, a surveyor for the US Coast and Geodetic Survey from 1862 to 1878. Chase was a major contributor to Stephen Powers's seminal work *Tribes of California.* (SI.)

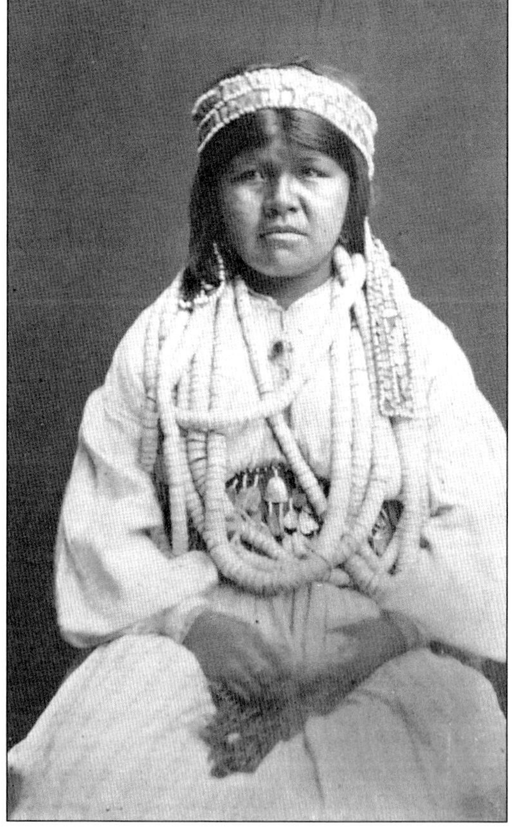

Captain Tom's Wife. This lady has been identified by elder Nisenan as Jane Lewis, or "Koto Jane." She lived over 100 years, dying in 1945. She might have been a second or third wife of Captain Tom. Jane was a skilled basket maker and a respected healer. She bestowed adult names to youths after coming-of-age ceremonies. Her 10-yard-long necklace of clamshell money beads was obtained through trade with coastal Indians. (SI.)

Captain Tom's Son. Over the years, the subject of this image has been identified as "boy," "Captain Tom's son," and "Captain Tom's grandson." He is wearing a combination of contemporary clothing and traditional dress. The headband is made from feathers of the yellowhammer bird, while the sash and gorget (throat piece) are made of abalone shell. (SI.)

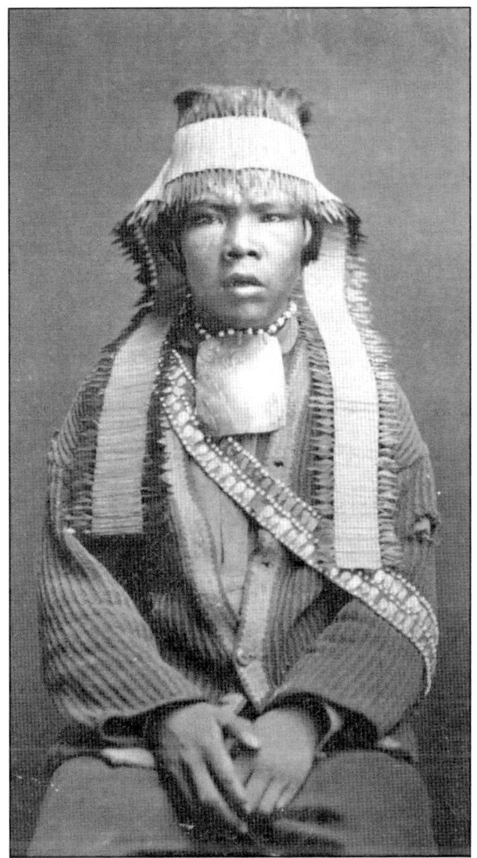

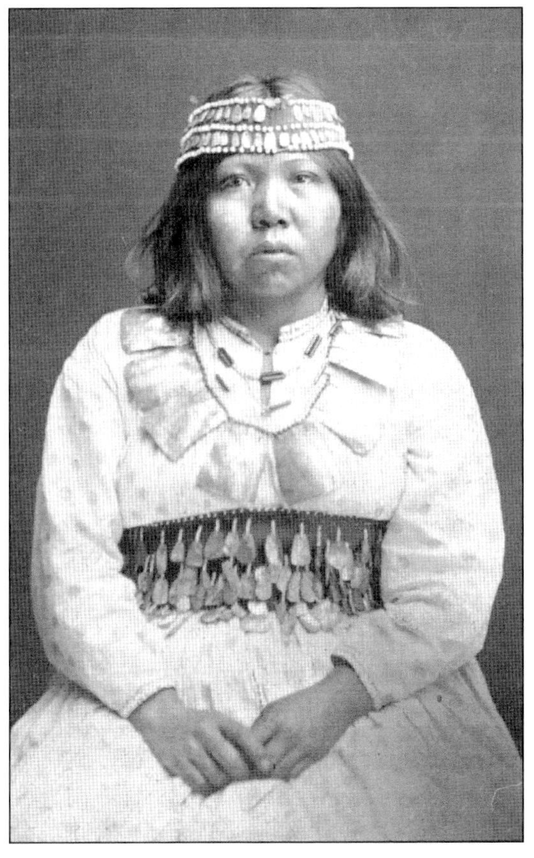

Captain Tom's Daughter. His daughter's adornment is part of Captain Tom's wealth. Ethnographer Stephen Powers listed Tom's wealth as including clamshell money, abalone shells, and bearskins. As a measure of Tom's skill as a leader, his band of Nisenan avoided the harsh treatment many other Indian groups endured from the influx of outsiders on their land. (SI.)

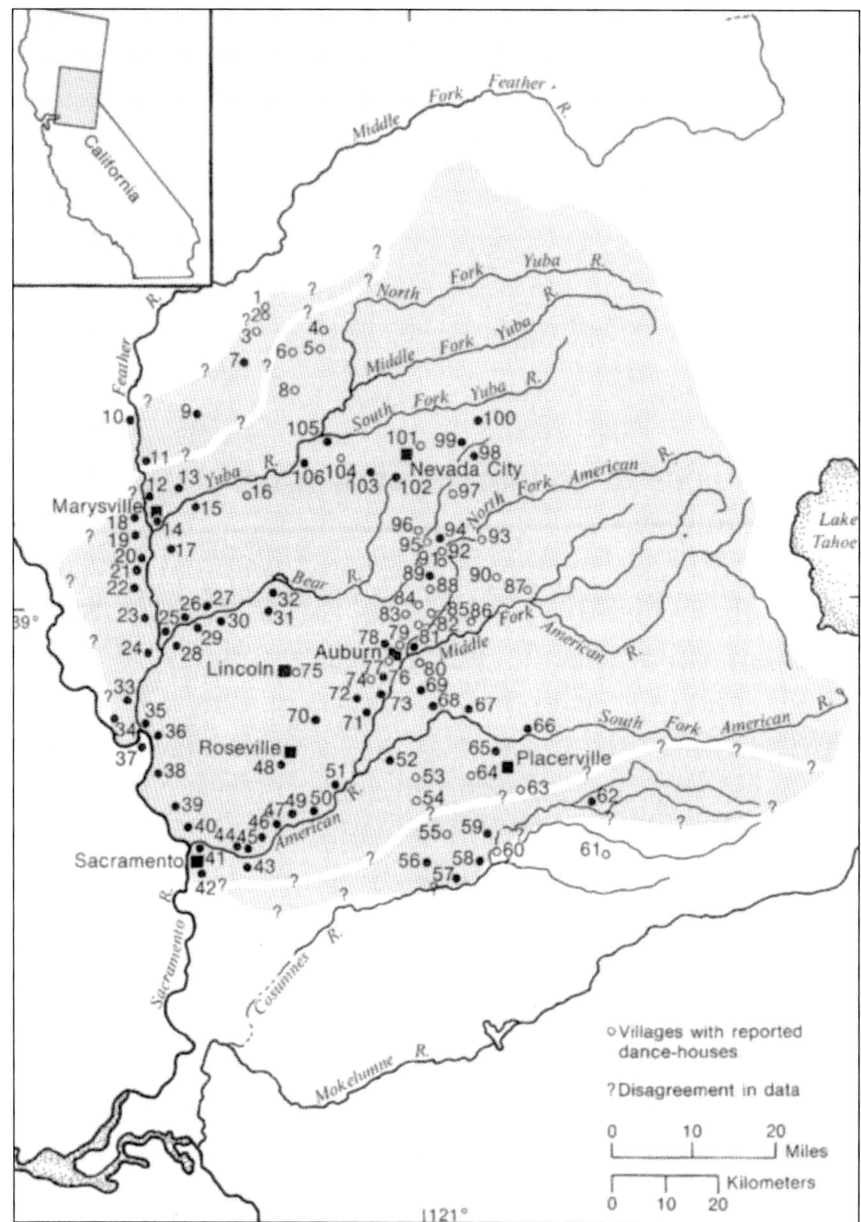

NISENAN, OR SOUTHERN MAIDU, TRIBAL TERRITORY. The Valley Nisenan lived along the shores of the Feather and Sacramento Rivers, while the Hill Nisenan inhabited the drainage basins and ridges of the Yuba, Bear, and American Rivers. The numbers depicted here represent the distribution of selected village locations. Many more have been lost to time. These villages might range in size from three or four family homes to nearly 50. The village was the smallest organizational unit, and a number of associated villages often affiliated under the leadership of a headman or captain for specific purposes, such as ceremonies, food gathering, and decision making on a variety of issues, including hunting areas and trespassers. As seasonal migrations of the Hill Nisenan were generally confined to a single drainage basin, the Nisenan in the Auburn area migrated seasonally along the American River drainage. (SI, *Smithsonian Handbook of North American Indians*, vol. 8.)

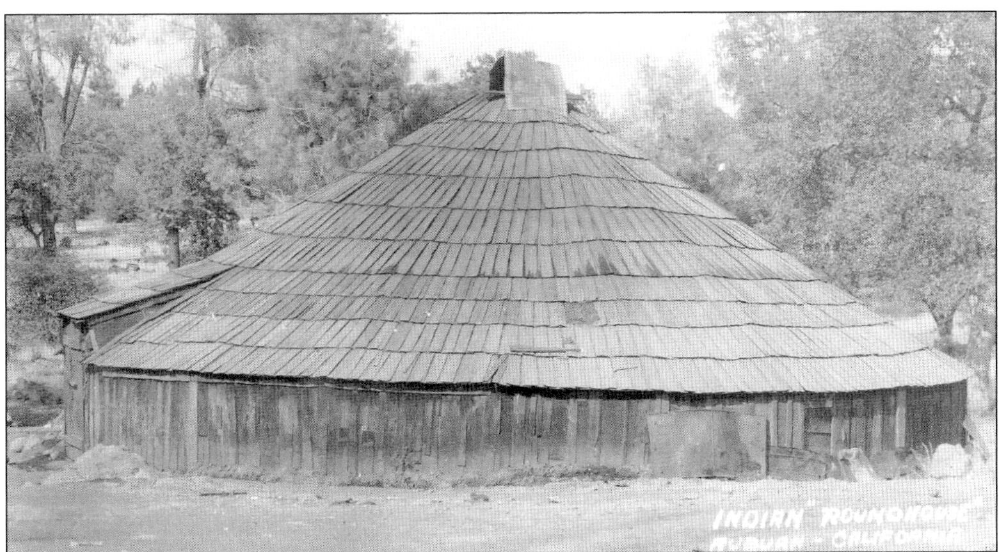

ROUNDHOUSE/DANCEHOUSE. This roundhouse was located on the grounds of the Auburn Rancheria. It was built under the direction of headman Jim Dick in about 1917. The roundhouse, or *kum*, was used for ceremonies called Big Times, or *lu mai*. The kum was decorated with bearskins, streamers of feathers, and garlands of acorns. Ceremonial dances and great feasts that would last for several days were held for seasonal events. (PCM.)

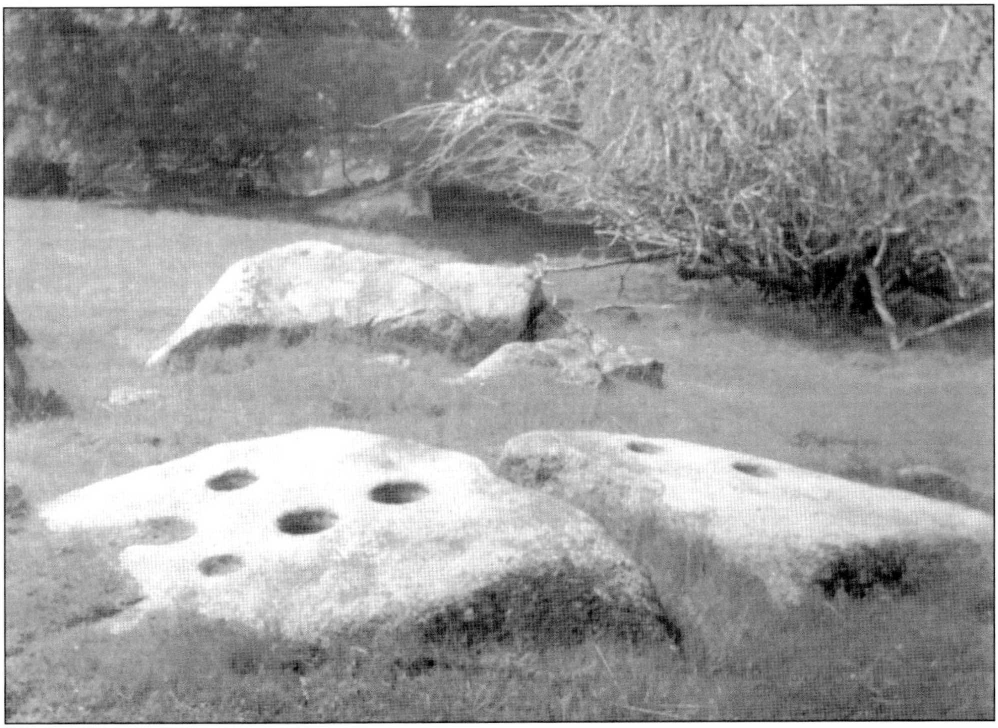

BEDROCK MORTARS. Acorn gathering was done by extended families or whole villages of Hill people. The acorns were knocked from trees, then shelled and ground into a meal using these bedrock mortars. Soup, mush, or fried cakes were made from the leached acorn meal. The acorn, called *ooti*, was a staple of the Nisenan diet that held spiritual and religious importance. (PCM.)

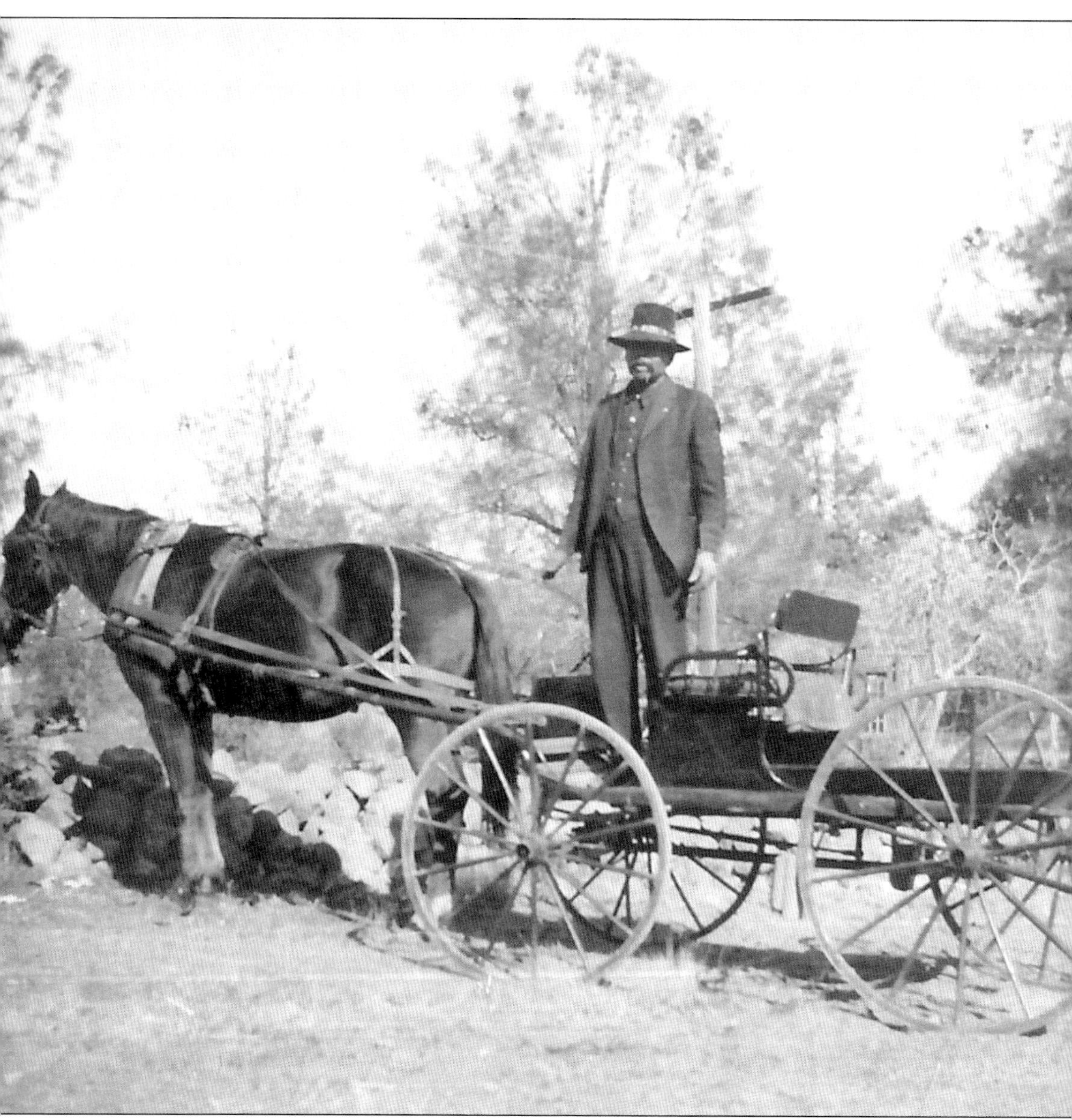

Headman Jim Dick. Dick was the last traditionally elected *huk* of the Auburn Nisenan. His territory covered parts of Placer, Nevada, and El Dorado Counties. He was responsible for organizing large rabbit hunts, communal gathering parties, and many ceremonial events. The position of headman or captain was generally hereditary, but he could be replaced if the villagers thought him unwise. It was even possible for a female to hold the position. Today, Dick's descendants are part of the United Auburn Indian Community (UAIC). An act of Congress federally recognized them in 1994 after years of contention and strife with the government. The UAIC has ownership of the enormously successful Thunder Valley Casino. Since its inception, the UAIC has donated more than $10 million to local nonprofit organizations throughout Placer County. (AM.)

Two

Before the Rush

A variety of hunters, trappers, and explorers came through the Auburn area in the pre–Gold Rush era; however, they left little evidence of their passage. Among the very few Americans and Europeans in this part of the sparsely settled Alta California province of Mexico were John Sutter, French sailor Pierre Theodore Sicard, former Hudson's Bay trapper John Sinclair, and William Johnson. Sutter was in present-day Sacramento, while Sinclair was on Rio de los Americanos (the American River) a few miles from Sutter's fort, and both Sicard and Johnson had ranches on the Bear River.

Sutter was by far the largest employer in the area, recruiting James Marshall, Claude Chana, and scattered remnants of the Mormon Battalion, as well as several hundred Indians and a contingent of Hawaiians.

James Marshall, working with several Mormons in Coloma (which means "beautiful" in Nisenan), found gold at the site of the sawmill he was building for Sutter in January 1848. After the discovery of gold, early settlers of Alta California had the jump on those who came into the area later. One of these early gold seekers was Frenchman Claude Chana, a cooper. Chana had worked for Sutter but was at Sicard's rancho when gold was discovered. Like most of Sutter's workers and everyone else in the area, he abandoned his job and set out to find gold.

Chana left Sicard's with Francois Gendron, Philbert Courteau, Eugene (last name unknown), 25 Indians, and 35 horses. On May 16, 1848, on their way to Coloma, they camped on the Auburn Ravine, and Chana tried his luck panning with a *batea* (a wooden pan). They stayed for about a week and found approximately three pounds of gold.

Several other groups came through Auburn in 1848; most, like Chana, did not stay long, lured away by news of big strikes farther afield. In late 1848, Joe Woods and Tuck Warner discovered large deposits at Rich Flat. In early 1849, gold was found in what would become the Old Town section of Auburn, and miners flocked to the area. Samuel Holladay later wrote that the streets in Auburn were so dug up that it looked like an earthquake had hit.

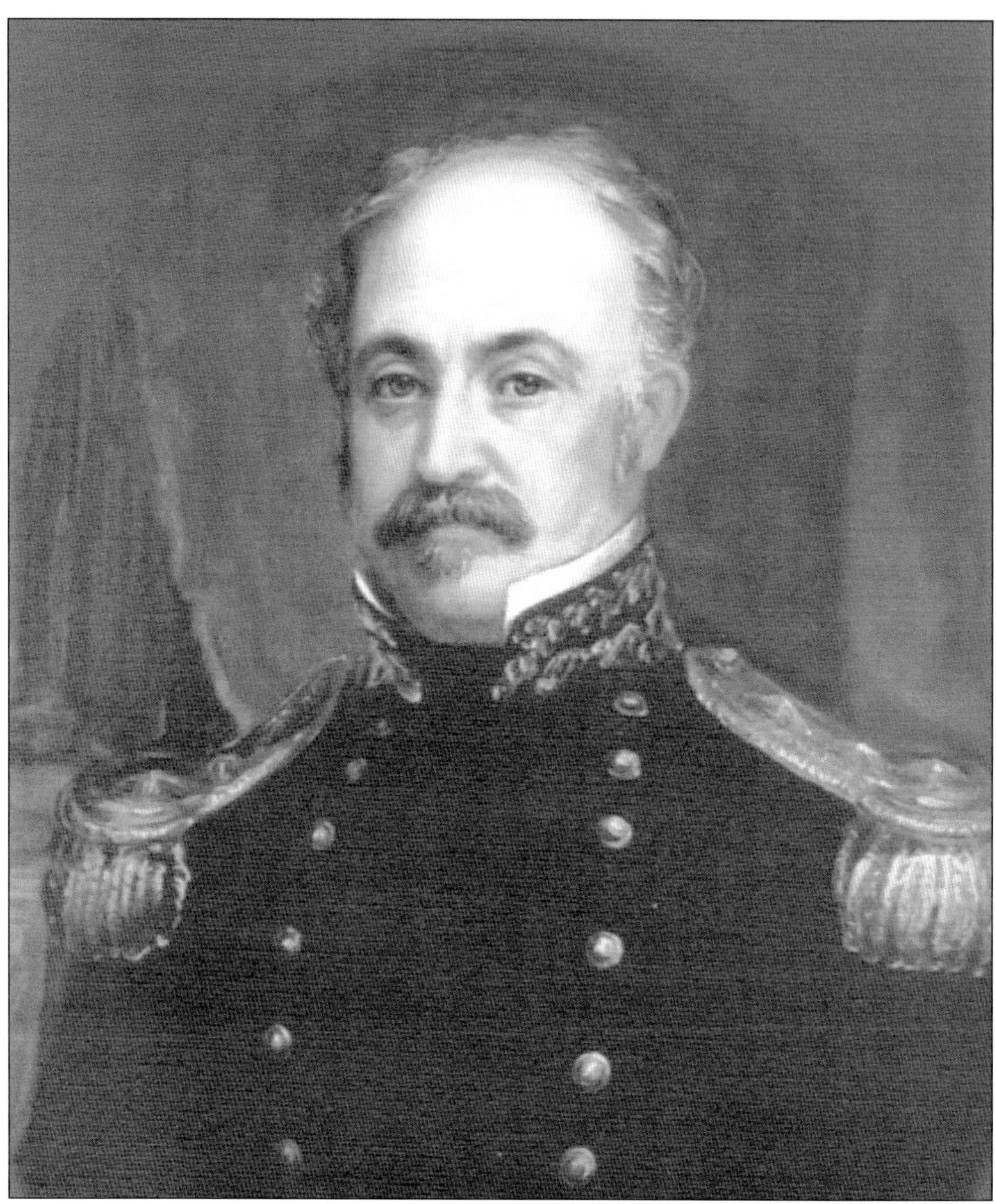

John Sutter. Johann Augustus Sutter arrived in Alta California by way of Hawaii in 1839, having abandoned his wife, their five children, and his debts in Bern, Switzerland. By 1841, he had persuaded Gov. Juan Bautista Alvarado to grant him 11 square leagues, some 48,400 acres for a rancho near the confluence of the Sacramento and American Rivers. Sutter's Nueva Helvetia, or New Switzerland, was a small empire. The ranch and subsequent fort was a welcome refuge for early American immigrants crossing the Sierra. In the winter of 1846–1847, the rescue parties for the Donner Party were organized at Sutter's Fort. While he was known to be generous to immigrants, Sutter's treatment of the local Native Americans was brutal. It is estimated that he enslaved 600–800 Indians to build his fort, raise his crops, and even serve in his private army. Sutter claimed to have been a captain in the Swiss Guards and is shown here in one of the formal uniforms he favored. (AJS.)

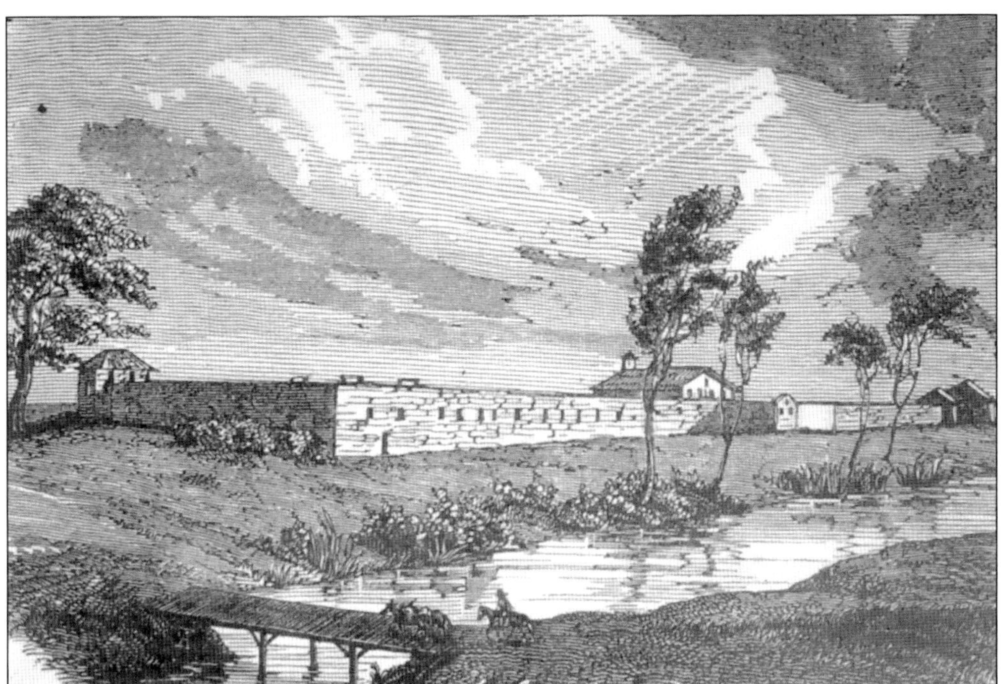

Sutter's Fort. Workers Sutter had brought from the Hawaiian Islands, along with local Native Americans, built this fort around 1841–1843. The fort was the center of a large empire managed by Sutter, who eventually owned over 150,000 acres. He raised wheat, grapes, cattle, sheep, and hogs, among a variety of other enterprises. However, the influx of men coming for gold destroyed Sutter's empire and left him bankrupt. He died nearly penniless. (PCM.)

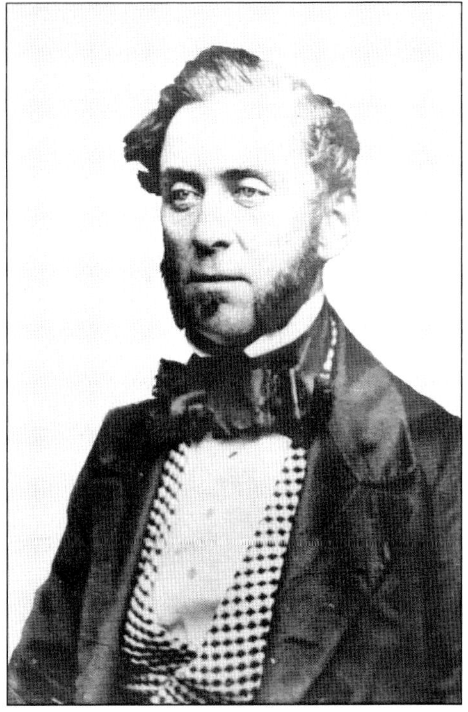

Samuel Brannan. Brannan was California's first millionaire. In 1848, after seeing customers at Sutter's Fort buying supplies with gold dust and nuggets, he quickly rounded up all the picks, shovels, buckets, and knives he could find, then headed to San Francisco, running through the streets and calling, "Gold! Gold from the American River!" In spite of his early success, a disastrous divorce left him nearly destitute at the end of his life in 1889. (CSL.)

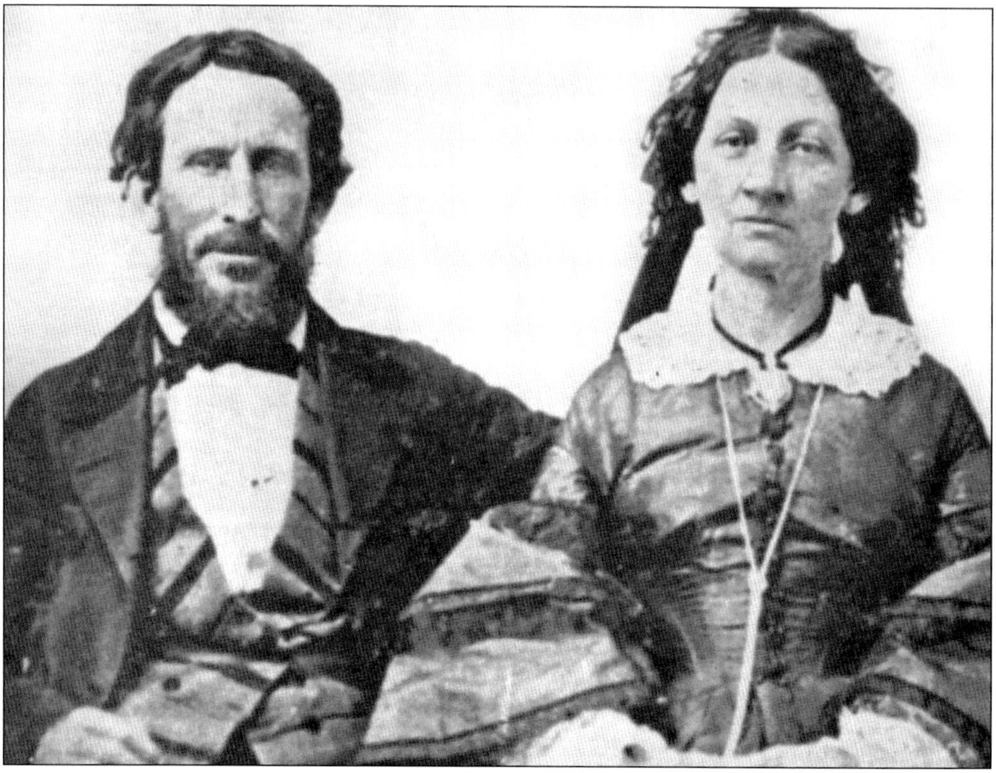

James and Margaret Reed. The Donner Party's experience of the dreadful winter in the mountains is a well-known story of suffering, privation, and cannibalism. James tried to rescue his family and the rest of the party. After months at Sutter's Fort, he made it back to Donner Lake. His stepdaughter penned the following advice in 1847 after the rescue: "Never take no cut offs and hurry along as fast as you can." (JK.)

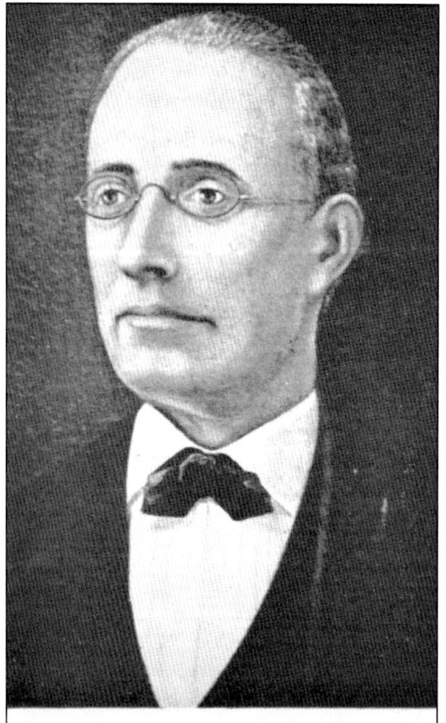

John A. Sutter, Jr.

John Augustus Sutter Jr. The son of the founder of Sutter's Fort was sent for by his father shortly before the gold discovery in Coloma in 1848. He and his father tried to capitalize on the influx of miners, including efforts to establish a store in Auburn, but failed dismally. The Sutters eventually lost their empire, but Sutter Jr., with the urging of Sam Brannan, is credited with laying out the town of Sacramento City. (CSL.)

Three

Discovery and the Forty-Niners

They abandoned families, farms, and stores, even law and medical practices, and they deserted from the military. They were mostly male and mostly young. They came from all over the globe to take part in an unprecedented migration. They were the forty-niners.

The first miners in the area were local men who were already in California; the next wave came from the established trade routes on the Pacific. Hawaiians were among the first to arrive, along with Oregonians. They were followed by argonauts (adventurers) from Mexico, Peru, Chile, and Australia. It took about a year from the initial discovery for those coming from the States to arrive.

Approximately 80,000–100,000 men from all over the world came to California in 1849, half by sea, half overland. Either way, it was not easy to reach California. From the East Coast, the voyage around South America was 18,000 nautical miles and took five to eight months. Rampant seasickness, rotten food, and boredom faced these argonauts. Three men who ended up in Auburn—John Boggs, Robert Gordon, and Edward Hall—came on the ship *Xylon* out of Baltimore in February 1849. The trio faced such hardships on board that they and other passengers mutinied in Rio de Janeiro and forced the resignation of the captain.

The land route was not any easier. The 2,000 miles overland from the Missouri River to California took about six months. Typhoid, cholera, hostile Indians, and lack of food and water afflicted these travelers. The Isthmus of Panama route was usually faster, taking three to five months, but it was not uncommon to be stranded on the Pacific side, waiting months for a ship to California. Tropical disease was the main threat on this route.

One distinctive pattern of the forty-niners was their restless movement once they arrived. Prospecting was hard work, and the payoff was sporadic. Any word of a rich strike would attract large numbers of men practically overnight. In Foresthill, just east of Auburn, two men found a rich claim in the early winter of 1849; just a few months later, there were thousands of men there.

For some, it was a great adventure; for others, it offered freedom or escape. Whatever the motive, it had universal appeal, and as historian J.S. Holliday wrote, "The world rushed in."

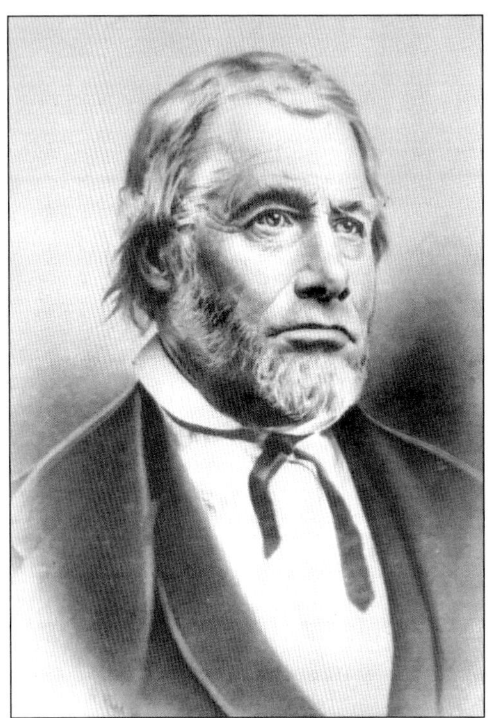

JAMES MARSHALL. Marshall came to Sutter's Fort in 1845. He was known to be an expert carpenter, but a little eccentric. On January 24, 1848, he found gold in the tailrace of the sawmill he was building for John Sutter. He spent some time in Auburn searching for gold, but Marshall never profited from his great find and ended up destitute. (AJS.)

SUTTER'S MILL. Sutter managed his fort and the large Hock Farm on the Feather River, as well as this sawmill at Coloma, some 50 miles from the fort on the South Fork of the American River. James Marshall was in charge of building the mill using native labor and several veterans of the Mormon Battalion. This sawmill is the site of the gold discovery that began the California Gold Rush. (LOC.)

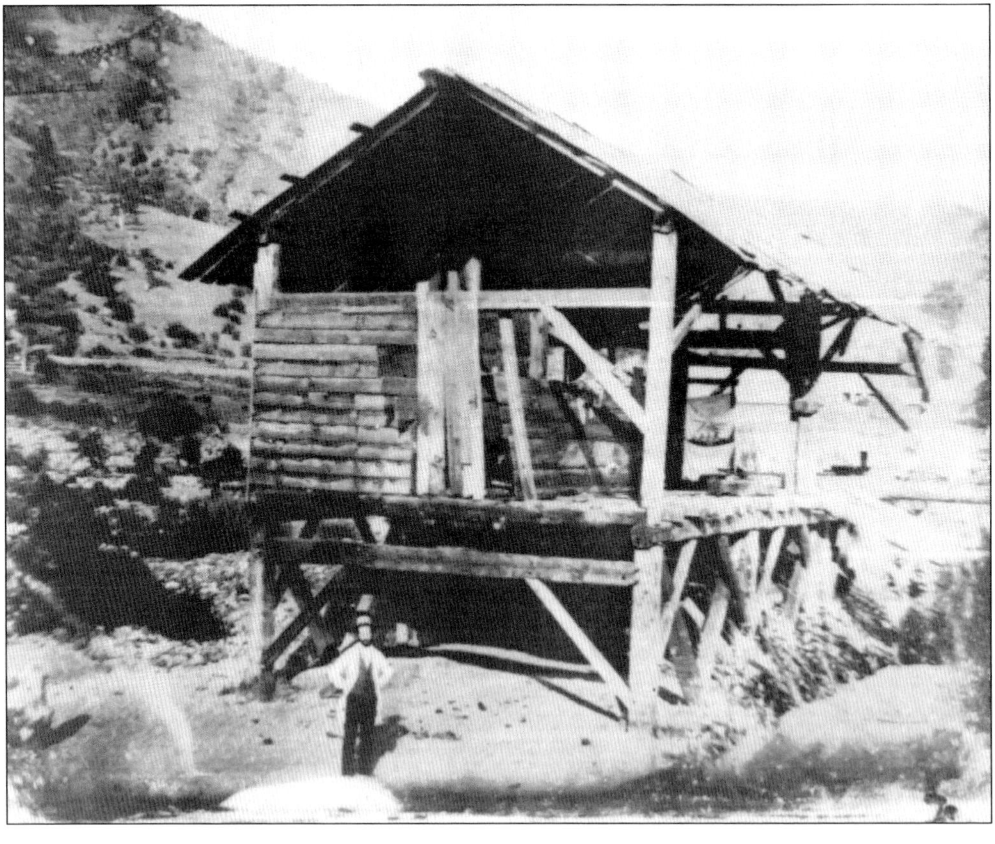

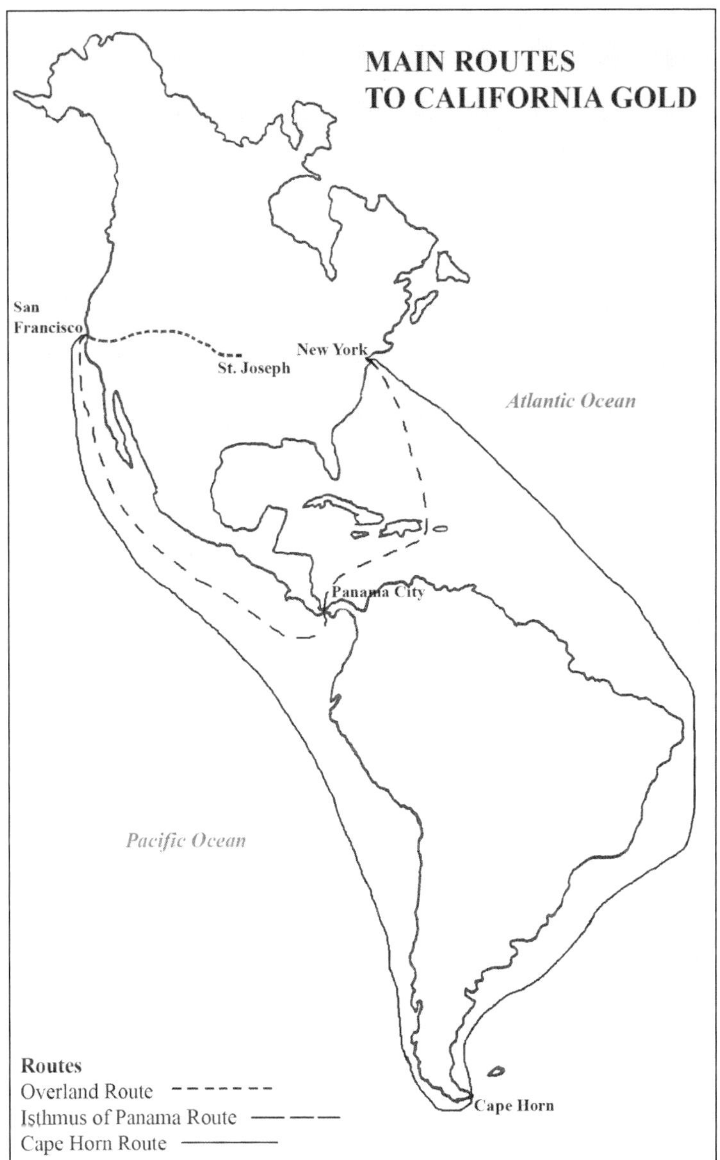

MIGRATION ROUTES. The mass migration to California was unique for several reasons. First was the tremendous distance traveled by the immigrants; second was the sheer number of arrivals. In 1849, approximately 80,000–100,000 came; by 1855, the total number had reached 300,000. The third factor was the ethnic variation. The Gold Rush seemed to offer the same opportunity for success to the Cantonese peasant as to the Boston lawyer. All of the early routes were fraught with danger and hardship. Robert Gordon, later an Auburn businessman, recorded these sentiments about his 1849 sea voyage: "Steerage is cold, damp and disagreeable. Nearly all the passengers are knocked over with seasickness. The meat is tainted and so salty that it cannot be used." Stephen Wing, who mined in the Auburn area, came via the isthmus route in 1852. He reported that hundreds were camped in Panama waiting for a California-bound ship, with most suffering from sickness and poverty. Chagres fever and dysentery were rampant. On the overland route, John Markle, who mined in Auburn, wrote, "Today we traveled 15 miles over sandy, mountainous, barren country, destitute of water or grass." (JK.)

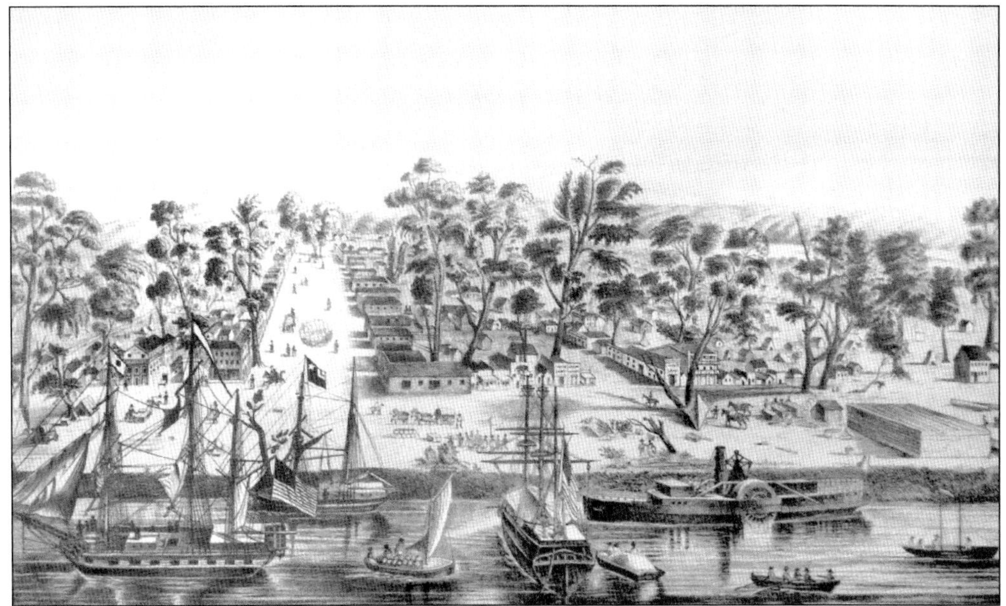

Sutter's Embarcadero. Built by John Sutter at the confluence of the American and Sacramento Rivers, this wharf was the main entryway for goods and argonauts during the Gold Rush. Every conceivable item, from oysters to boots, arrived here and was loaded onto freight wagons to supply the northern mines. Much of the freight came into Auburn, where it was transferred to mule trains or men's backs to continue the journey to the remote mining camps. (CSL.)

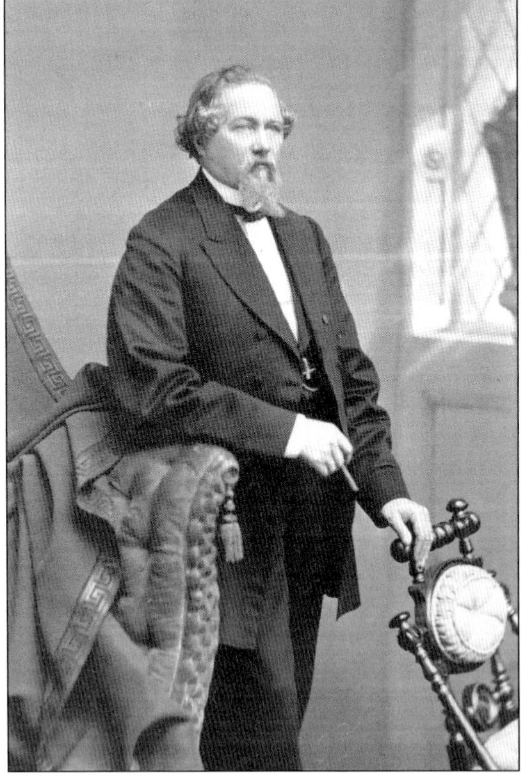

Julius Wetzler. Wetzler came to California by sea in 1849 with the party that included Samuel Holladay, who later became Auburn's first alcalde, or mayor. From 1849 to 1851, Wetzler and John Sutter Jr. had a store in Auburn called the California Exchange. By 1870, Wetzler had become president of a bank in Sacramento. (PCM.)

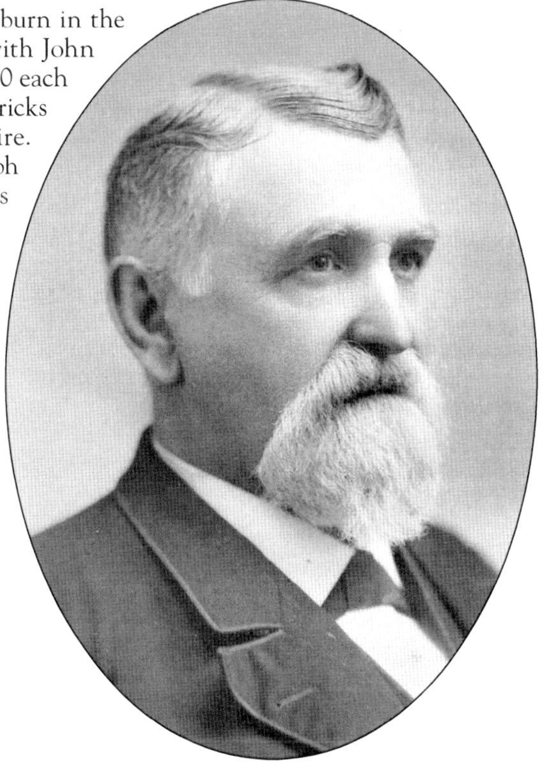

Henry T. Holmes. Holmes arrived in Auburn in the summer of 1849. He went into business with John Gwynn, and by 1852, they were netting $200 each per month. He built a brickyard, and his bricks helped rebuild the town after the 1855 fire. Holmes and his partners built the first telegraph line in California, from Auburn to Grass Valley. He was later known for his vast lime enterprises in Northern California. (CSL.)

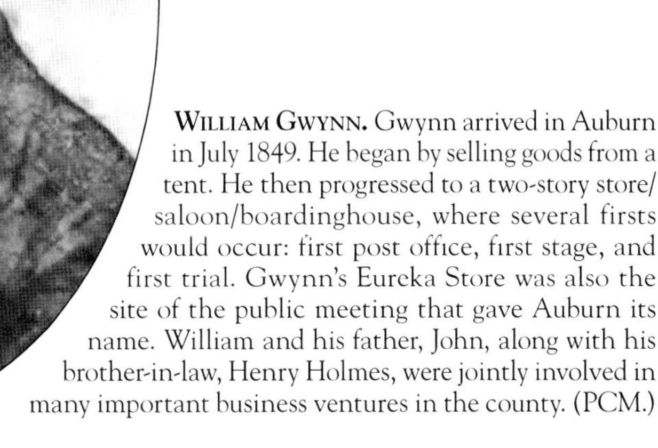

William Gwynn. Gwynn arrived in Auburn in July 1849. He began by selling goods from a tent. He then progressed to a two-story store/saloon/boardinghouse, where several firsts would occur: first post office, first stage, and first trial. Gwynn's Eureka Store was also the site of the public meeting that gave Auburn its name. William and his father, John, along with his brother-in-law, Henry Holmes, were jointly involved in many important business ventures in the county. (PCM.)

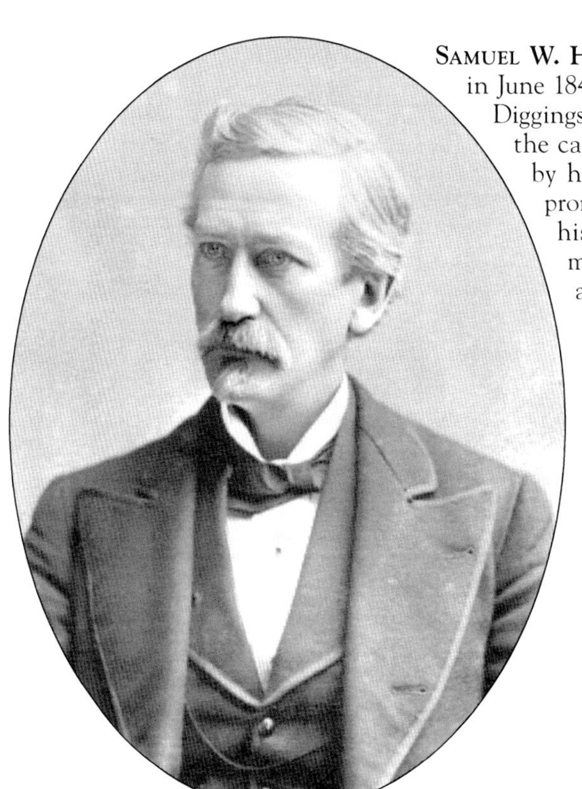

SAMUEL W. HOLLADAY. Holladay arrived in Auburn in June 1849, when it was still called Wood's Dry Diggings. In addition to helping formally name the camp as Auburn, he was elected alcalde by his fellow miners. Holladay became a prominent San Francisco lawyer. Later in his life, he wrote of his time in Auburn, mining in front of the American Hotel and on the American River. (CSL.)

MAHLON D. FAIRCHILD. Mahlon and his father, David, arrived in Auburn in August 1849; they were penniless but managed to get credit from a storekeeper. Mahlon did not repay the debt until 1851. Both father and son were involved in the newspaper business and combined that occupation with their mining endeavors. Later in life, Mahlon and his cousin Myron Angel collaborated in writing the esteemed *History of Placer County* and the *History of Nevada*. (CSL.)

NANCY (SIX) MCCORMICK GREEN. Nancy and John McCormick and their children arrived in Auburn in September 1849. The McCormicks were the first white family to settle in Auburn. Later that winter, John set out to Sacramento for supplies and drowned in a river flood. Left with five children, Nancy sold all the leather goods they had brought and opened a hotel on the corner of Commercial and Main Streets. (SHS.)

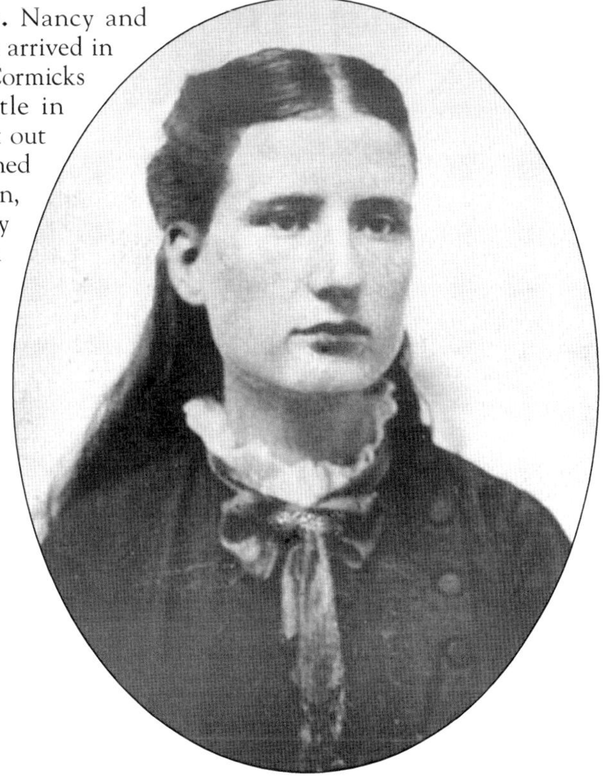

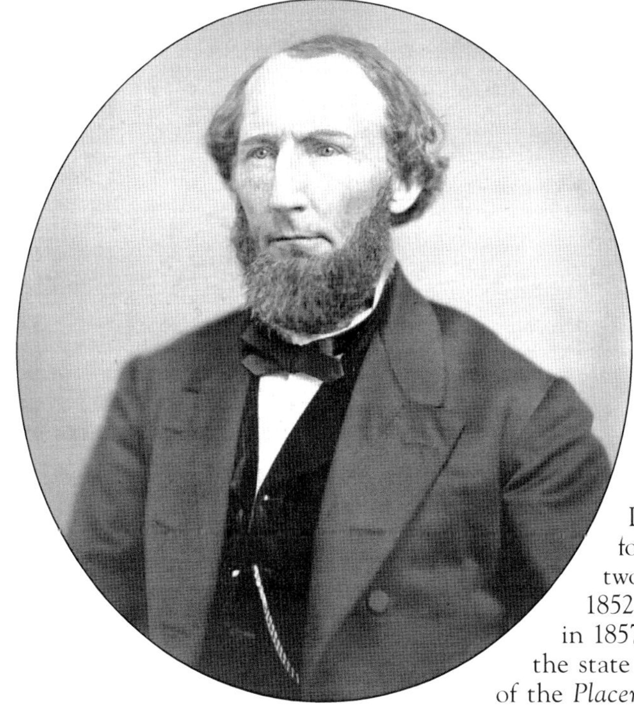

JOSEPH WALKUP. Walkup came to Auburn in August 1849. He and Samuel Wyman opened one of the first mercantile stores in the camp. Later, he was on the commission that formed Placer County, and he served two terms as a state senator starting in 1852. He was the lieutenant governor in 1857 and was credited with reforming the state prison system. He became editor of the *Placer Herald* newspaper in 1868. (JD.)

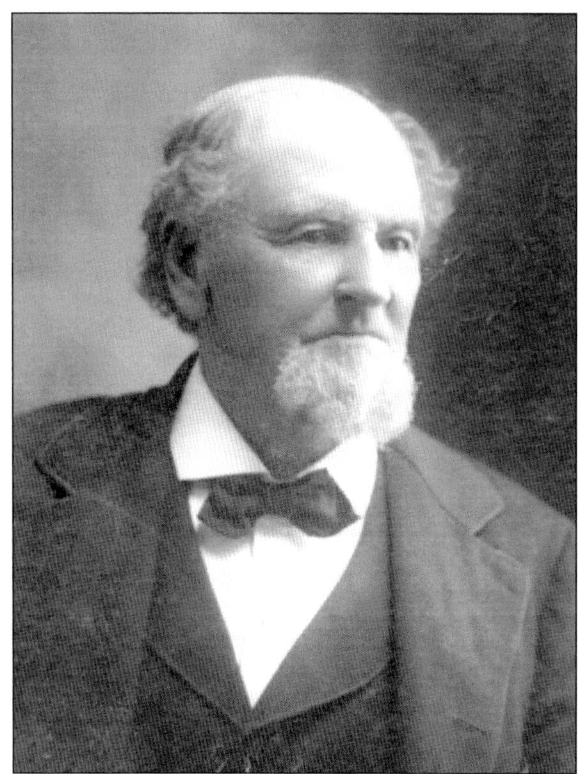

John Craig Boggs. Boggs arrived in Auburn in September 1849 and became one of the most famous law enforcement officers in early Placer County. He was deputy sheriff from 1855 to 1865, then was elected sheriff in 1879. He relentlessly pursued Rattlesnake Dick, the region's most notorious outlaw. As he was dying from a gunshot wound, Dick wrote in a note, "If J. Boggs is dead, I am satisfied." Boggs outlived Dick by many years. (CSL.)

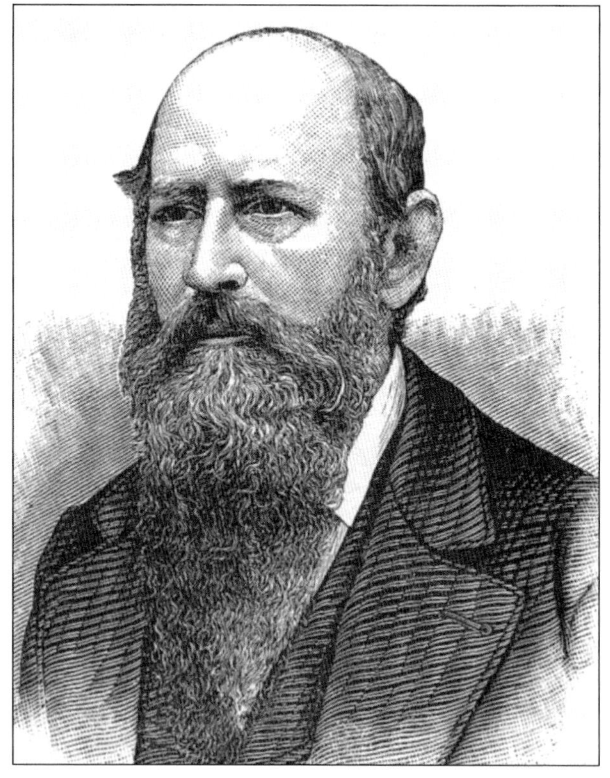

Moses Andrews. Andrews came to Auburn in 1849. He mined there for a few years, then partnered on two stores and owned the Wild Cat House in Secret Ravine. He was elected to the state assembly in 1854, but by 1857, he had moved back to Auburn and returned to his previous occupation as a watchmaker. He and Henry Hubbard also ran the only bank in town. Andrews was one of the first to plant citrus trees in the county. (TW.)

Robert Gordon. Gordon arrived in Auburn in November 1849 after a harrowing sea voyage that lasted over seven months. He brought goods to sell, but upon arrival in San Francisco, the ship's crew deserted, headed for the gold fields, and Gordon could not get his freight unloaded. He tried mining for a year, with sporadic success, before opening a store in Auburn, which he ran for over 25 years. (CSL.)

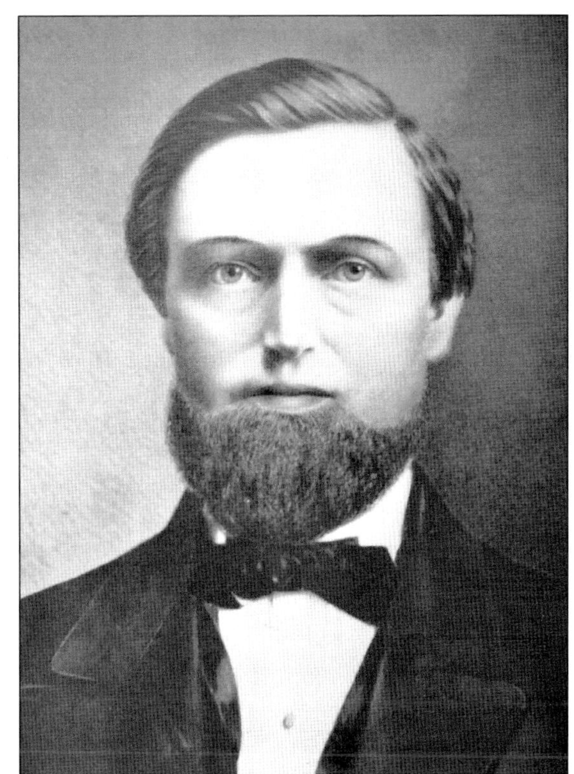

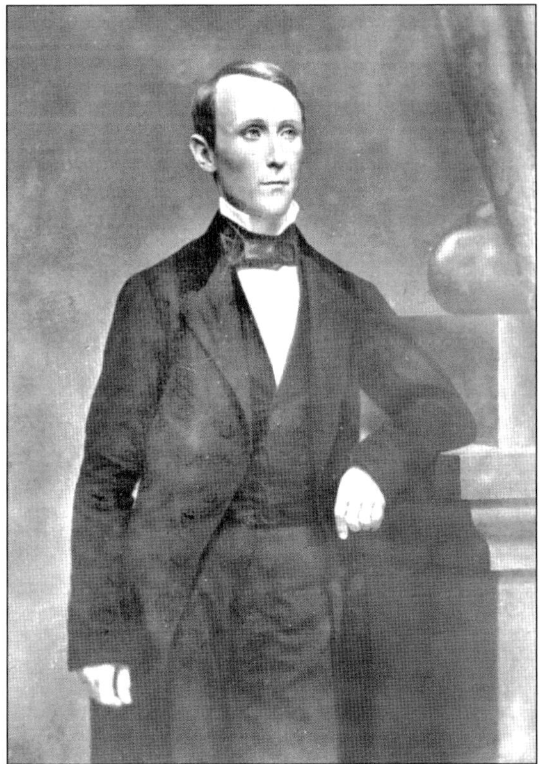

Gen. William Walker. Born in Tennessee, Walker was a "freebooter" seeking to expand the boundaries of slave territories in the United States through military conquest. In early 1852, he was a forty-niner at Spanish Flat in Auburn, where he formulated his "Auburn enterprise" to conquer the territories of Baja California and Sonora in Mexico. He was unsuccessful in Mexico but had more, although short-lived, success in Nicaragua in 1855. He was executed in Honduras in 1860. (LOC.)

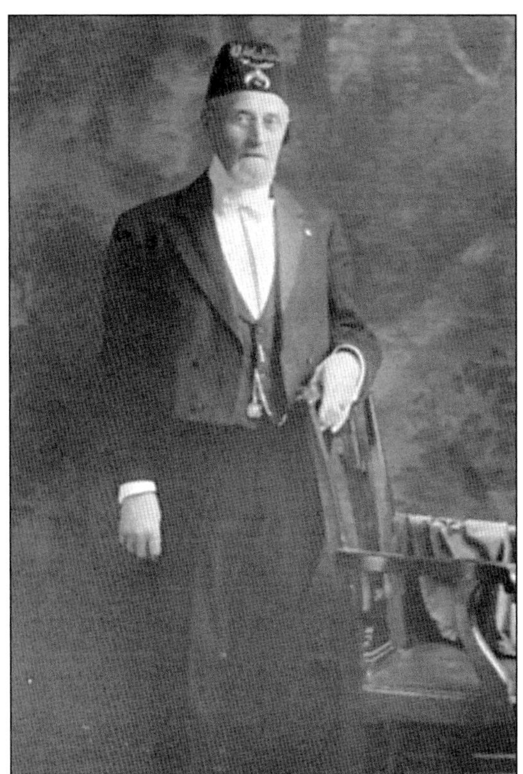

Abner Graves. Graves was only 15 years old when he mined in Auburn with his father in 1849. They claimed 20 square feet right in the center of Main Street. Isaac Annis, in town at the same time, later wrote, "Thare is so manney people here . . . wee are all in a heap. The gold diggings is full of miners. Tha are diggin all around me." (PCM.)

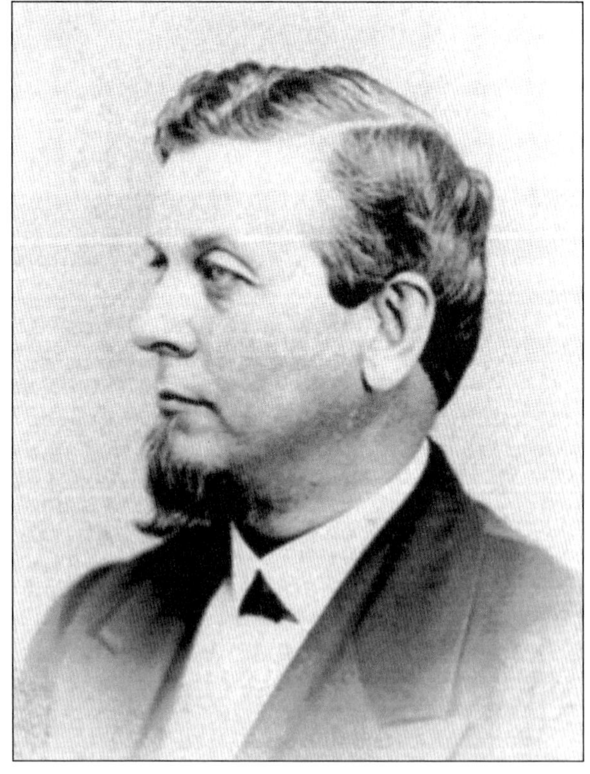

Frederick Ferdinand Low. Low mined in Auburn and on Horseshoe Bar in 1849 and was successful. He formed the California Steam Navigation Company in 1854 and controlled river transportation to the gold regions. As the ninth governor of California, he established the state park system and the university system. He was an advocate of equal rights for Chinese and Native Americans, and he served as minister to China from 1869 to 1874. (JK.)

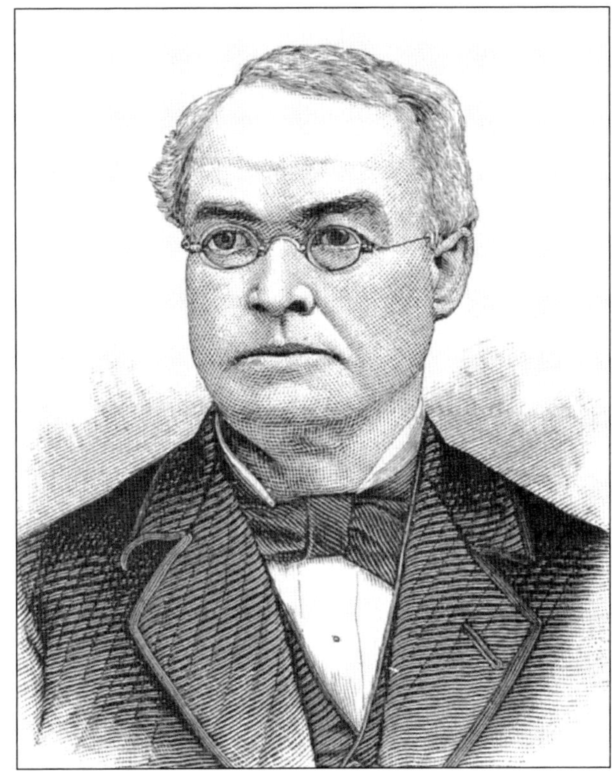

James Ellery Hale. Hale was already a lawyer before arriving in Auburn in the winter of 1849. He was county judge from 1855 to 1859. Active in politics, he served in the state senate and as reporter for the state supreme court. He held a pivotal role in the 1878–1879 Constitutional Convention and was credited with successfully recovering the state's war claims for expenses during the Civil War. (TW.)

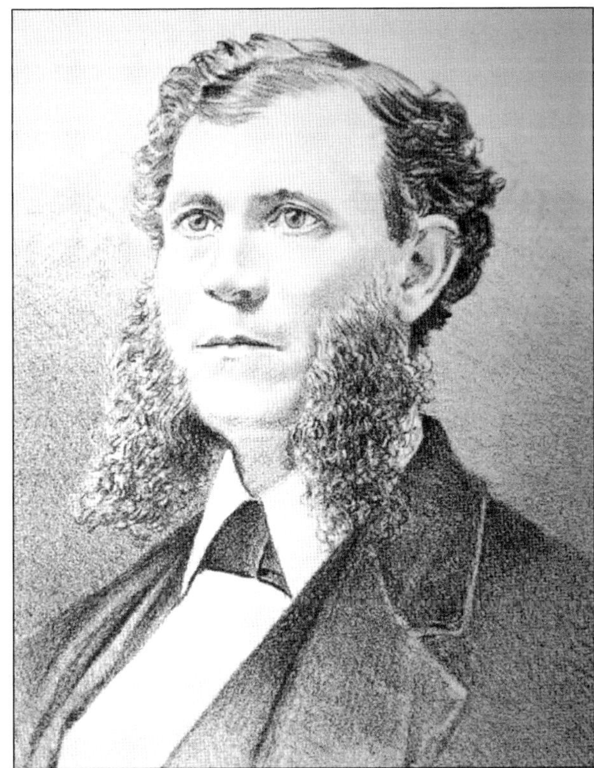

Charles Frederick Reed. When Reed mined in the streets of Auburn in May 1849, he was one of only about a dozen men who were looking for gold. He did not stay long, and he eventually settled in Knights Landing, where he became known as "the Wheat King." He returned to Auburn and mining in the 1880s and built a country villa in Aeolia Heights that included an aviary on the front lawn for singing birds. (PCM.)

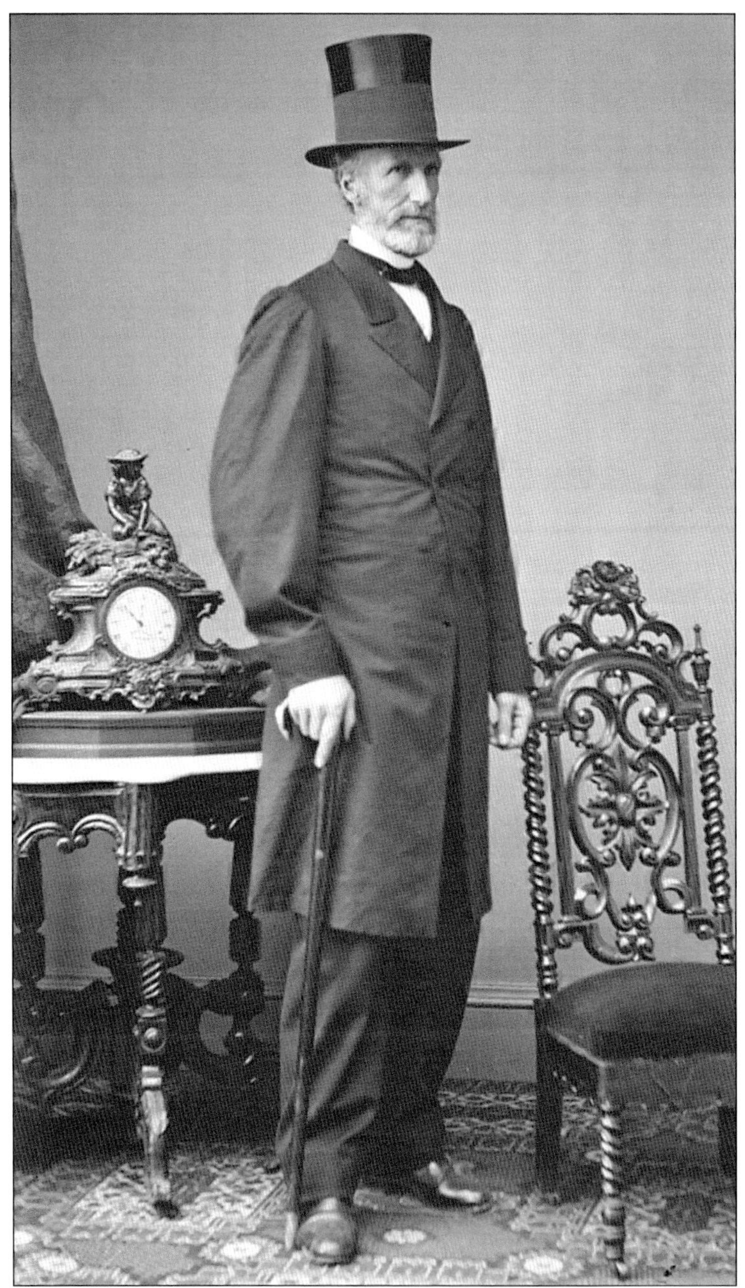

Gordon Newell Mott. In addition to serving as a volunteer during the Texas Revolution and as a captain in the Mexican-American War, Mott had already been admitted to the Ohio State Bar before joining the Gold Rush. In 1849, he was mingling law and mining in Auburn. He was a Sutter County judge before the formation of Placer County. He moved to Nevada in 1861 and was appointed associate justice of the Nevada Territory Supreme Court. As part of the controversial Comstock Ledge case, he sided with the single-ledge faction of the large corporations over the individual miner's assertion that the ledges were discrete, separate bodies of ore, not unified. The hostility over this ruling followed him throughout his later career and forced his resignation as a congressional delegate in 1863. (LOC.)

Four

Mining

There were three quite distinctive periods of the Gold Rush. The first was the mining season of 1848, when surface gold was abundant and the pickings were easy. The second lasted from 1849 to the early 1850s. During this period, mining became much more labor intensive. In the third period, after 1852, most mining became industrialized and capital intensive.

In the first period, those men who were already in California and those coming down from Oregon reaped the rewards of the easy pickings. Using picks, shovels, butcher knives, and even frying pans, they could literally pick up large nuggets from the ground or pry them out of crevices in rocks. In August 1848, one man found $16,000 worth of gold in only five cartloads of dirt in Auburn.

The second period was marked by the reality of serious mining. In July 1849, Samuel Holladay noted, "About the center of Auburn where the ravines converge, some splendid lumps were found, as high as twenty ounces pure. Many of these I sought and saw but never found." Mining became hard, repetitive work—digging, carrying, and washing, usually in ice-cold, swiftly moving water. Men banded together to work the rockers and Long Toms. They shared hastily built cabins and took turns cooking.

The winter of 1849–1850 was particularly difficult for the greenhorn miners. Exposure, sickness, scurvy, and typhoid fever were prevalent. Isaac Annis, in Auburn that winter, noted, "They ware dieng all around me. Tha wrap them up in blanket and put them in the ground for lumber is so high it would cost $200 fully for a coffin."

By the time the third period of mining arrived, most solitary miners had given up and returned home or fallen back on their previous occupations. Many went to work as day laborers for large mining companies. The expense of hydraulic and hard rock mining required vast amounts of money, which was supplied by East Coast and European capitalists.

The dream of getting rich quickly never materialized for a large percentage of men; on the whole, they were unsuccessful, disillusioned, and embittered. Only one in 20 returned home richer than when he left.

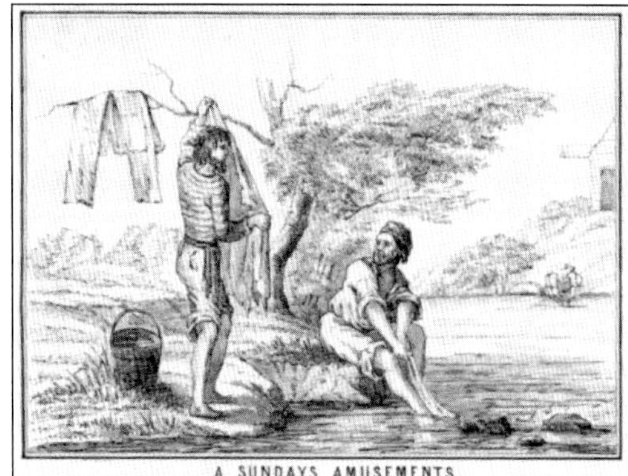

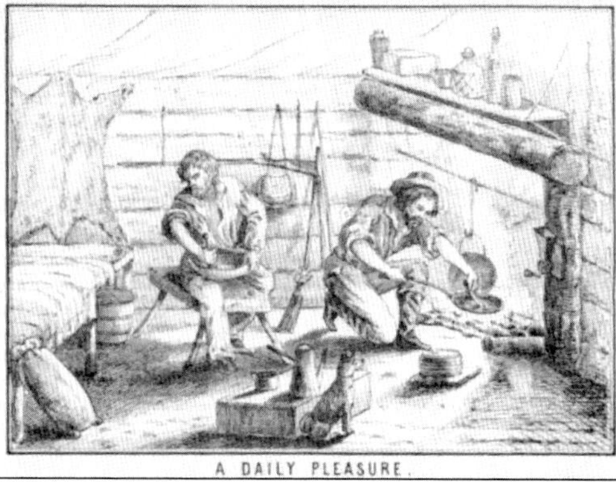

THE MINER. The myth of the rugged individual miner gave way to the reality and necessity of having partners in the quest to find gold. Men counted on each other to share the labor and household chores, as well as for companionship. John Markle, in Auburn with his partners in the winter of 1849, wrote, "Robbins and Sampson had built the chimney . . . and by noon we had part of the roof on." (LOC.)

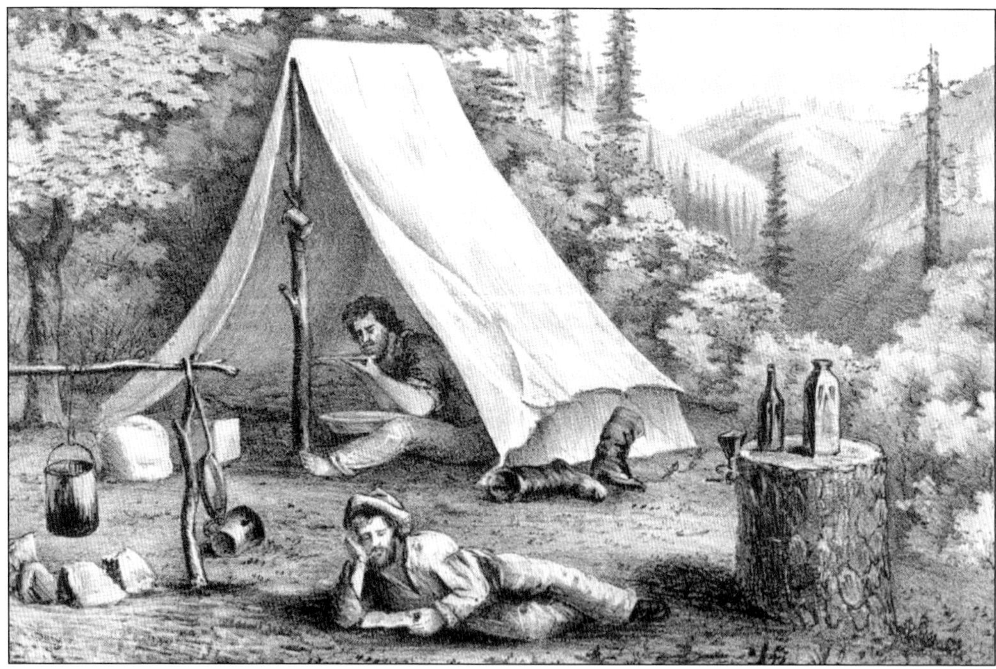

CAMP LIFE. Lithographs provide visual images from the time before the widespread use of photography. These striking images show the simplicity of the miner's life: a few possessions, a good book, and a supply of liquor. One miner wrote home that he was "fully provisioned . . . with a slab of bacon, a few pounds of flour, a little sugar, coffee, tobacco, a frying pan, a butcher knife and spirits." (LOC.)

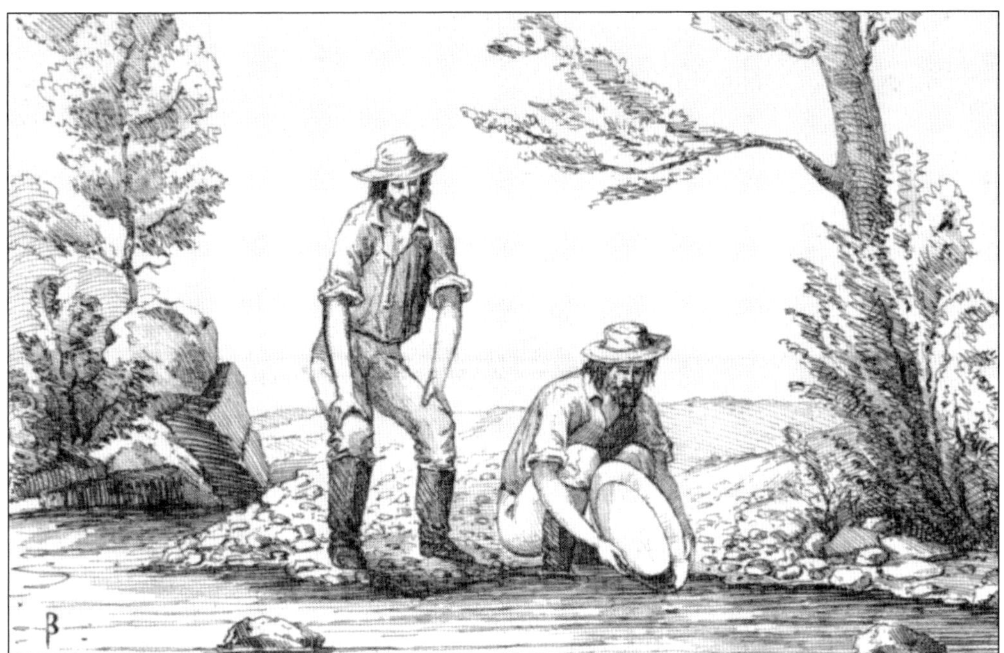

Gold Panning. Panning was the oldest and simplest way to separate gold from gravel. The early miners used the Mexican batea or tightly woven Indian winnowing baskets. Panning was also one of the most exhausting forms of manual labor; it required squatting or stooping in the burning sun, either beside or in icy water, for hours at a time. (LOC.)

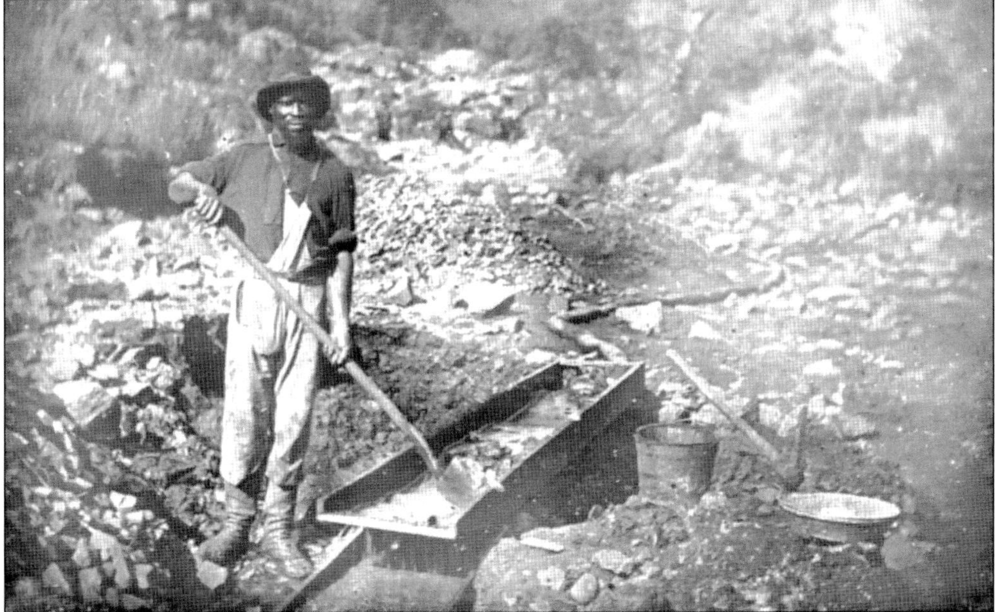

African American Miner. Joseph Blaney Starkweather took this photograph in Auburn in 1852. California came into the Union in 1850 as a free state, not so much because of any abolitionist stance but because miners did not want to compete with slave labor in the search for gold. It is estimated that blacks in California sent about $750,000 to the South to purchase the freedom of loved ones. (CSL.)

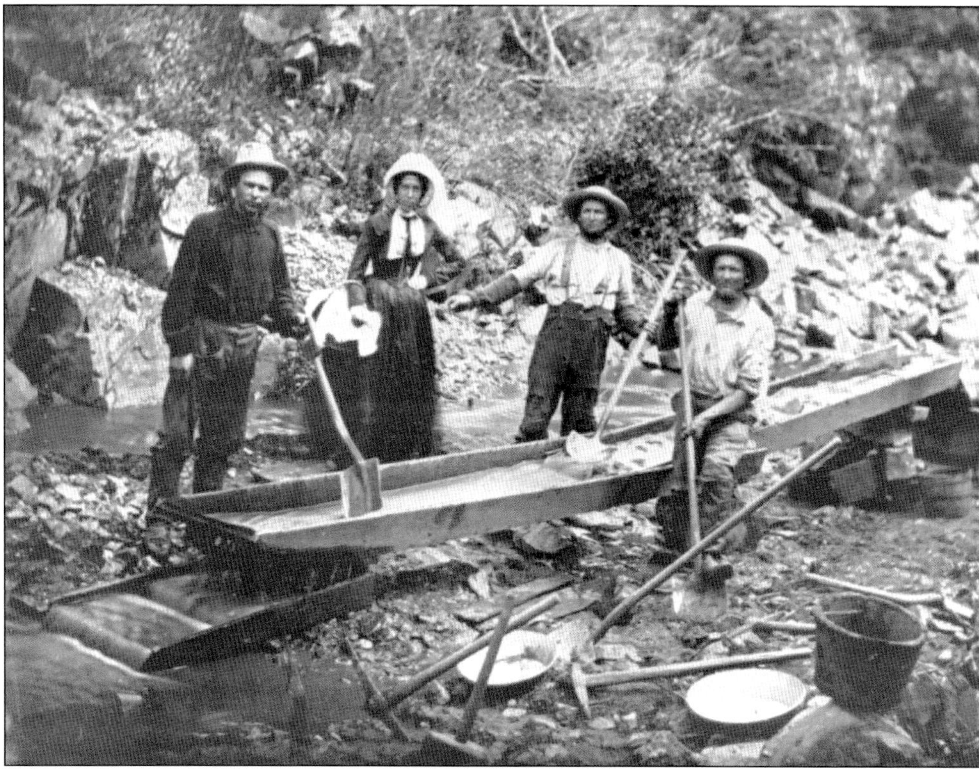

Long Tom. The Long Tom is a larger version of the rocker or cradle. At least two men shoveled dirt, rocks, and gravel into the top while a third removed the large debris. The gold and sand caught in the riffle was removed and panned. The woman in the photograph is most likely delivering lunch to this Auburn location. Women started arriving in Auburn in numbers in the early 1850s. (CSL.)

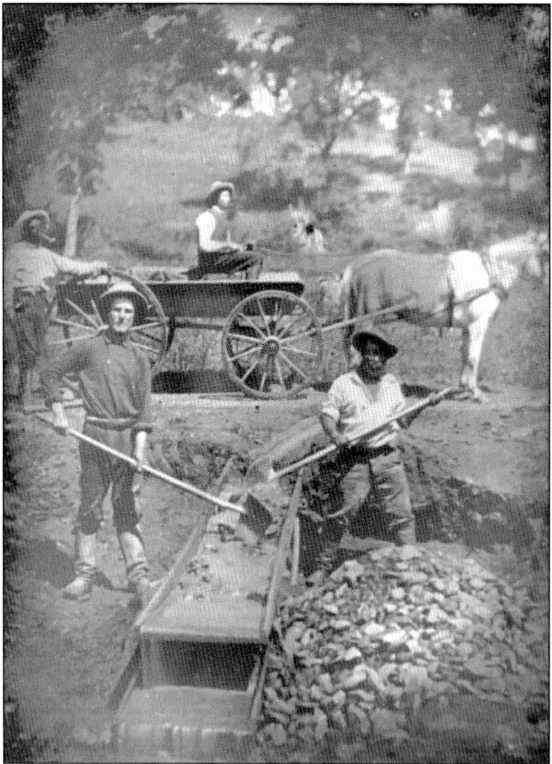

Mining at Spanish Flat. This famous photograph was taken in 1852 on Spanish Flat, near the present-day post office on Nevada Street. It perfectly captures the second phase of the Gold Rush, featuring the use of the Long Tom by several men. It also exhibits the ethnic diversity of the Gold Rush, with the Caucasian and African American miners working the same claim. (CSL.)

MINING IN OLD TOWN. This iconic photograph was taken in the heart of Old Town Auburn. The large building at right is John Echols's National Hotel. About this same time period, Isaac Annis wrote home from Auburn: "There is six men digging with[in] 2 rods of my door that tuck out yesterday $516. All this region is full of people." (AJS.)

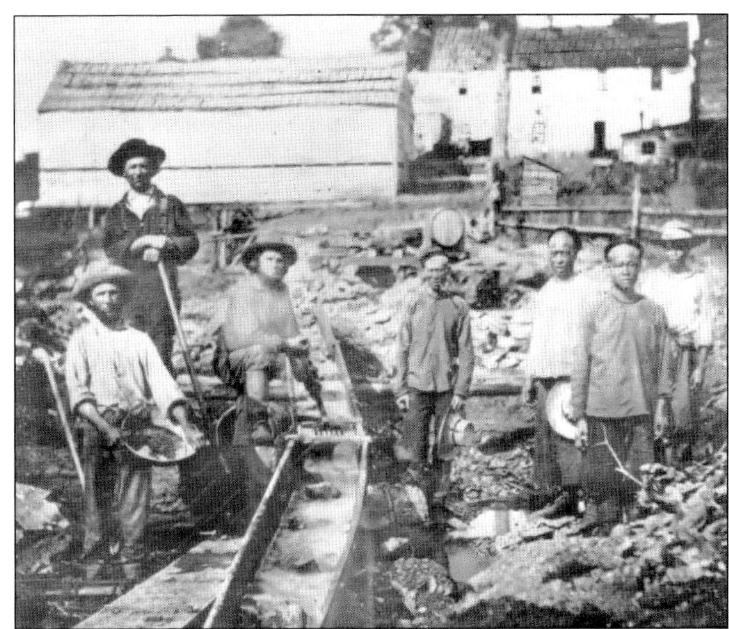

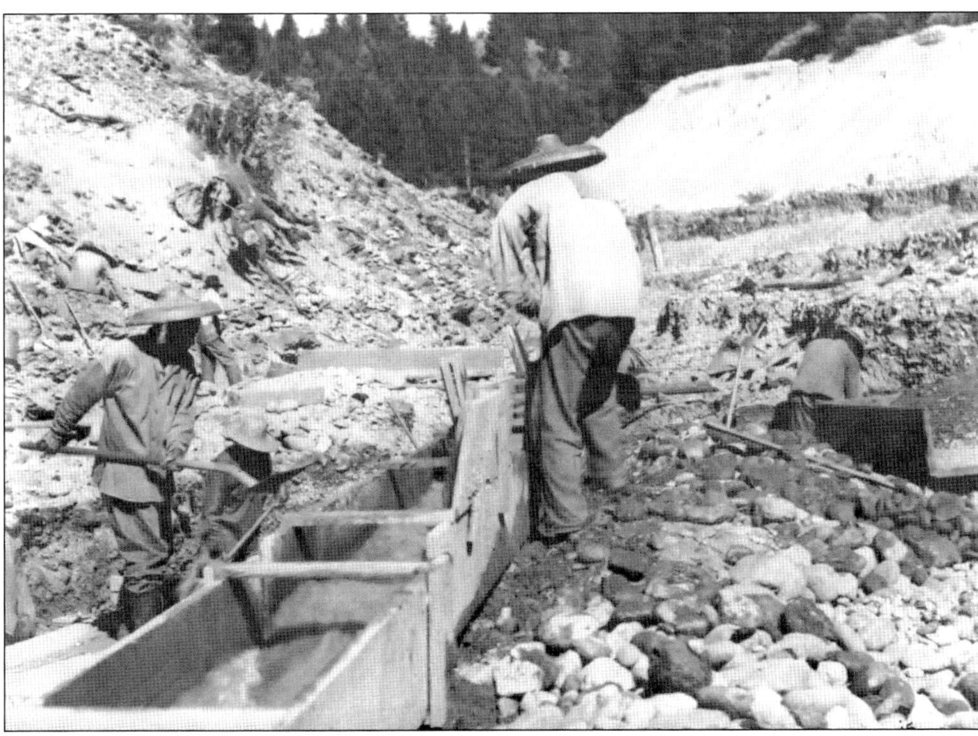

CHINESE MINERS. This photograph illustrates the use of the Long Tom by unidentified Chinese miners. Most Chinese miners came to California, or "Gold Mountain," under the credit ticket system, an indenture program promoted by the Chinese Six Companies. Chinese miners were noted for taking over played-out claims and, with hard work and patience, making them pay again. (PCM.)

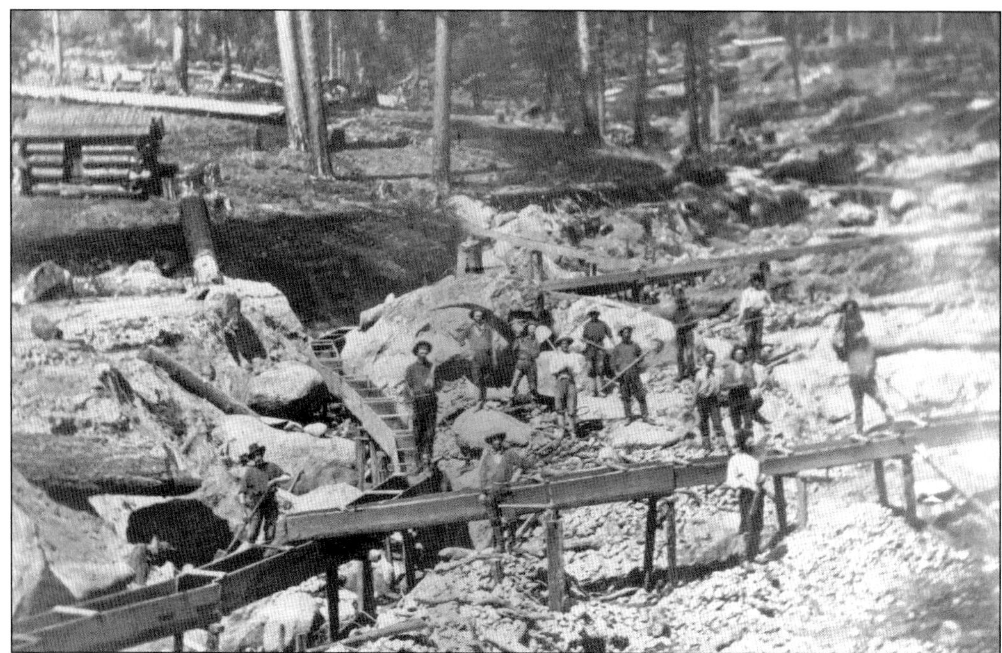

Flumes. Flumes and dams required vast amounts of capital and a large workforce. Given the capriciousness of the river flow, many saw months of work swept downstream during a winter flood. In 1874, Auburn miner George Reamer lost the fortune he had made from his New Jersey mine when the $200,000 dam he was building was swept away. (AJS.)

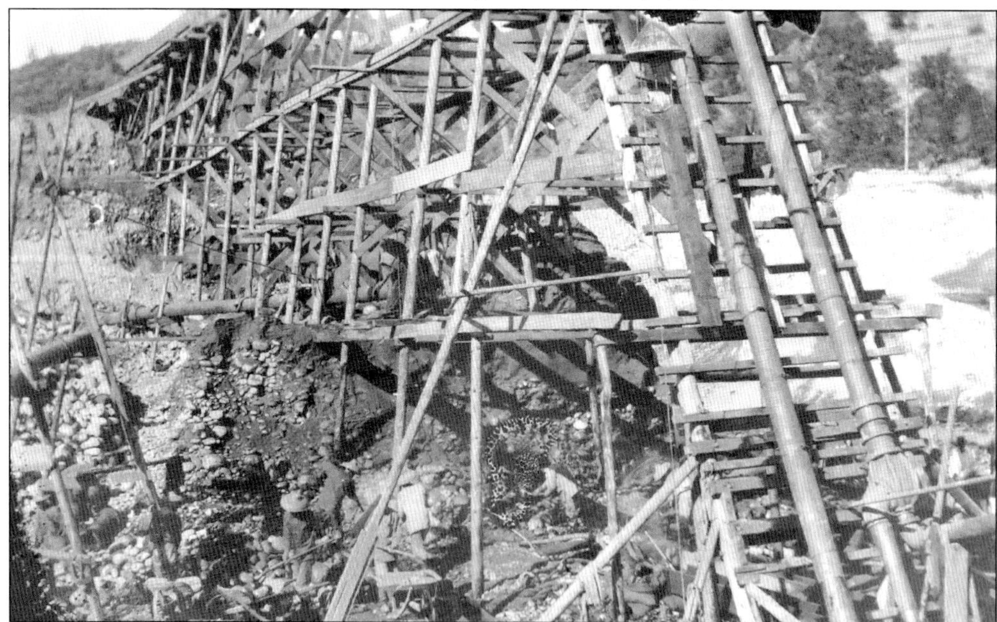

Chinese Miners. Note the Chinese miners wearing their trademark conical hats as they work underneath this flume. The Chinese started coming to the Auburn area very early in Gold Rush. By 1852, they made up about one-third of the male population in Placer County. Following the fire of 1855, Chinese were encouraged to come to Auburn, and houses were built for them. By 1860, Chinese made up 25 percent of Auburn's population. (PCM.)

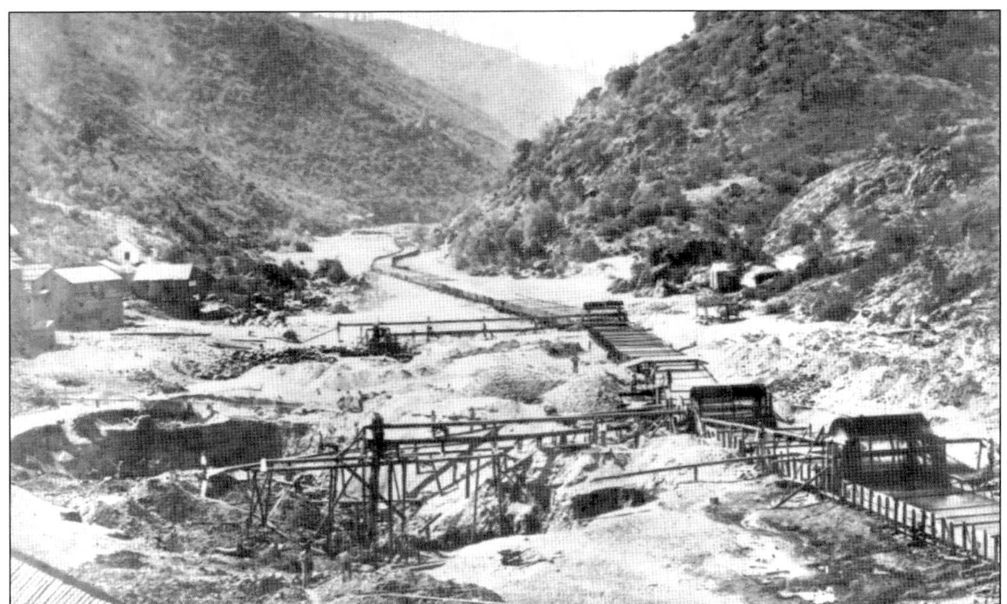

LAYING BARE THE RIVERBED. Gold deposits lay in the ancient riverbeds, and channeling the river became an enormous challenge. William Bickham wrote home in 1850 about moving the river: "We have not, nor are we able to procure machinery, consequently huge stones have to be lifted and carried away by main strength." He went on to describe working in the river, saying, "One party goes in and remains for 16–20 minutes and comes out at the expiration of that time shivering and chattering like a man with ague." Both the 1850 image of Maine Bar above and the 1977 image below show the same landscape and illustrate the extent to which miners went to change the natural course of the river. (Both, PCM; album created by Charles Weed.)

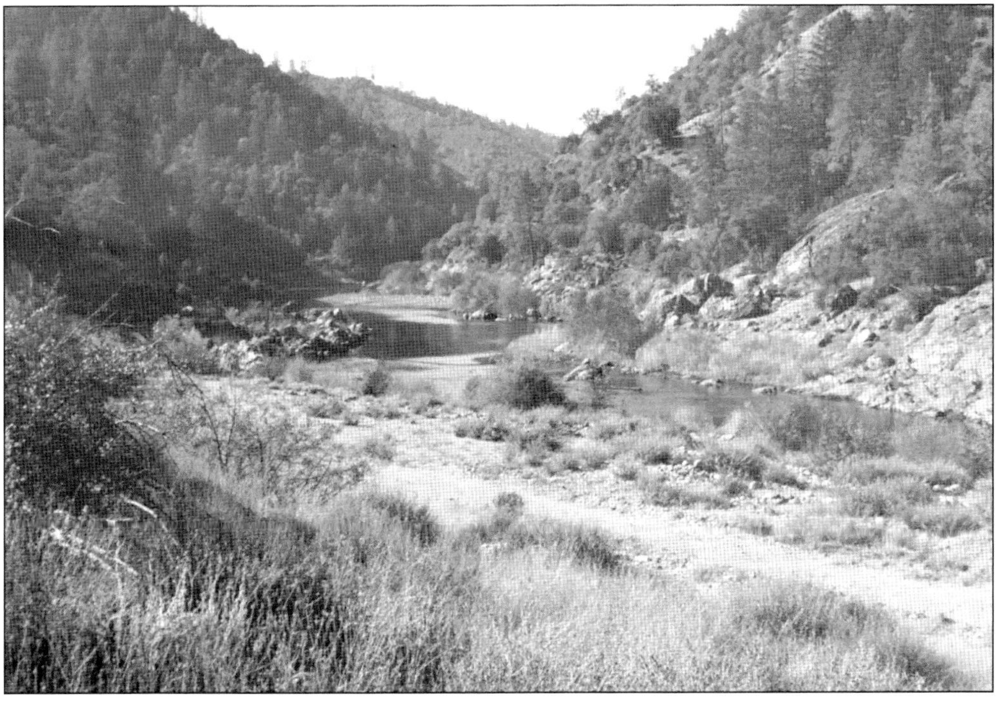

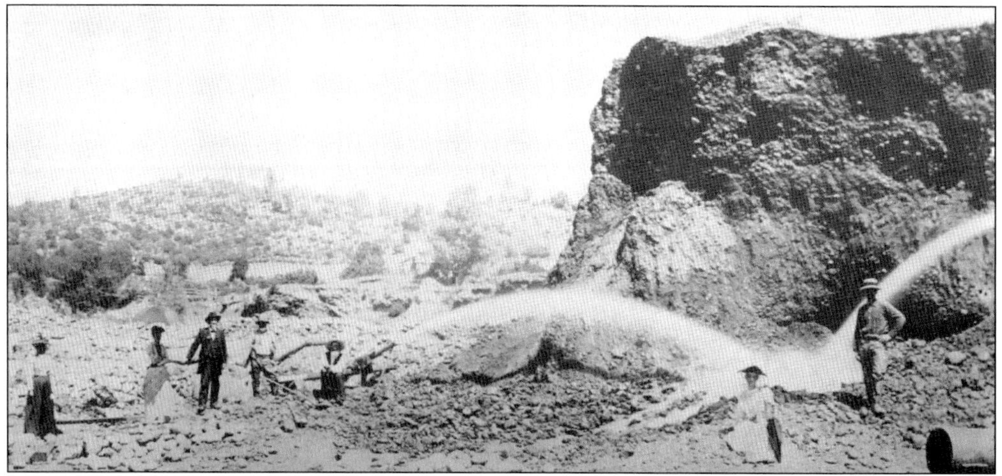

Rattlesnake Bar. The town of Auburn and the practice of mining on nearby rivers and the Foresthill Divide were inextricably intertwined. This illustration of hydraulic mining on Maurice Kelly's claim at Rattlesnake Bar shows an unusual scene that includes women of the Kelly family. This gold mining family still has descendants in Auburn. (PCM.)

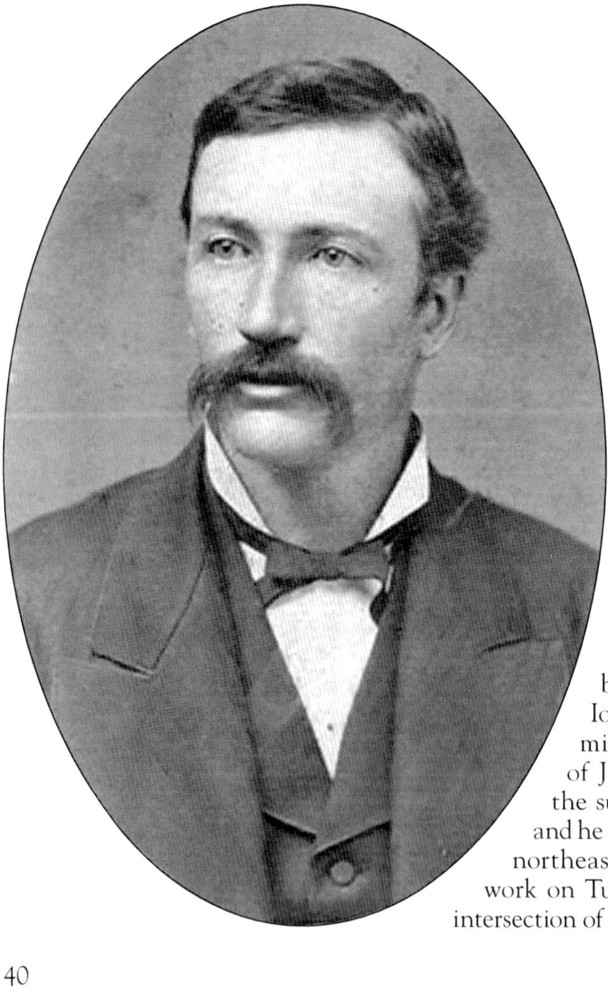

John B. Hobson. Hobson arrived in California in 1849. By 1869, he had become the acknowledged expert on Iowa Hill and had mapped the entire mining district. He was an associate of Jacob H. Neff in the operation of the successful Morning Star drift mine, and he had a hydraulic mining claim slightly northeast of Auburn. The remnants of his work on Tunnel Hill are visible north of the intersection of Luther Road and Interstate 80. (DB.)

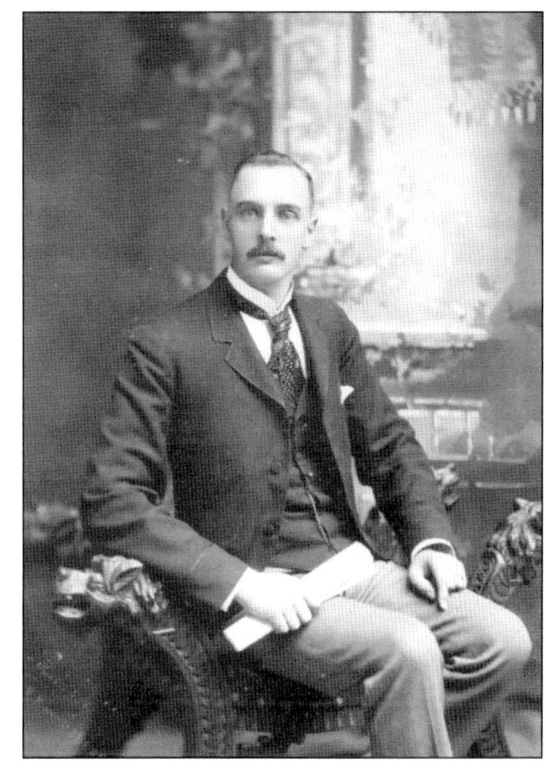

Harold Thomas Power. Harold was the second generation of the Power family involved with the fabulously successful Hidden Treasure mine on the Foresthill Divide. Harold's mother, Isaline, was a major real estate mogul in Auburn, buying and selling many properties and holding mortgages. In 1901, Power bought the Huntley mansion, one of the finest homes in Auburn. (AJS.)

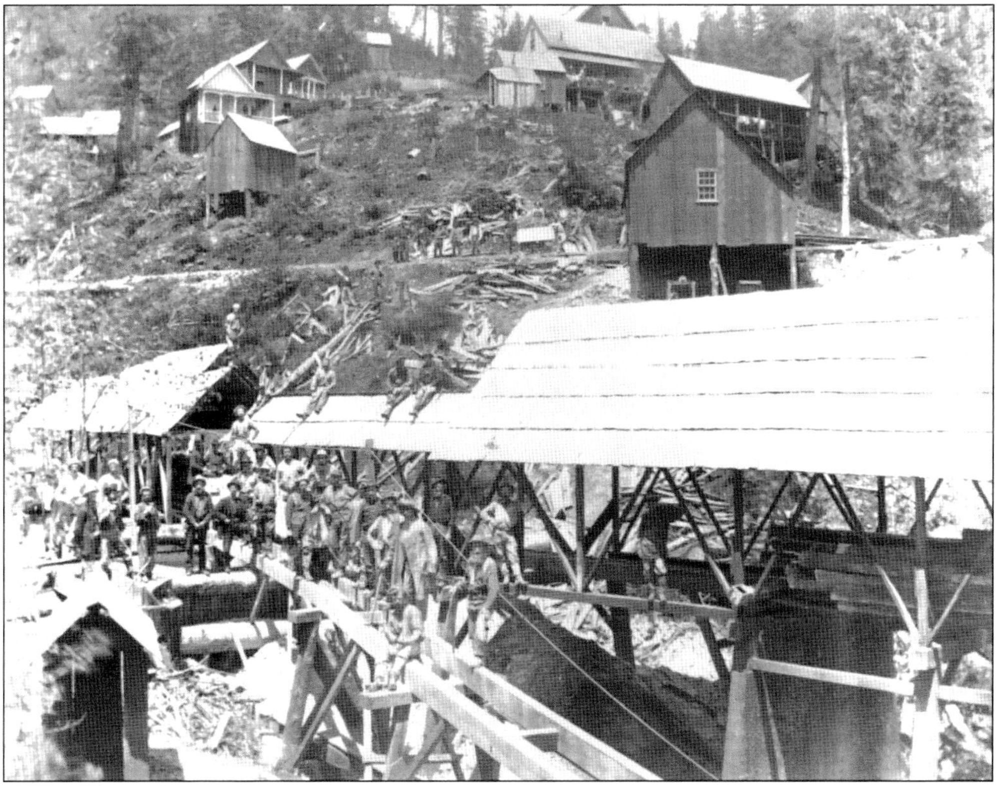

Hard Rock Mining. The scope of the mining operation at Power's Hidden Treasure mine in 1877 is illustrated here. Mining required men, equipment, and capital. Digging and blasting through the earth to reveal gold-bearing quartz rock was labor intensive. The rocks needed to be crushed, and then the gold was separated. (AJS.)

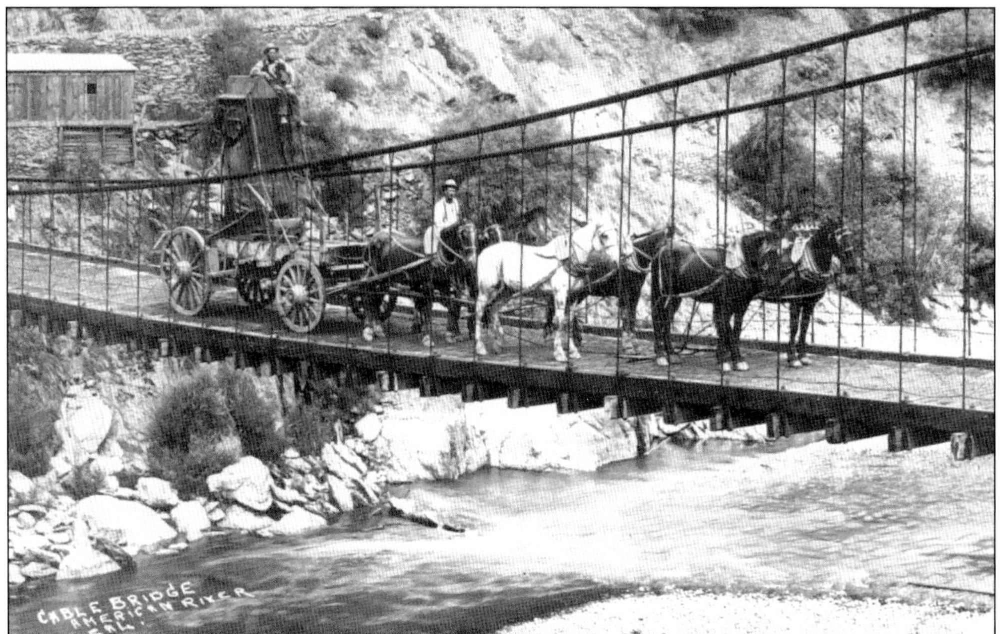

Mining Equipment. This freight wagon drawn by a six-mule team is crossing Lyons Bridge on the road from Auburn. Lyons Bridge was one of the many over the North Fork of the American River. As mining became industrialized, heavy equipment like this steam donkey engine was needed. (AJS.)

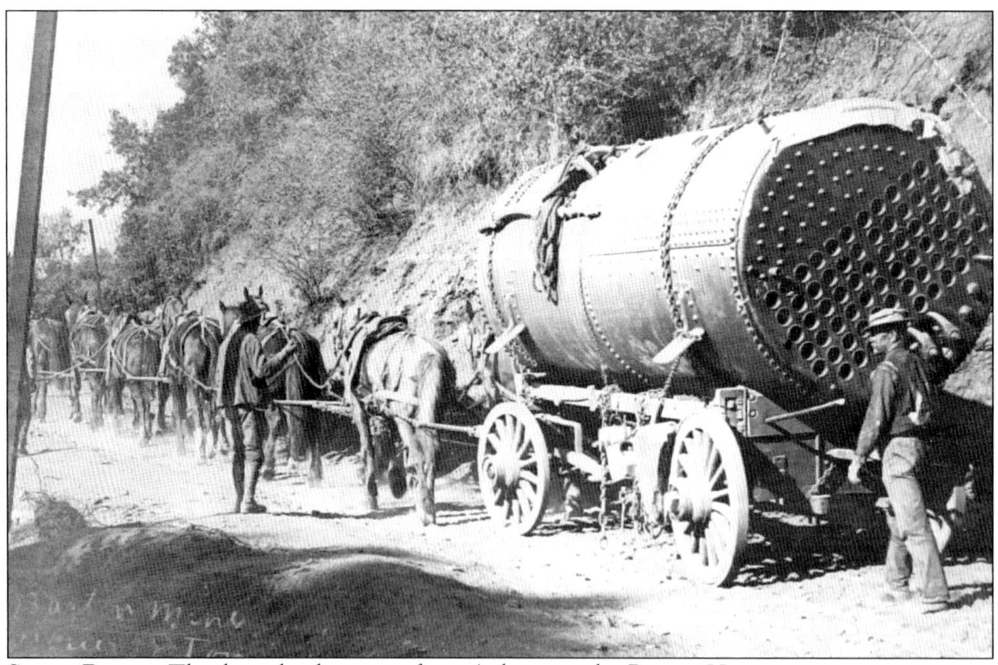

Steam Boiler. This large load coming from Auburn to the Barton-Herman mine operation on the Foresthill Divide is another illustration of how the mining practices had evolved from an individual with a pan to large companies with machinery and capital. Will Patrick, the head driver, headquartered in Auburn. (AJS.)

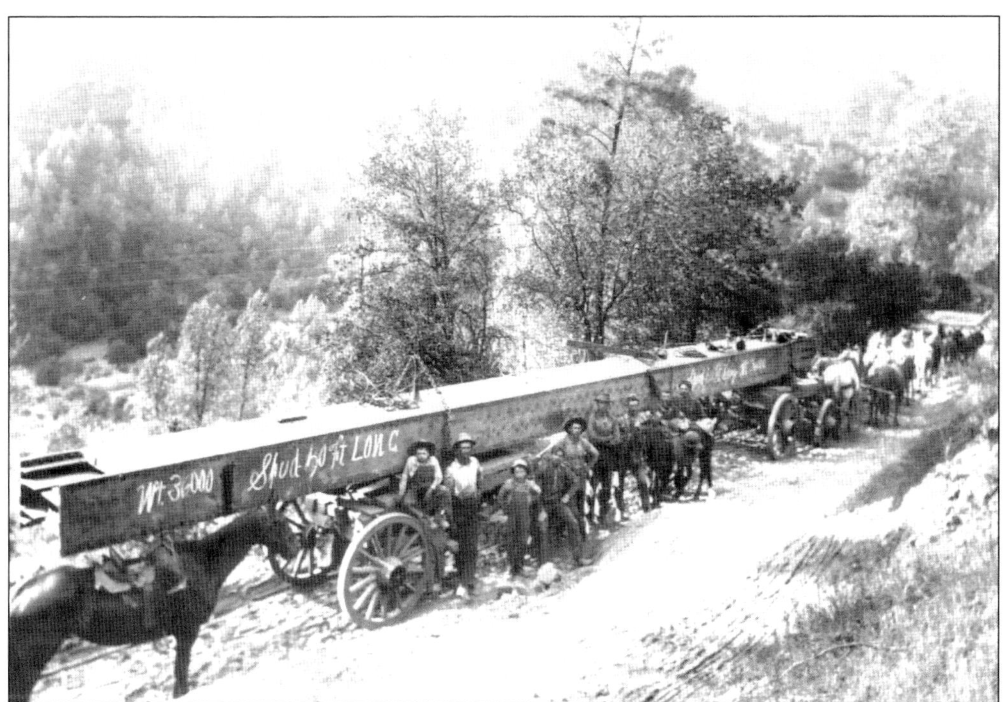

Mining the River. As late as 1913, freighting from Auburn to the mountain towns and the river canyons was done by mules, horses, and oxen. The above photograph shows part of the dredge headed to Mammoth Bar. Below is the massive dredge in operation. Despite its Pacific Gold Dredging Company ownership, it was commonly called the Guggenheim Dredge, after company owner Solomon R. Guggenheim. (Both, AJS.)

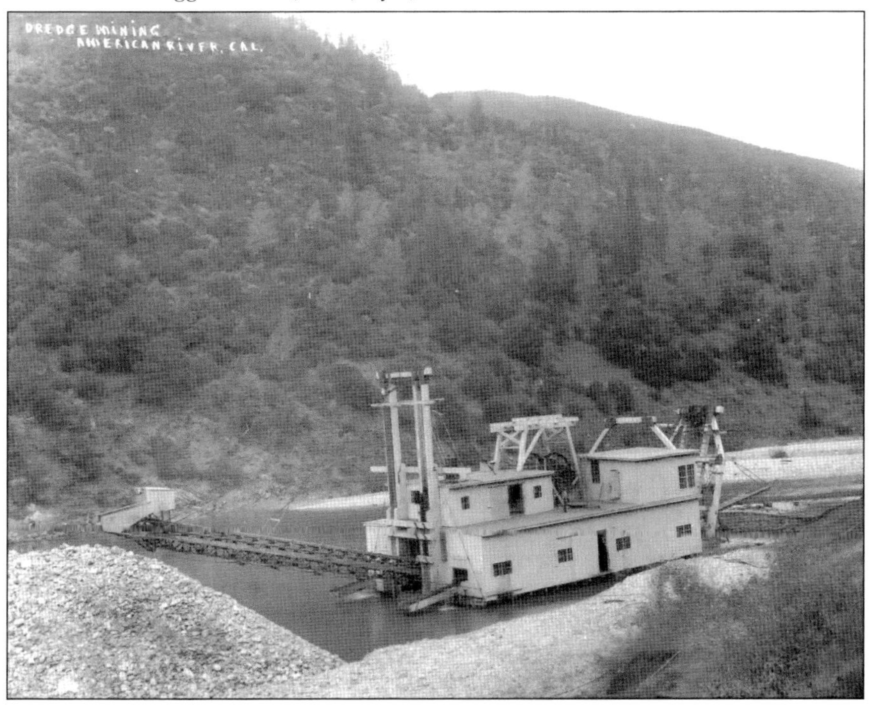

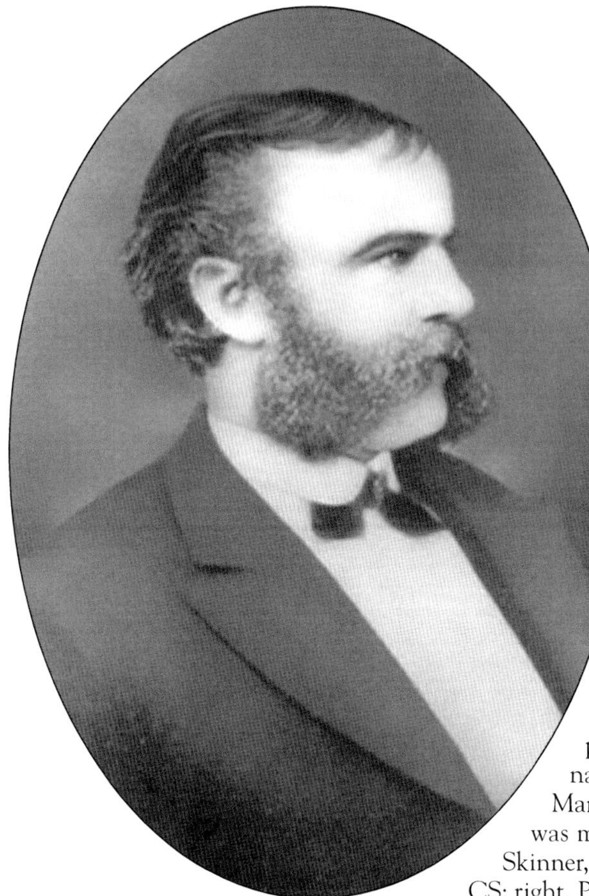

Gustavus Frederick Deetken. Deetken represents the third stage in the mining evolution. He was educated at a mining school in Germany and came to California in the early 1850s. He patented a chlorination process for extracting gold and was highly regarded in the mining world as "one of the most noted metallurgists and mining chemists of the coast," according to his obituary in the *Placer Herald*. In 1885, he owned and operated the Marguerite Mine, one of the few mines within Auburn city limits, on present-day Marguerite Mine Road. It was named after one of his daughters, Helene Marguerite, pictured here on her pony. He was married to Catherine Augusta "Gussie" Skinner, also shown here. (Left, above and below, CS; right, PCM.)

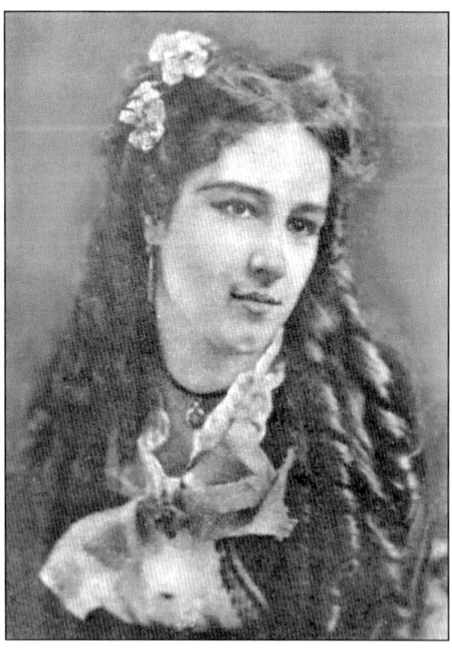

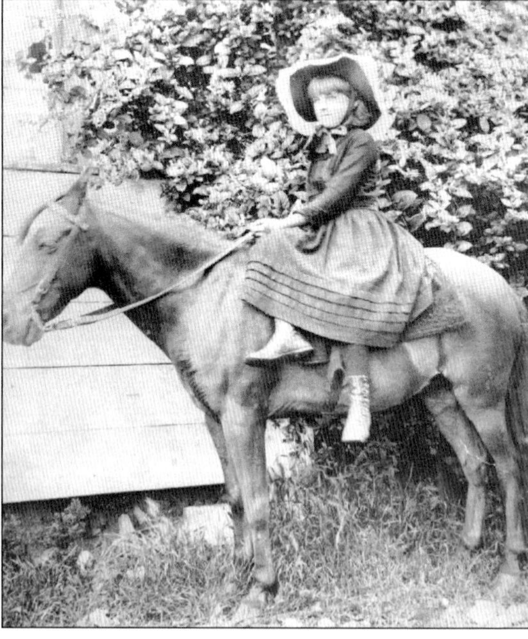

Five

Grain over Gold

The miners coming into the Auburn area in 1848 and 1849 brought very little with them to a region that was nearly devoid of any agricultural products. Several entrepreneurs quickly established trading posts, and a few even began farming. Joseph Walkup and Samuel Wyman, who opened one of the first mercantile/saloon/boardinghouses in Auburn, also began growing wheat. Claude Chana, who found gold on the Auburn Ravine, established a farm along the Bear River and eventually became a successful vineyardist. Northeast of Auburn, miners E.T. Mendenhall and Lisbon Applegate both established very successful orchards and tree nurseries in about 1850. Some of their tree stock came from Oregon and as far away as France.

In a very short time, others followed their example. In Auburn, John Russell, John Gwynn, John Crandall, Edward Loving, Charles Tuttle, George Bishop, and James Collins planted small orchards, vineyards, and/or market gardens. Others raised sheep, cattle, swine, and milk cows. There was a ready market for all local produce.

As more and more miners discovered the discomforts and uncertainties of mining, many returned to agriculture. By the 1860s, additional factors had influenced the change in focus from gold to grain. The primary element was the existence of the expansive canal and ditch system designed to bring water to mining areas that were turned to the use of irrigation. In Auburn, the Bear River and Auburn Water and Mining Company was the most important water delivery system. Bolstering the turn to agriculture was the coming of the transcontinental railroad in 1865. The railroad had the ability to transport huge amounts of fresh agricultural products. In the Auburn area, fruit production became paramount as the premier crop for many years.

As large-scale farming was developing, it came into conflict with hydraulic mining. Debris devoured land and filled the rivers and creeks with silt. Flooding downstream was rampant, and agricultural land was inundated. Claude Chana was a victim of the effects of hydraulic mining; debris covered and ruined his fine farm. The Sawyer Decision of 1882 severely limited hydraulic mining. This first environmental protection law set the standard for the rest of the country and vastly increased water available for irrigation.

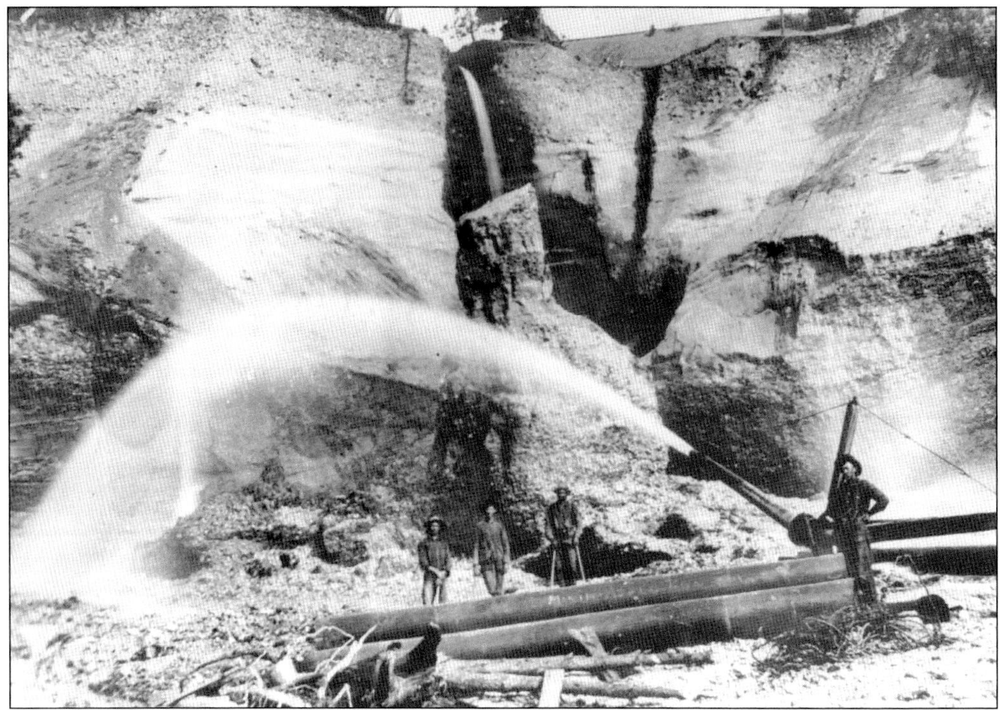

Hydraulic Mining. The destructive nature of this type of mining set miner against farmer. The damage done to the landscape is clearly shown in this photograph. Acres of land were destroyed by the high-pressure water cannons. After the landmark Sawyer Decision of 1882, hydraulic mining went into decline, and agriculture became the mainstay of the local economy. (PCM.)

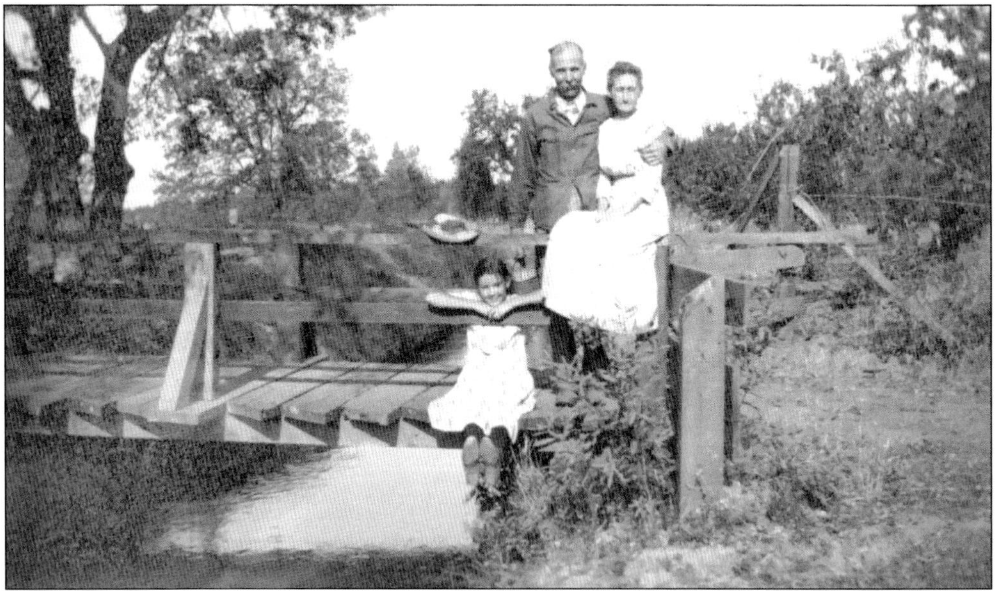

Water Ditch. Ditches like this one were hand dug. Initially, they were built to bring water to dry diggings, but as mining waned, the water was used to irrigate the burgeoning agricultural industry. The Luther family is pictured here by the ditch (part of the Bear River ditch system) that ran through their dairy farm on present-day Luther Road. (PCM.)

John Riggs Crandall. Captain of the Peoria Pioneers, Crandall came to California in 1849. He was the founder of the Bear River and Auburn Water and Mining Company, one of the first of the massive projects to bring water to the miners; it later provided farms and orchards with irrigation water. He owned the successful toll road that ran from Auburn's Junction House to Newcastle and was an early promoter of "fruit culture." (TW.)

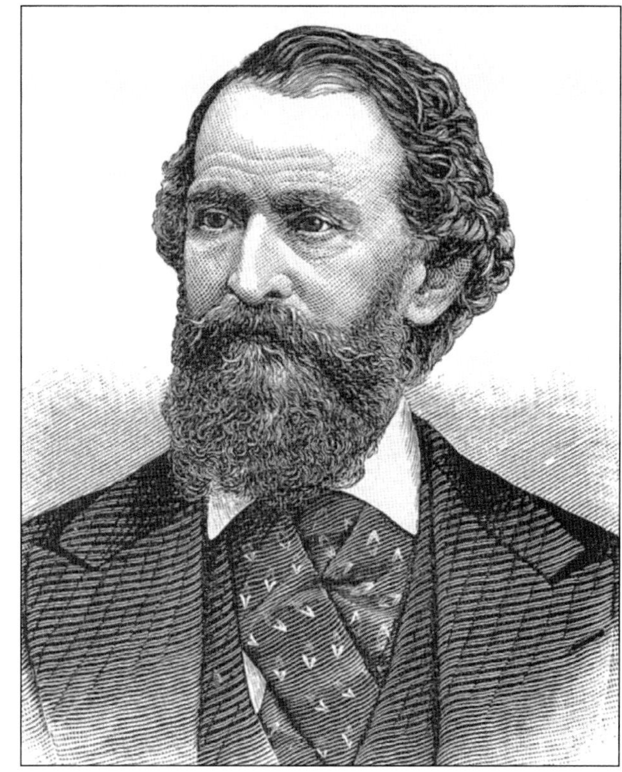

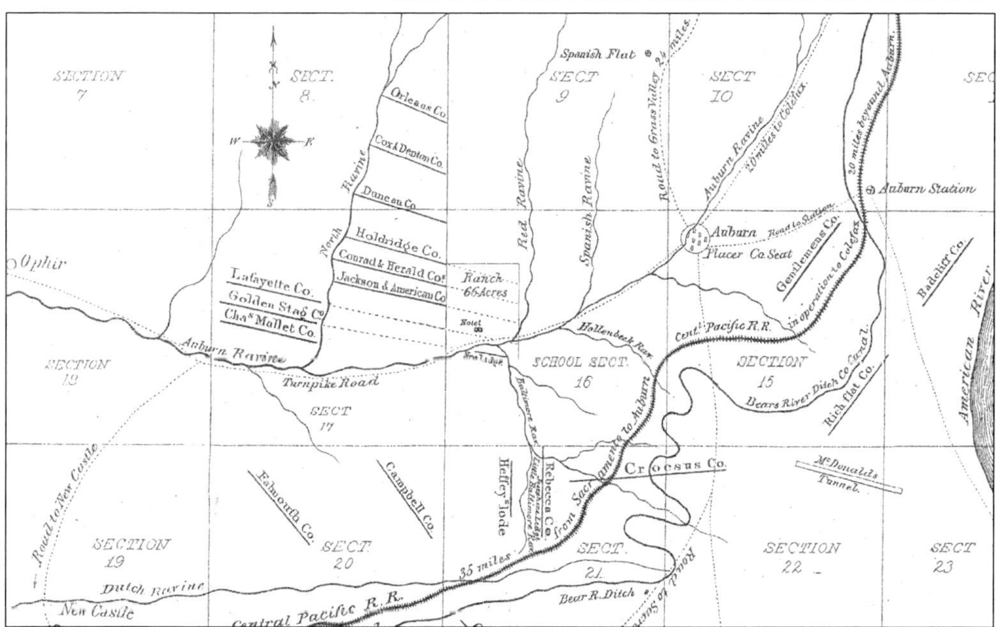

Bear River Ditch. While not to scale, this map provides a visual representation of a segment of the ditch. It runs from the top right corner to the bottom left corner of the map. The ditch eventually extended almost 200 miles. Recognizing the change from mining to agriculture, the company offered free water for five years to anyone in Placer County who planted 50 orange or lemon trees in 1878. This ditch still supplies all of Auburn's water. (PCM.)

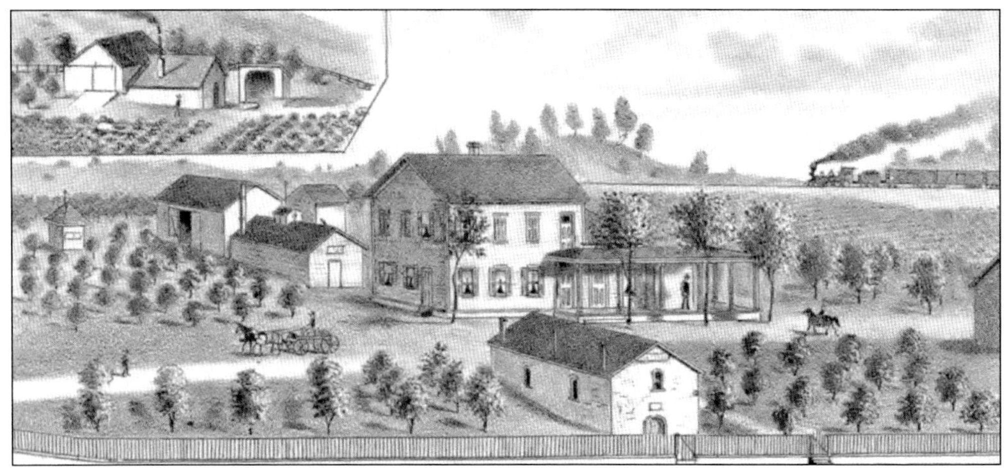

The Traveler's Rest. This hotel and tavern was built in early 1851 for George Bishop and John Long. It is the oldest surviving building in Auburn. In 1858, Bishop converted the hotel into his residence and planted the surrounding orchards and vineyards. In 1868, teamster Bernhard Bernhard sold his 10 mules and purchased the property. Members of the Bernhard family owned the house until 1958. A portion of the property is now home to the Bernhard Museum. (TW.)

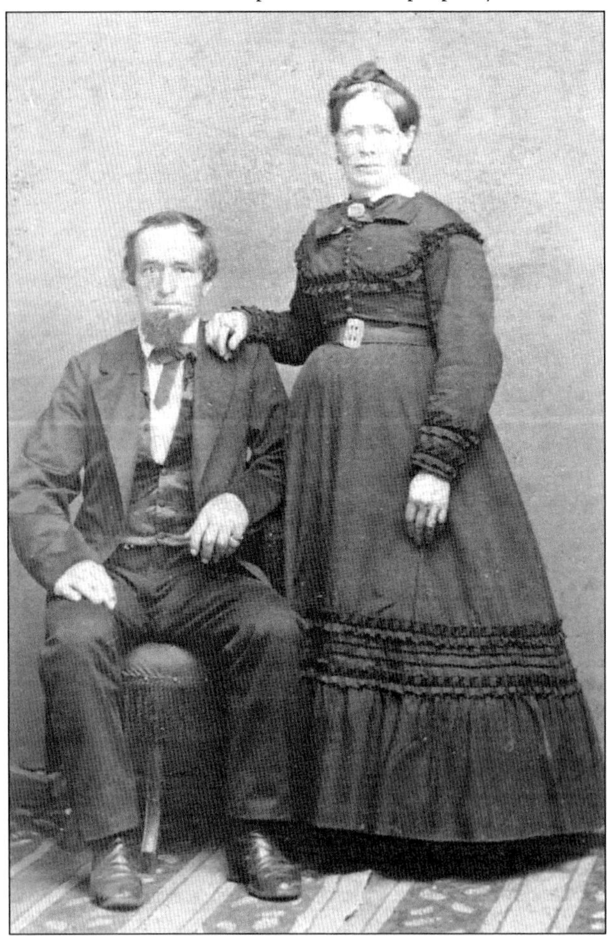

The Bernhards. Bernhard Bernhard and Rosa Hau were born in the same village in Germany, and in 1846, they immigrated to America, where they were married. Bernhard came to California in 1852. He was already a successful teamster when Rosa joined him in Auburn in 1855 or 1856. When the new railroad crossed the Sierra summit, Bernhard gave up hauling for farming. Hard work made their orchard and vineyard among the very best in the community. (PCM.)

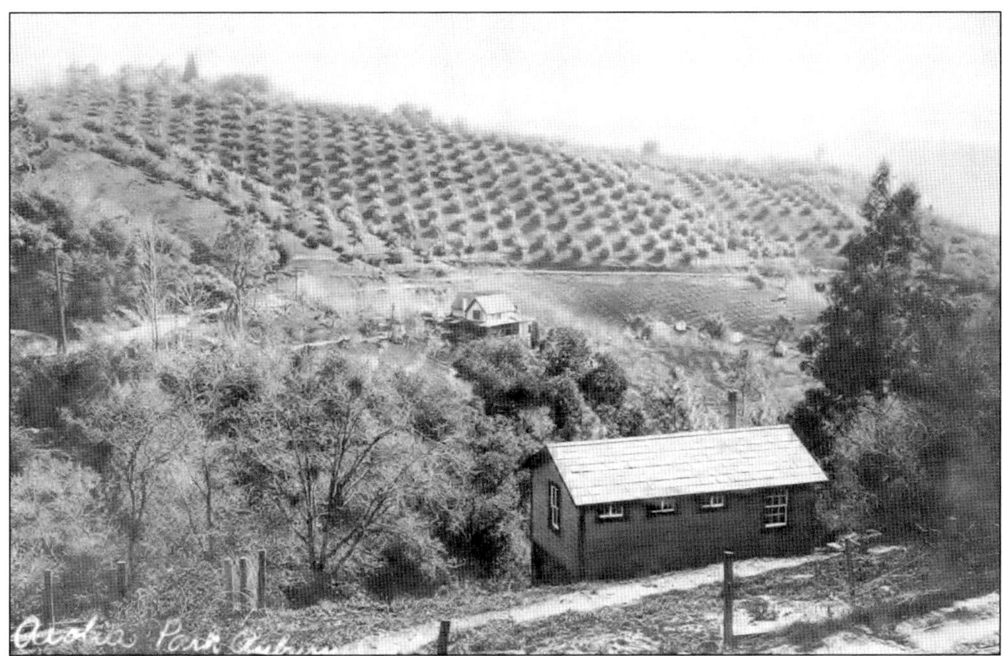

Aeolia Heights. Frederick Birdsall purchased 70 acres in Auburn in the 1880s and planted thousands of olive trees. His ranch, Aeolia, was named for the Greek god of winds. At the peak of the enterprise, the Birdsall Olive Oil Company produced 1,500 gallons of pure olive oil and 500 gallons of pickled olives per year. The company remained in business until the 1970s. (PCM.)

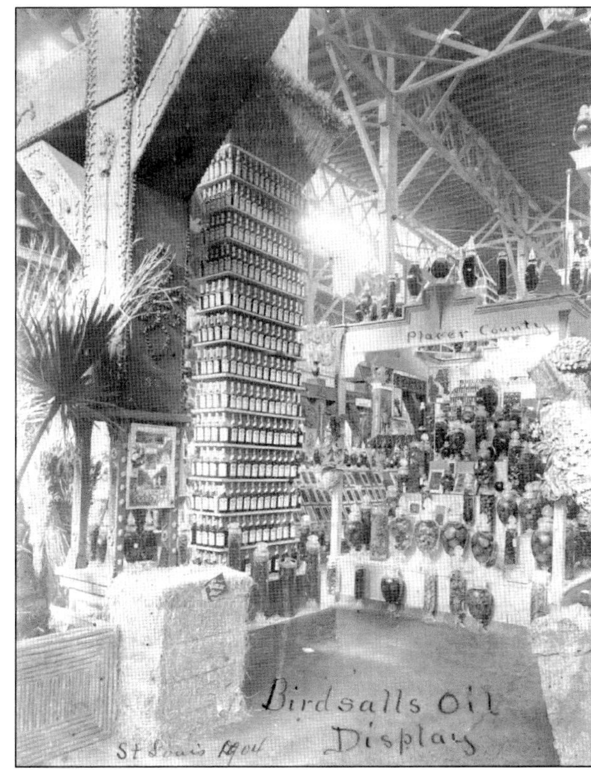

Birdsall Olive Oil. In 1904, the Birdsall Olive Oil Company used this display to advertise its oil and olives at the St. Louis Exposition, where the oil won first prize. As advertised, "Birdsall Olive Oil is now prescribed for throat, lung, liver, stomach, kidney, rheumatic and nervous troubles." The company's products were shipped all over the country. (PCM.)

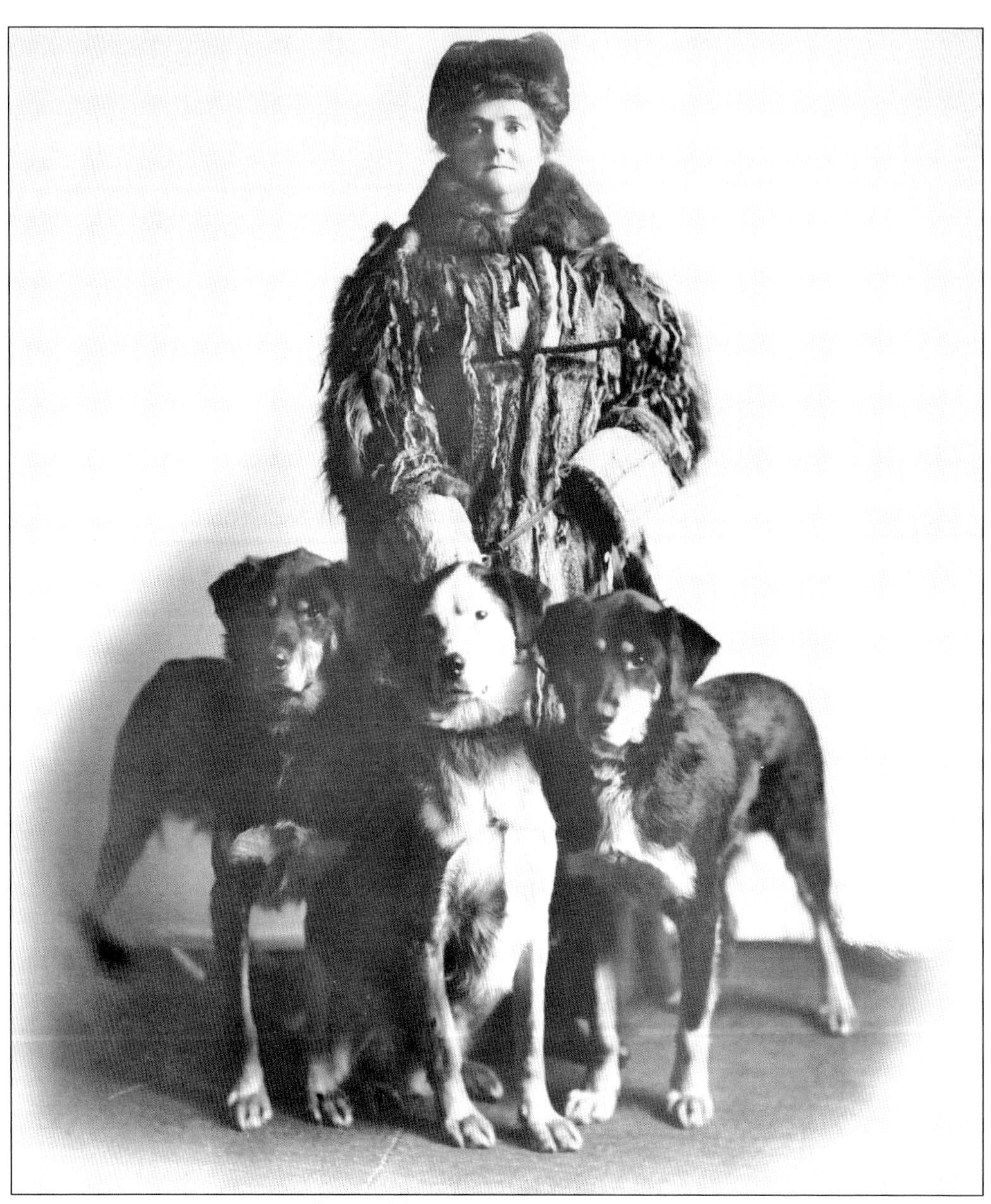

Esther Birdsall Darling. The wealthy Frederick and Esther Birdsall family divided their time between their Aeolia Heights ranch in Auburn and their mansion in Sacramento. Rather late in her life, their daughter Esther (named after her mother) married Charles Edward Darling, who ran a hardware and expedition outfitter company in Nome, Alaska. Esther Darling became fascinated by the sled dog teams used in Alaska for hauling. In 1908, she, along with her husband's partner, Scotty Allen, established the Nome Kennel Club and organized the first long-distance sled dog race. The Allen-Darling teams of dogs dominated the All Alaska Sweepstakes for years, with the mixed-breed dog Baldy in the lead. Beginning in 1913, Esther Darling wrote seven novels about the dogs, including the acclaimed *Baldy of Nome*. Esther received the French War Cross in 1917 for the heroic feats of Baldy's descendants in World War I. Esther Darling returned to Aeolia Heights, spending her last years in Auburn until her death in 1965. (ASL, Dr. Daniel Neuman Photograph Collection, P307-1088.)

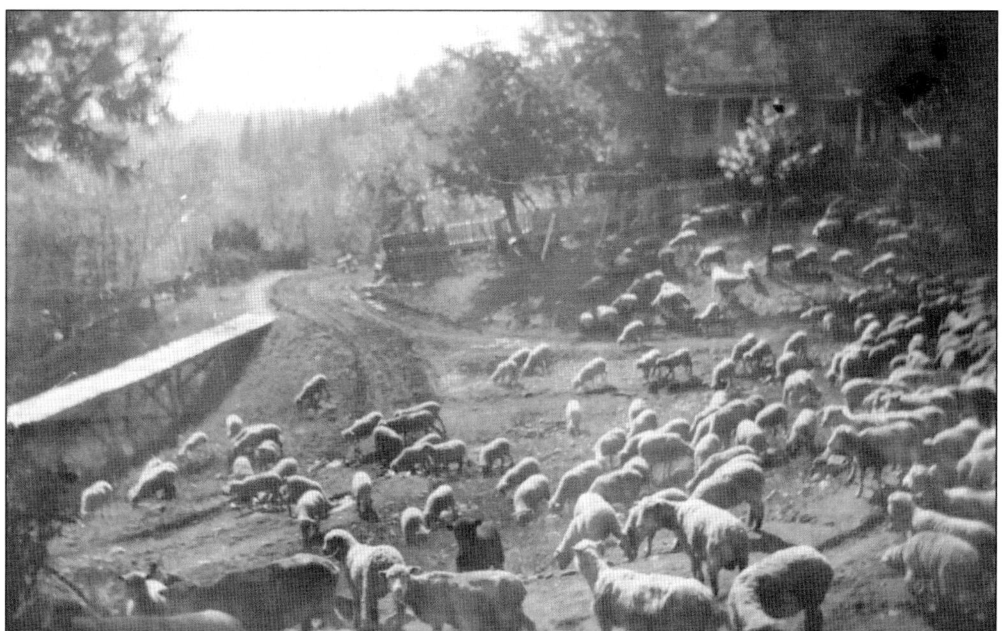

Sheep. Raising sheep (and cattle) was an important industry. George Bishop and John Long had more than 2,000 sheep at the former Traveler's Rest property in 1861. Typically, sheep were pastured at the "home" ranch in the winter, then herded through Auburn twice a year on their way to and from the mountain summer pastures. (PCM.)

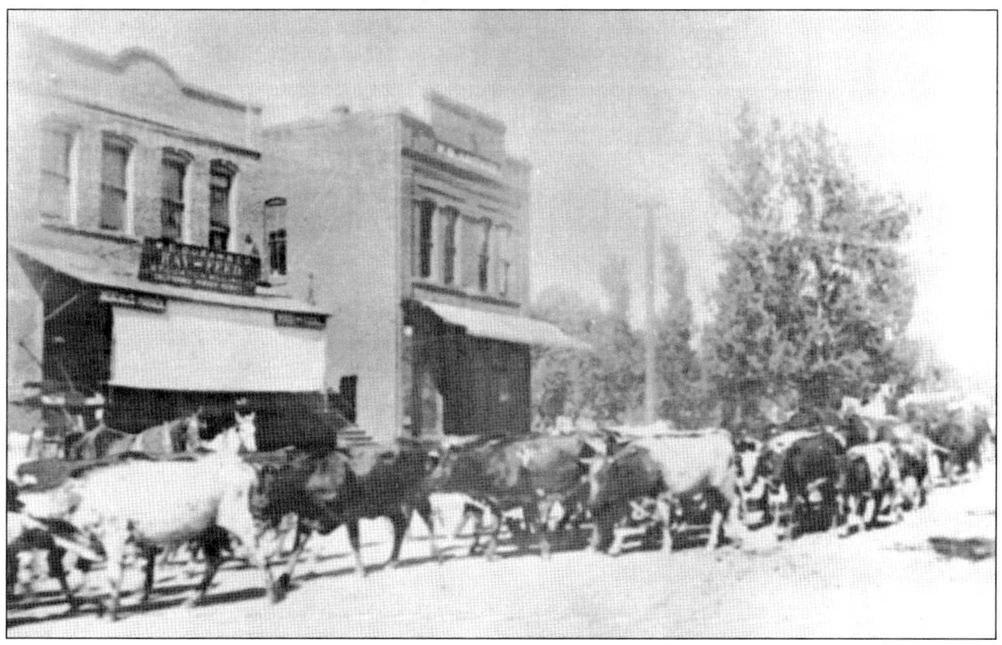

Cattle. When the argonauts first arrived, many pre–Gold Rush Californios were quick to turn their herds into a food source. The price of cattle went from $3 a head to $75 a head. George Bishop and John Long were the early stock raisers in Auburn, having more than 250 head of cattle in 1860. Seen in front of the still-standing Arthur building, this cattle drive is passing through Auburn on Lincoln Way. (AJS.)

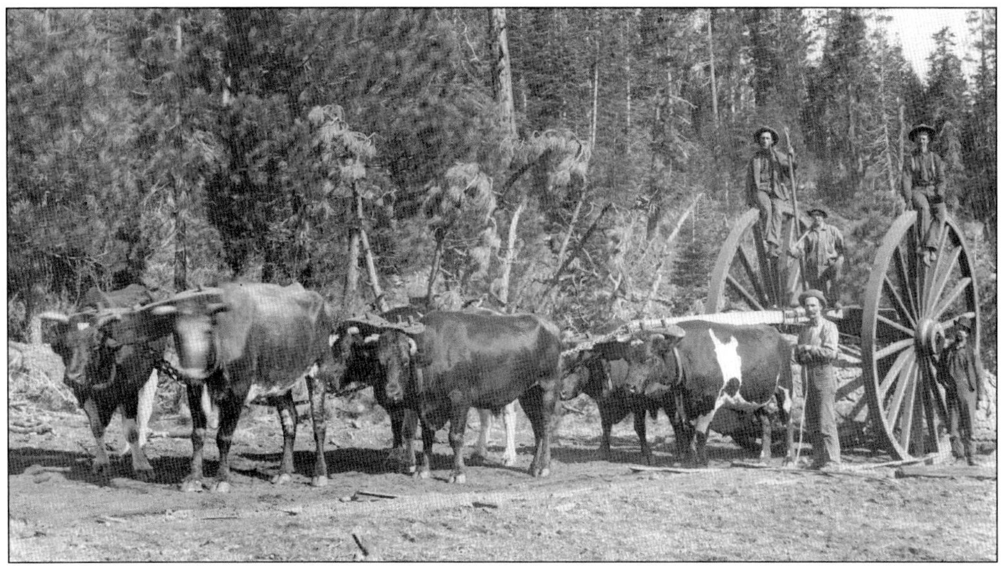

Logging. This unusual rig was used for hauling logs. The logging industry developed along with the mining industry. In the earliest days, from 1850 to 1860, lumber was needed for housing, mines, and the construction of mining flumes. From the 1860s to the 1870s, the railroad was a voracious consumer of wood products for ties, snow sheds, and fuel. In later years, lumber was used for general construction and to make shipping boxes for fruit. (PCM.)

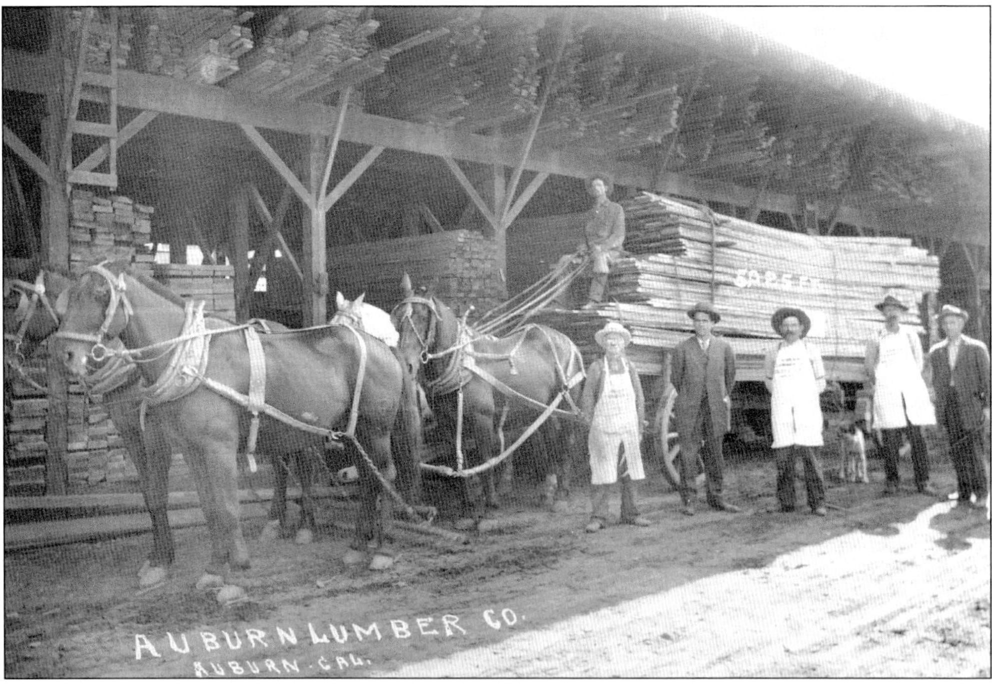

Putnam Planing Mill & Box Factory. Samuel Putnam established the mill in 1877. It was sold to the Towle brothers in 1883 and became part of the retail portion of their hugely successful lumber company. In 1900, it was sold to John Robie (their nephew) and Lathrop Huntley. It became the Auburn Lumber Company in 1902. Standing from left to right are John Robie, Edwin Robie, Andy Anderson, H. McCombs, and Lathrop Huntley; the man at the reins is unidentified. (PCM.)

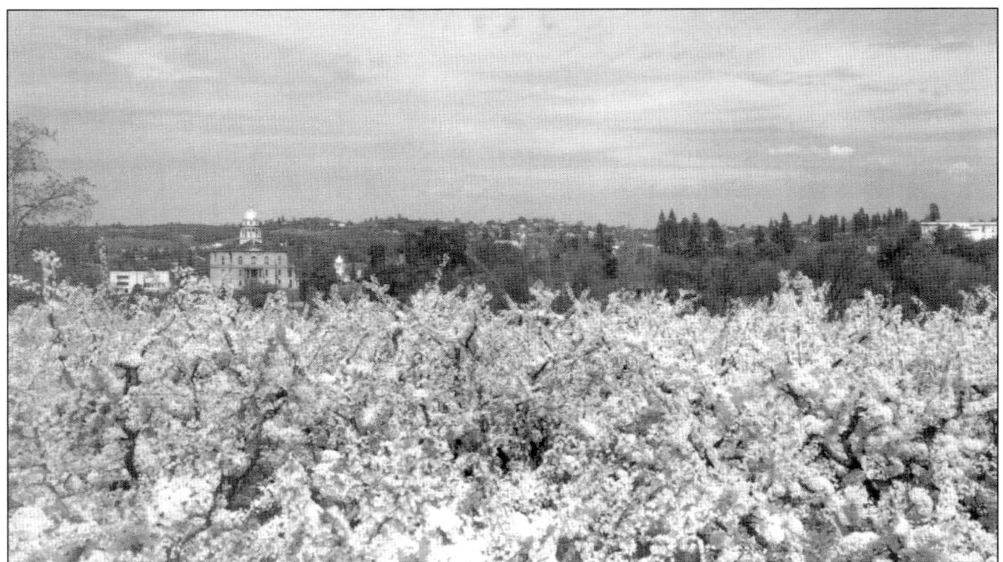

Blooming Orchard. The Placer County Courthouse is visible beyond this blooming orchard. This unusual perspective was taken from the racetrack area west of Auburn-Folsom Road. Beginning in the 1850s, this area was known as "China Garden," as it was one of two areas producing garden produce for the local Chinese community. (PCM.)

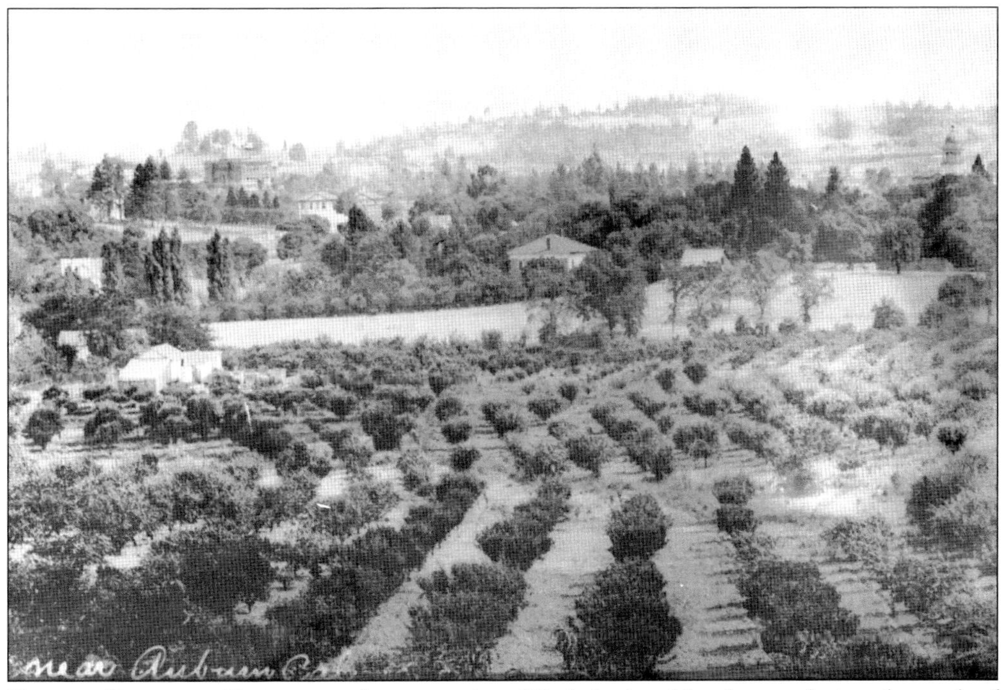

Collins Orchard. Fruit trees of every variety filled the local landscape during the peak of fruit production in the 1920s. This is the Collins family orchard on present-day Nevada Street. The Placer High School building is visible in the distance at left, and the dome of the county courthouse is seen at right. (PCM.)

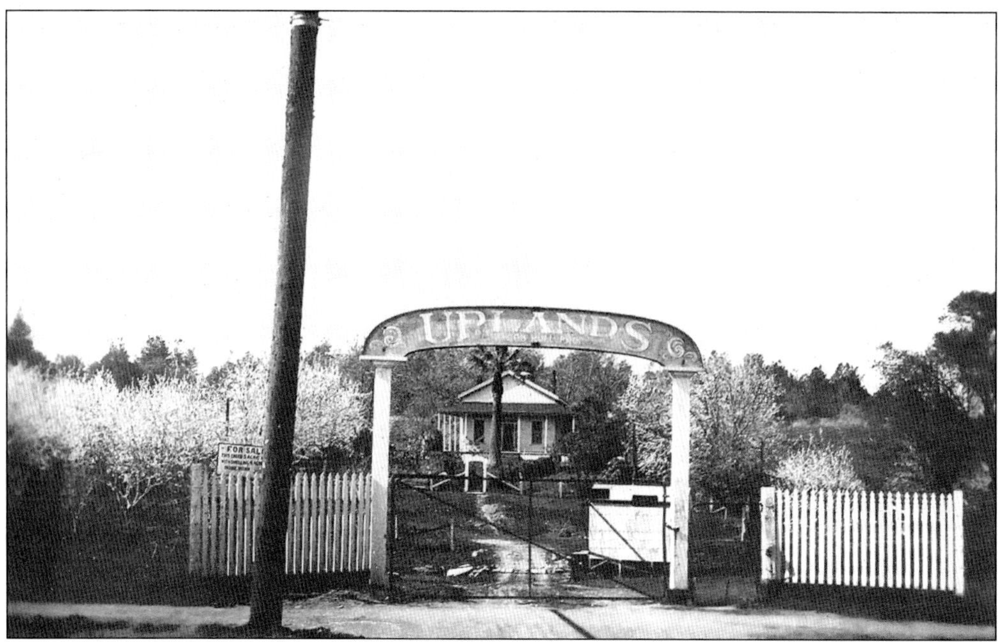

UPLANDS. Jacob Roll bought five acres at the corner of Auburn-Folsom Road and Sacramento Street in 1889. Like many property owners in town at that time, he planted an orchard. Roll was fortunate to have his own spring with crystal clear water to irrigate his land. That same spring water was used in his nearby Auburn Brewery, where he brewed superior lager. (GD.)

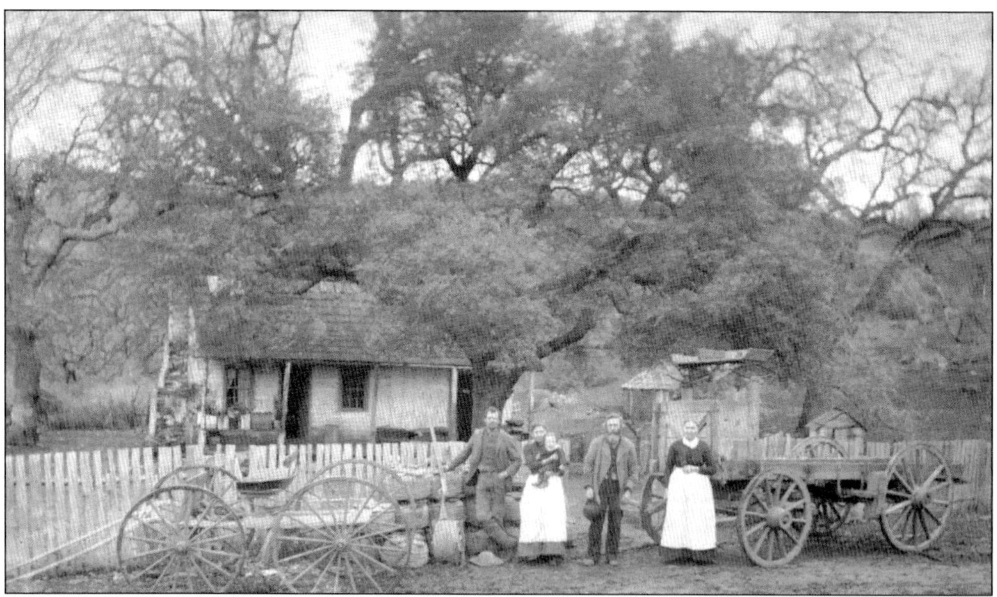

BABCOCK HOMESTEAD. Isaac Babcock, a forty-niner, started out farming and dairying in Sacramento on the flood-prone American River. As stated in a family diary, Babcock was tired of "living with a rowboat tied to the second-floor window," thus he moved his family and farming operation to this ranch at the present site of the Auburn Valley Golf Club in 1871. From left to right are Tiffin "Tip" Cannon; his wife, Ida Cannon, holding their daughter, Clara; and Ida's parents, Isaac and Evaline Babcock. (BL.)

Six

Moving Goods and People

As the miners flooded into the area, the need for provisions quickly followed. Supplies from all over the world arrived, first by ship in San Francisco, then to the Embarcadero near Sutter's Fort. The Sacramento-to-Auburn road was a main artery for freight coming into the gold region. From Auburn, supplies were transferred to mule trains or men's backs to traverse the steep canyons along the river.

The winter of 1848–1849 was pivotal for the growth of Auburn. Miners who had arrived with little in the way of supplies found themselves unprepared for the harsh, wet winter. Robert Gordon later wrote of his time down at the river in 1849: "The condition of many along this river is truly pitiable, their light summer tents have been but a very inadequate shelter from the incessant and drenching rains." Miners flocked to the nearest settlements to spend the winter. As a transit hub, Auburn already had some rudimentary hotels in place, along with mercantile shops, gambling halls, and saloons. By the end of that winter, Auburn had been well established as a trading center and thriving social center.

The amount of freight that came through Auburn is barely conceivable. On October 17, 1860, the *Placer Herald* reported, "[On] Thursday, seventy one teams, carrying 267 tons of freight, passed through town on the Auburn Ravine Turnpike."

Without government funding, citizens turned to private enterprise to build toll roads and bridges. By 1859, a half dozen toll roads had been built to facilitate freighting in the Auburn area.

Beyond serving as a hub for provisions and gold shipments, Auburn was a center for passenger travel. By 1852, there were eight stage lines running to and from Auburn. In 1854, the *Placer Herald* reported 120 passengers a day arriving from Sacramento.

The arrival of the transcontinental railroad in Auburn in May 1865 did little to change the dynamics of trade and supply to the remote mountain regions. Instead of large freight wagons arriving from Sacramento carrying goods destined for the far-flung mining camps, the iron horse now brought the goods to Auburn for transshipment.

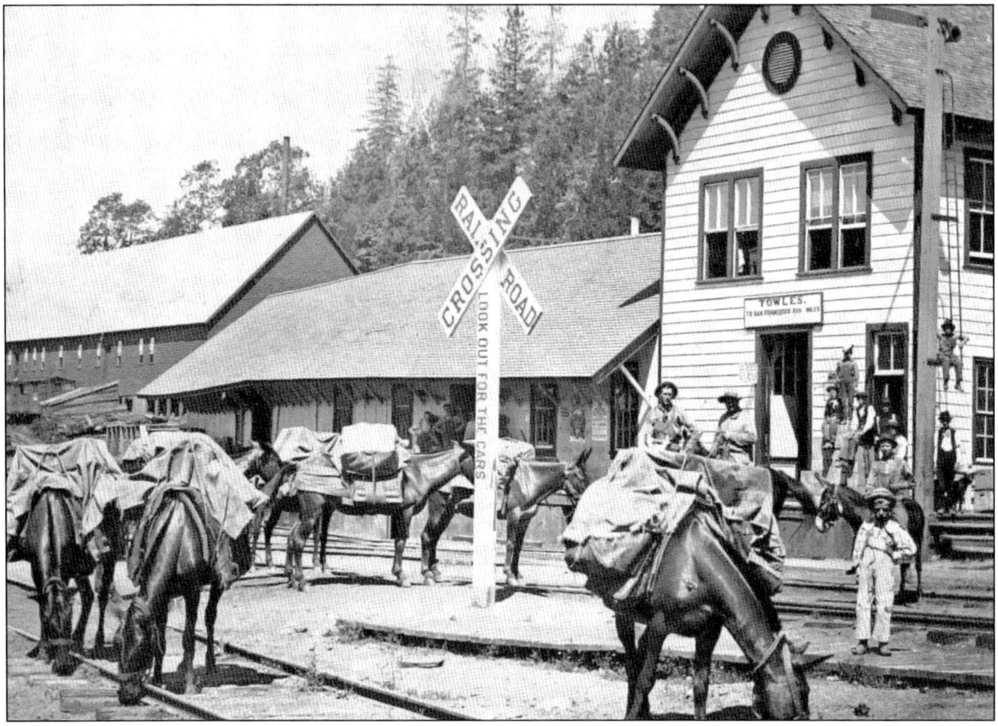

Pack Mule Train. Miners needed food, liquor, clothing, bedding, tools, medicine, and hardware, and every conceivable item needed to be transported. Mexican mules were considered far superior to mules arriving from the eastern states. The average mule train out of Auburn consisted of 40–50 mules with two muleteers. Smaller mule trains, such as this one at Towles, would venture to the more remote camps. (AJS.)

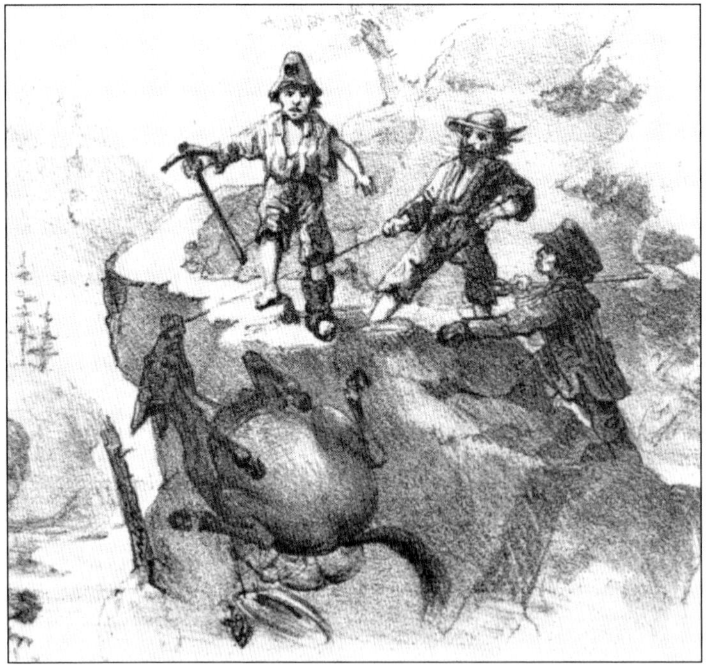

Mules. Packing was dangerous on the steep trails of the canyons. In a report to the *Daily Alta California*, a traveler stated, "During the day we passed along the steep and craggy side of mountains, where a single misstep would be a rapid journey to eternity. A great many mules and horses were lost here: their carcasses, with sometimes the pack, could be seen hundreds of feet below." (LOC.)

Henry James Monk. Hank Monk was a legendary stagecoach driver. He was one of the drivers to run the Auburn-to-Sacramento route in 1852. He later took over the Sacramento-to-Placerville route. He was called "Knight of the Lash" and "King of the Coachman." Mark Twain immortalized Monk in his novel *Roughing It*. (AJS.)

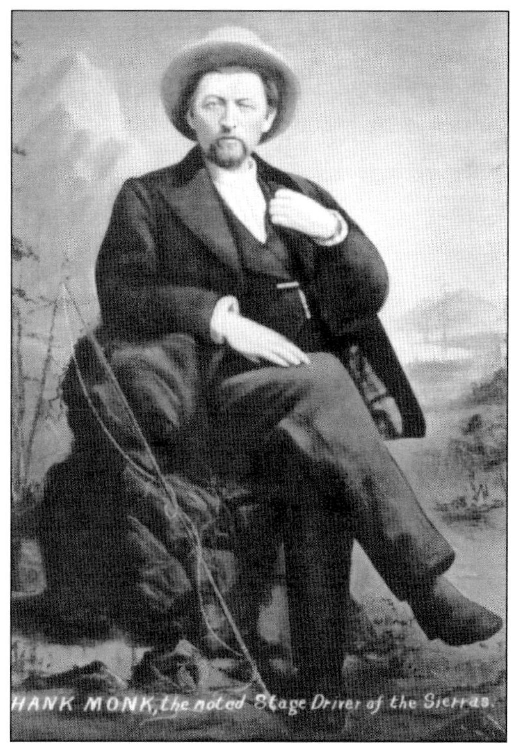

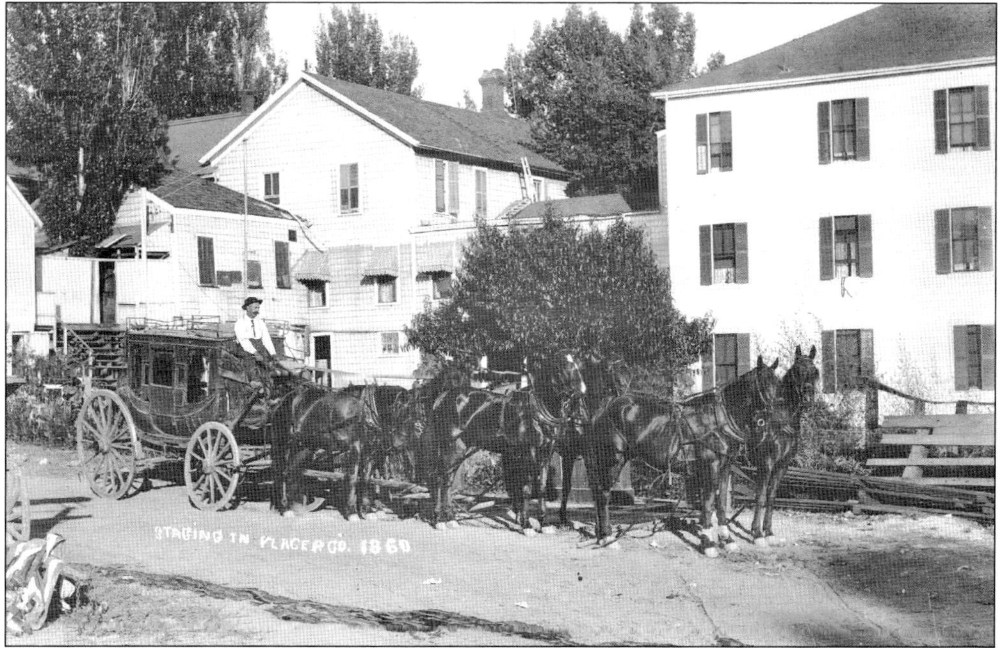

Stagecoach. Stagecoaches were the main mode of transportation in Auburn's early days. From Auburn, stages went to the Foresthill Divide towns, Illinoistown, Grass Valley, Georgetown, Sacramento, and Marysville. Even after the railroad's arrival in 1865, stagecoaches still served the mountain towns until the early 1920s. This is driver John McAnnich and his team behind Auburn's Freeman Hotel. (PCM.)

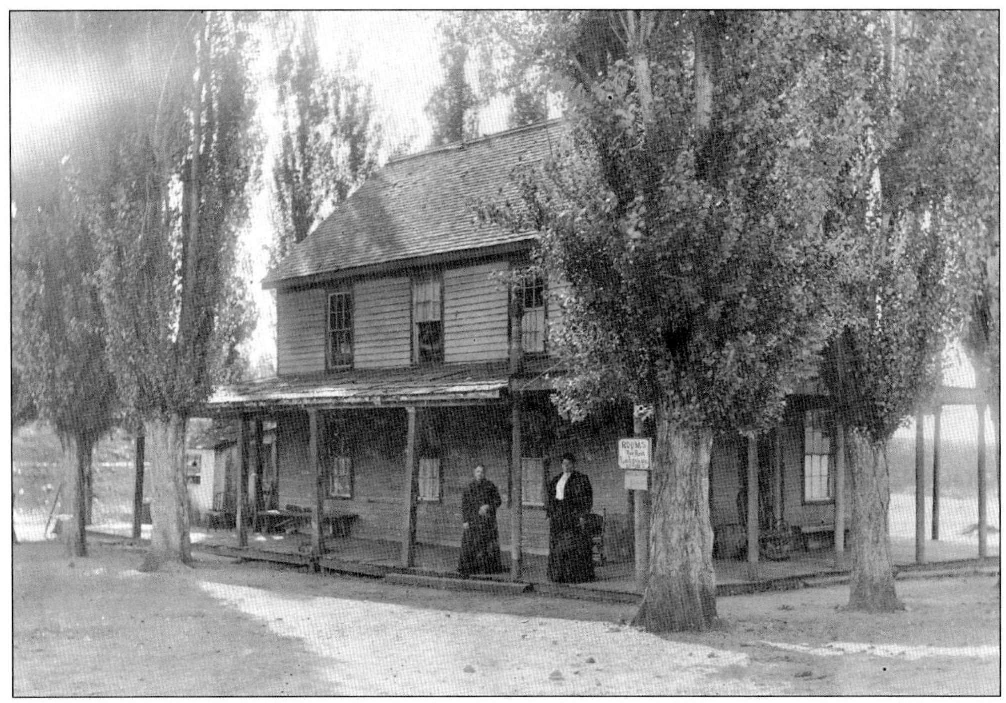

Way Station. This hotel just south of Auburn in nearby Long Valley is representative of the many stops along the route from Sacramento to Auburn. On his way from Sacramento City to Auburn in 1849, John Markle reported passing the Blue Tent, the Halfway House, the Oregon Tent, and the Miner's Hotel. From tents and rough cabins, these way stations grew to comfortable, well-supplied hotels. (PCM.)

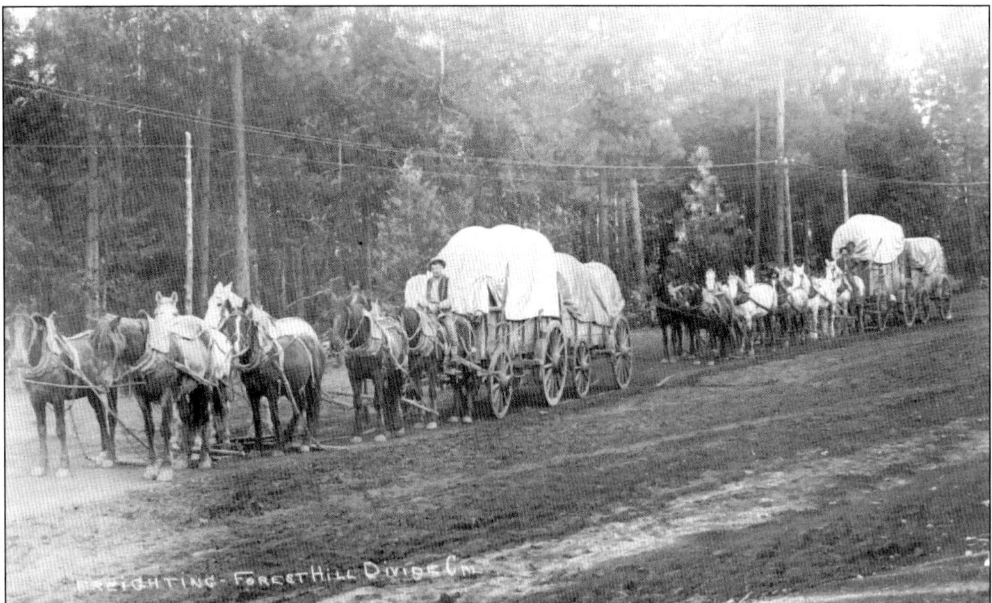

Jim Sheridan. Based in Auburn, well-known local teamster Jim Sheridan made regular runs to the Foresthill area. These double wagons drawn by teams of eight horses are equivalent to the modern-day semi truck in that they could carry huge amounts of freight. (AJS.)

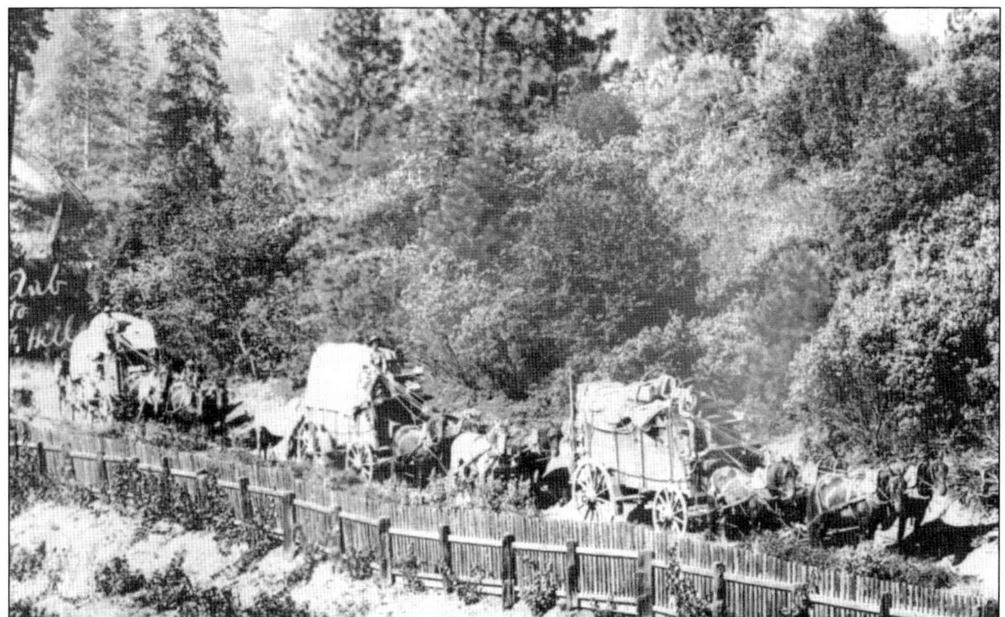

AUBURN-TO-FORESTHILL ROAD. Massive amounts of freight and passengers traveled this road. It has been estimated that of all the goods arriving at the port in Sacramento in the 1850s and 1860s, three-quarters were destined for the mining camps of the American River watershed. According to William Bickham, who wrote home in 1850, "The road is thronged with miners and teams, some going to the mines, some returning to the city for provisions." (PCM.)

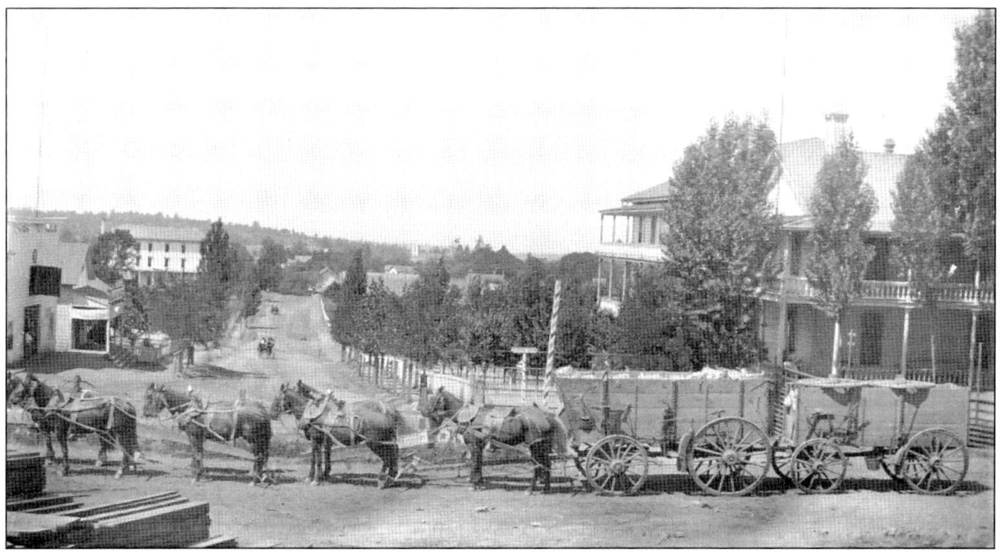

LIME WAGONS. There were several productive lime quarries just outside Auburn, including one discovered by John Gwynn in 1853. Lime was an important natural resource. It was used in construction, as an aggregate for roadbeds, and to make cement. Gwynn's quarry, later run by his son-in-law Henry Holmes, produced most of the lime used in Northern California. These wagons filled with lime are parked in front of the Freeman Hotel. (HF.)

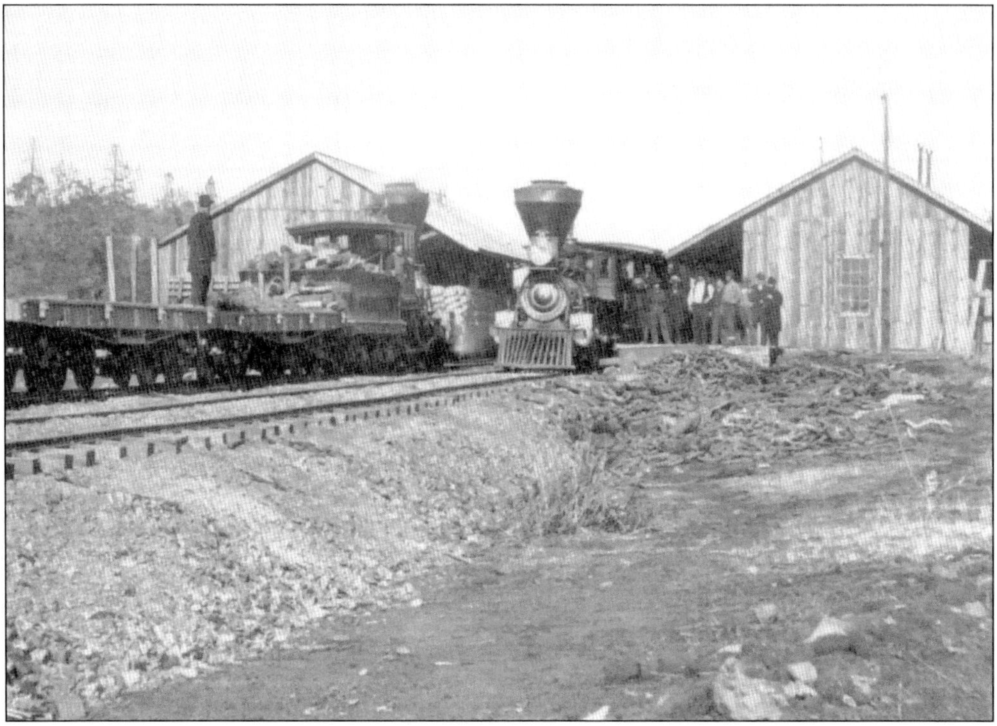

TRANSCONTINENTAL RAILROAD. The Central Pacific Railroad reached Auburn in May 1865. Alfred Hart took this photograph in 1865 or 1866. While this was a major improvement in the way goods moved north from Sacramento, Auburn remained the supply center for the mountain mining camps. For many years, fruit from El Dorado County was also shipped through the Auburn station. (AJS.)

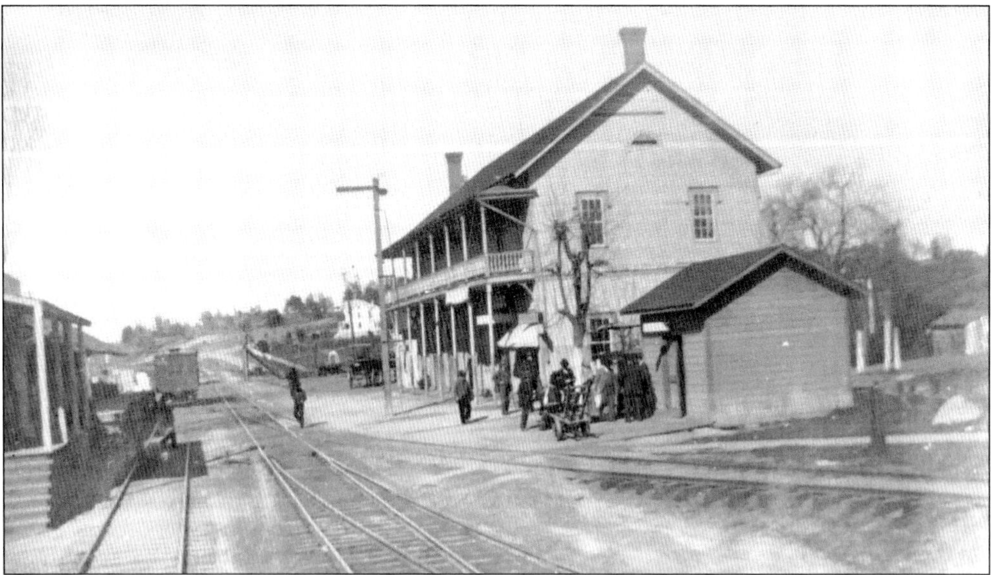

DEPOT. This is the second depot building in Auburn. Run by Thomas Curley and James Mahon, it contained the Depot Saloon, the ticket office, and the telegraph office. The second floor held a dining room with a large hall used for balls and other social events. (PCM.)

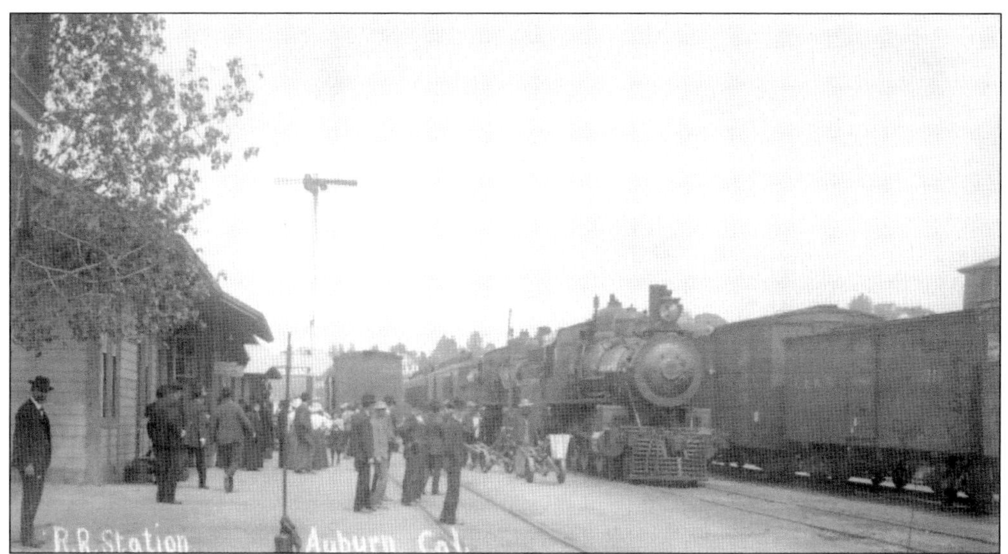

Railroad Station. The many sidings and crowds of people shown in this image illustrate the importance of rail traffic through Auburn. From its beginning in 1865 until the advent of the automobile, the railroad was the major mode of transportation for passengers and freight. At one time, the Auburn station was claimed to be the busiest depot in the Northstate region. (PCM.)

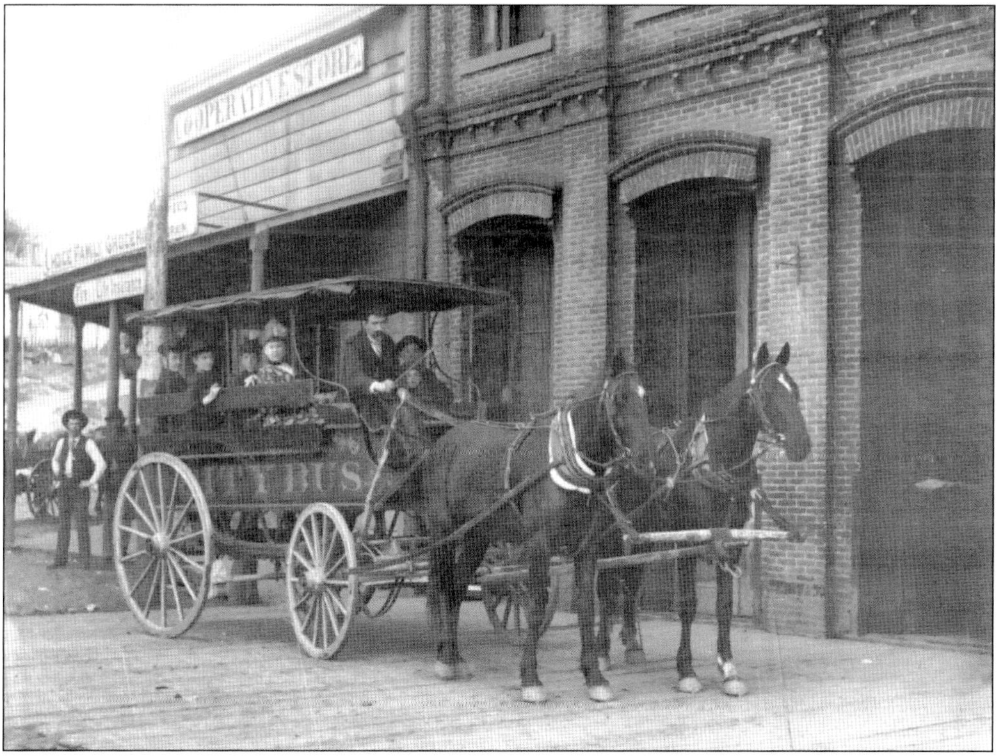

City Bus. This city bus provided citizens and visitors with transportation from the downtown train depot to Old Town beginning with the railroad's arrival in 1865. This bus is parked in front of the American Hotel. Note the hotel's planked entryway that is juxtaposed with the unpaved street. (PCM.)

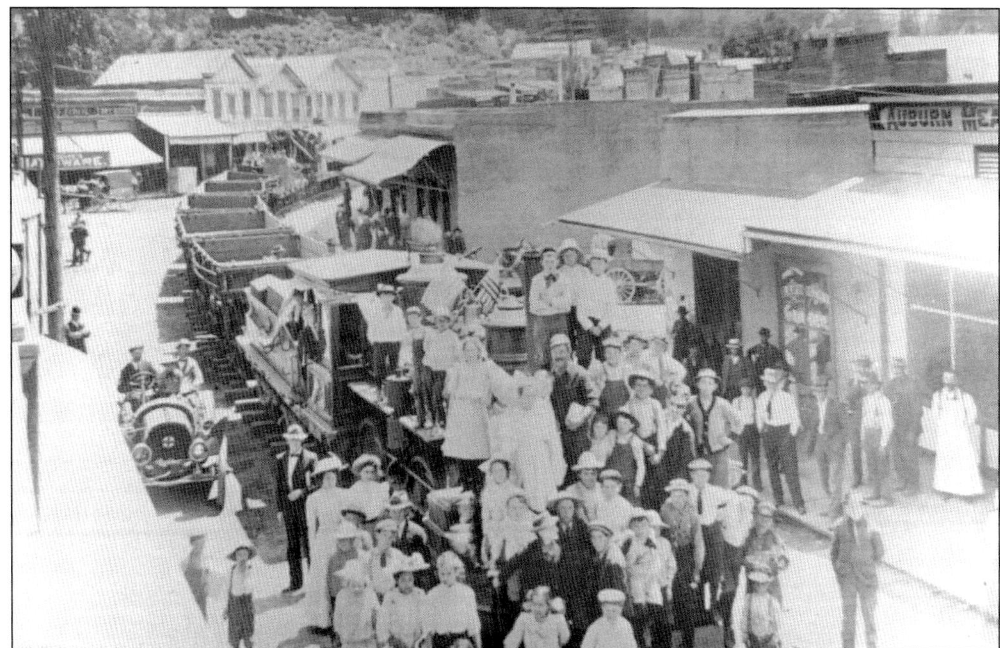

DOUBLE TRACKING. To lay a crucial second track over the Sierra Nevada mountain range, the railroad company needed to route its construction train right through the heart of Old Town, much to the delight of the schoolchildren shown here catching a ride. (PCM.)

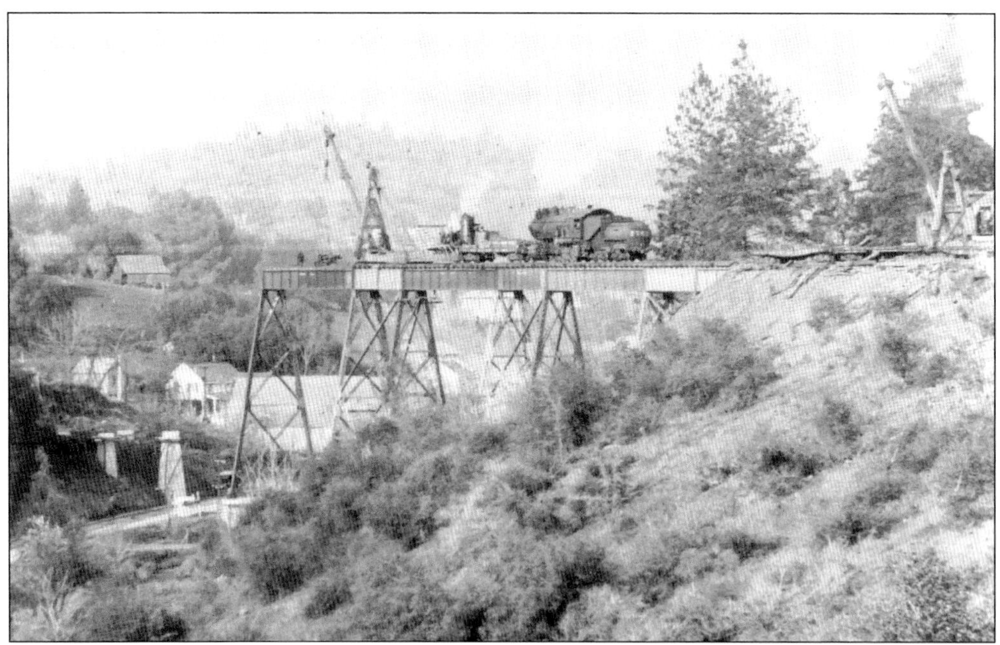

TRESTLE. Double tracking between Rocklin and Colfax began in 1909 and was completed in 1912. This half-completed railroad trestle at the entrance to Auburn was part of the effort to improve east-west traffic over the Sierra Nevada. Now modernized, this is the same trestle that stands today. (AJS.)

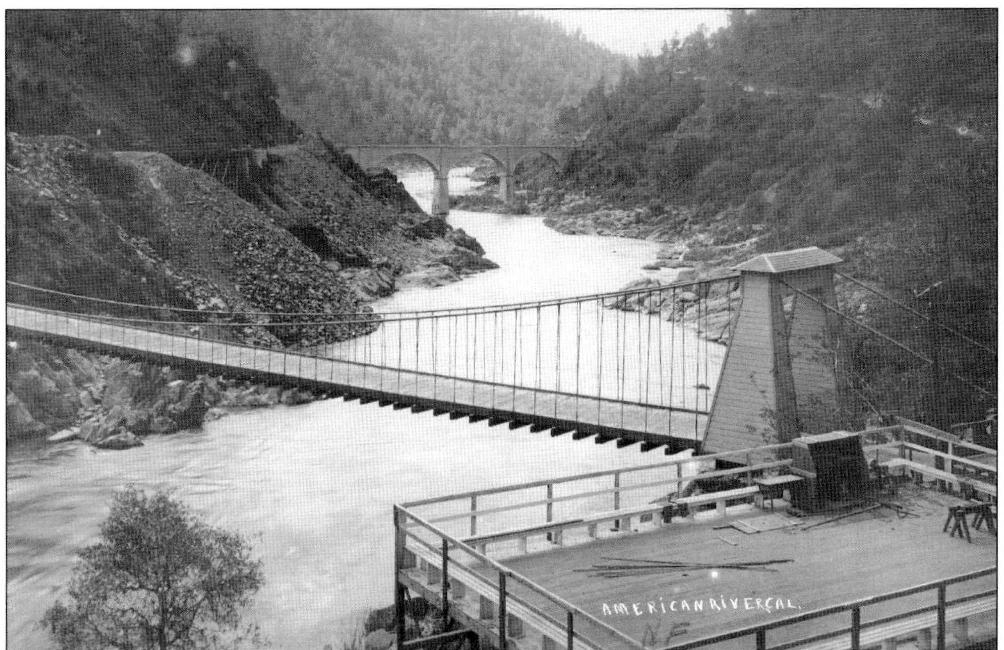

Lyons Bridge. Charles Lyons and John Mollett built this suspension bridge across the North Fork of the American River in 1865. Auburn served as the transit hub for mining camps on both sides of the river. Mountain Quarries Bridge, also known as "No Hands Bridge" by locals, is visible downstream. (PCM.)

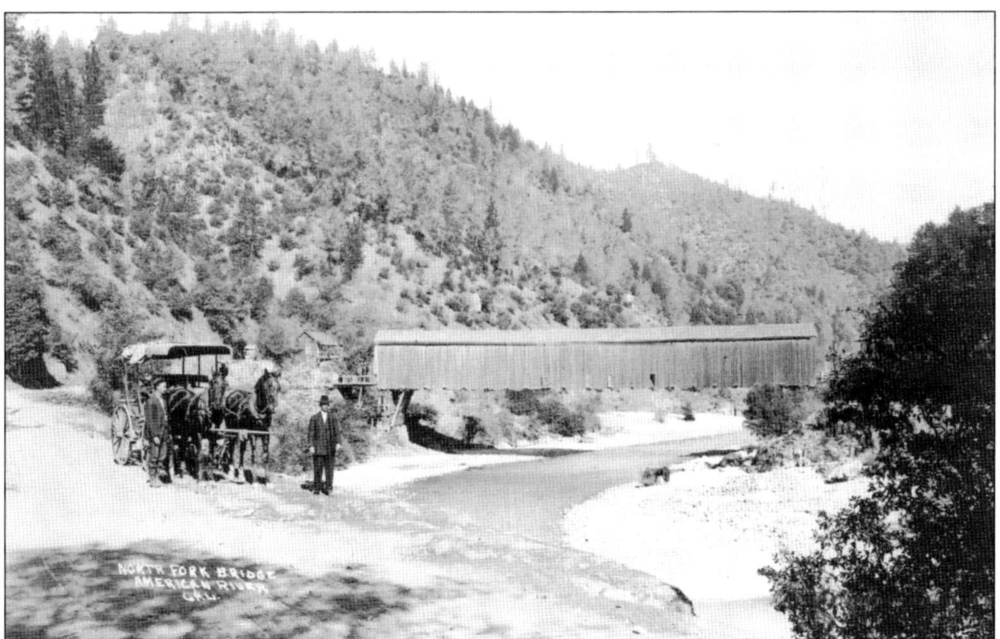

North Fork Bridge. This unusual covered bridge over the North Fork of the American River was constructed in 1875. It was a privately built toll bridge. In today's dollars, tolls were typically $10 per horse and rider or $30 per horse and wagon. To the left is the Auburn and Foresthill Stage. (PCM.)

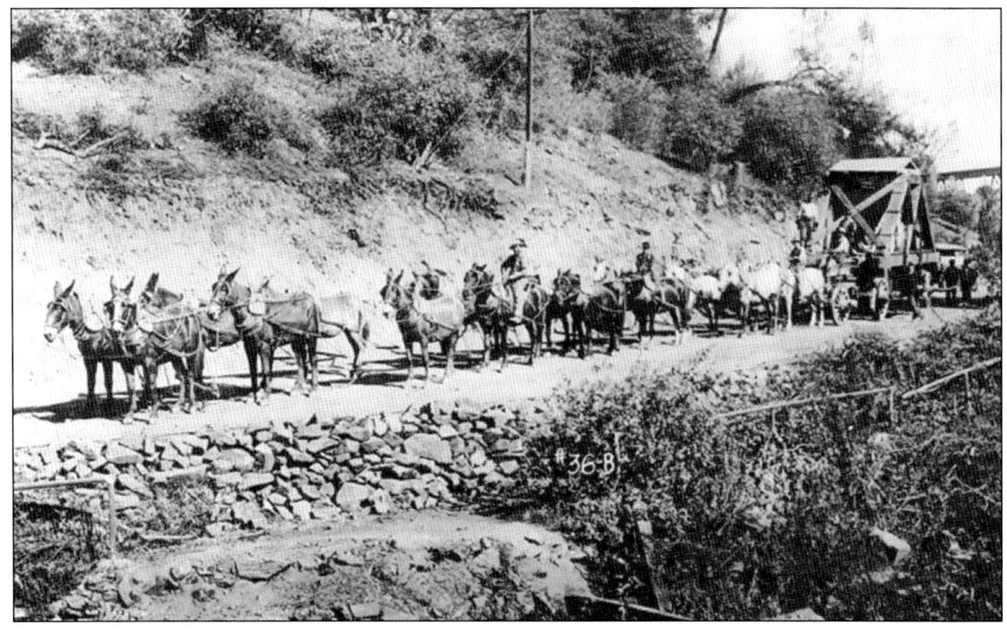

Auburn-to-Ophir Road. These photographs of the road along the Auburn Ravine, about a half mile below Auburn headed toward Ophir, show the approximate location of the first gold strike by Claude Chana in 1848. Though train travel was available as early as 1865, the horse and buggy remained the mainstay of personal transportation for many years. Hauling huge pieces of machinery via a mule team also lasted until well into the early 1920s. (Both, PCM.)

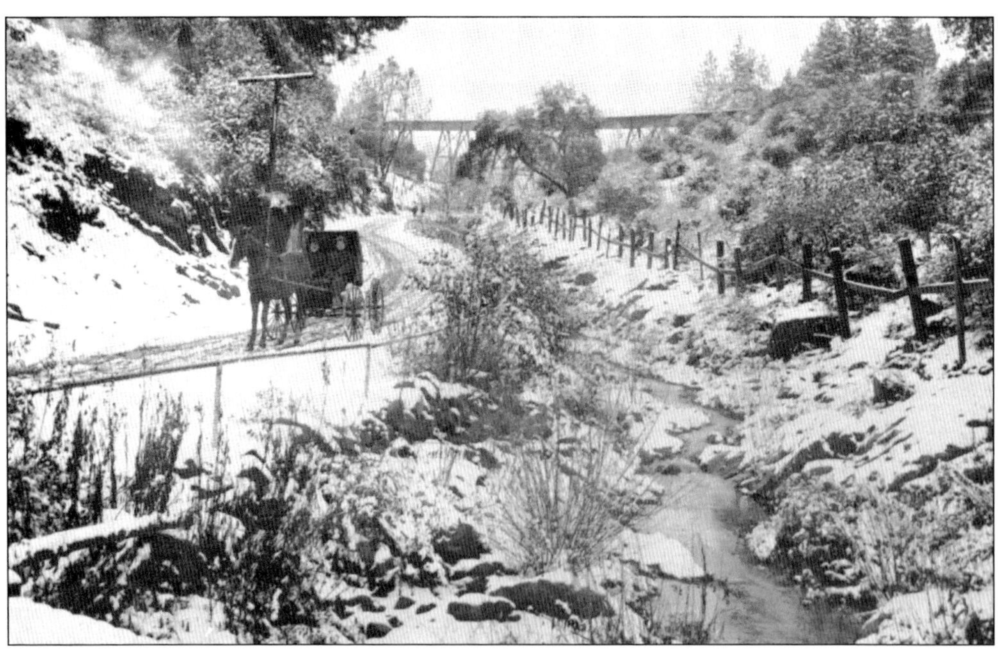

Seven

BUSINESS

Samuel Brannan, California's first millionaire, was the first to start "mining the miners." He rounded up all the picks, shovels, and buckets he could before announcing the discovery of gold in Coloma on the streets of San Francisco. Over a 70-day period in 1848, his store at Sutter's Fort sold $36,000 in equipment, an astounding $950,000 in today's dollars.

Very few of the gold seekers came to California with any thought of carrying on their past professions as lawyers, store clerks, or farmers. Most thought they would spend a few weeks or months acquiring their pile and return home wealthy men. This was called "the Bonanza mentality."

Hudson House arrived in Auburn, still called Wood's Dry Diggings, in the summer of 1849. He was accompanied by his manservant Elias and eight other men, including Samuel Holladay. Holladay and House set to work mining, but as Holladay recalled of House, "Work was not his strong suit." Like many argonauts, House was unprepared for the backbreaking physical labor of mining. He went into merchandising and opened one of the first trading posts in Auburn. Holladay also reported that another one of his companions, a Mr. Elliard, "went to dealing Monte—easier and more remunerative than mining."

Forty-niner Charles F. Reed, who was in Auburn at the same time as House, described the store he bought provisions from as "made of pine poles, covered with blue drilling." He bought $180 worth of supplies on credit and returned that same evening to repay his debt with enough gold dust left to buy a round for the house.

Most miners arrived with little or no supplies. As Edward Tuttle wrote home, "I was afoot with a roll of blankets on my back, a little grub, a tin can to make coffee and a fry pan." The miners needed everything, and some farsighted early arrivals realized they could capitalize on fulfilling those needs. When he was in Auburn, Isaac Annis recalled buying picks and shovels from miners leaving the area for $2 each and reselling them to newcomers for $10–$15 apiece.

Over time, many a disheartened miner returned to his former occupation, and the town grew more sophisticated in its business houses and hotels.

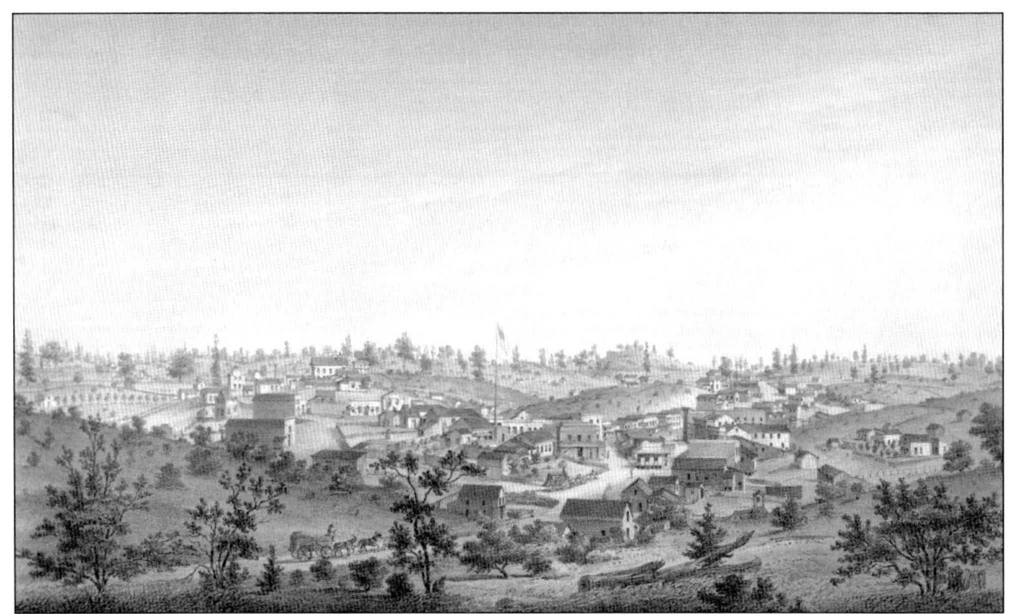

Express Companies. Wells Fargo & Company, Adams Express Company, and Gregory's Express were among the first express companies in Auburn. The Wells Fargo office was located near the flagpole in the heart of Old Town Auburn, as shown in this 1857 lithograph. The safe transfer of gold was a major problem for the early miners. Express companies like Wells Fargo were quick to fill the void. (JK.)

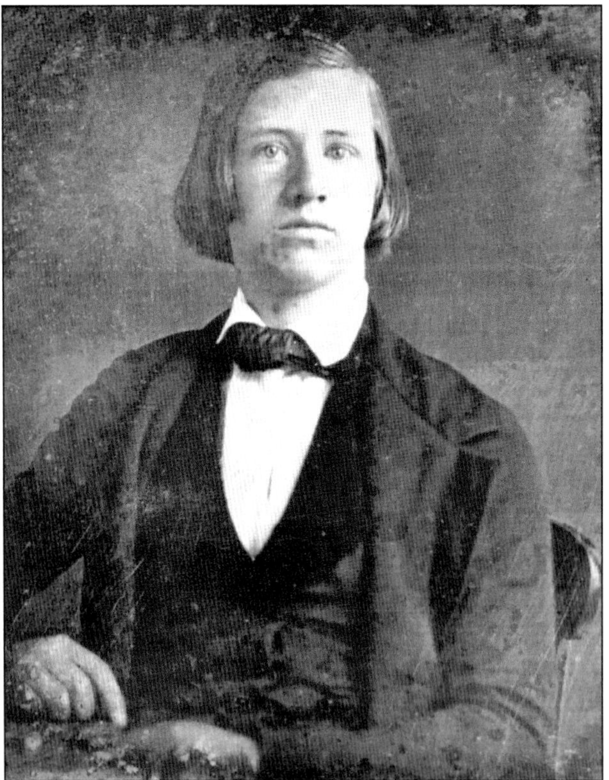

John Quincy Jackson. At age 23, Jackson was Auburn's agent for Wells Fargo. He presided over the Auburn office during the bank panic of 1855 with the help of his "friend, counselor, and safeguard," a 120-pound mastiff named Jack. He was able to satisfy the local depositors and even send surplus gold to San Francisco. He also wrote home to his father that managing the crisis was "certainly the proudest time in my life." (WFC.)

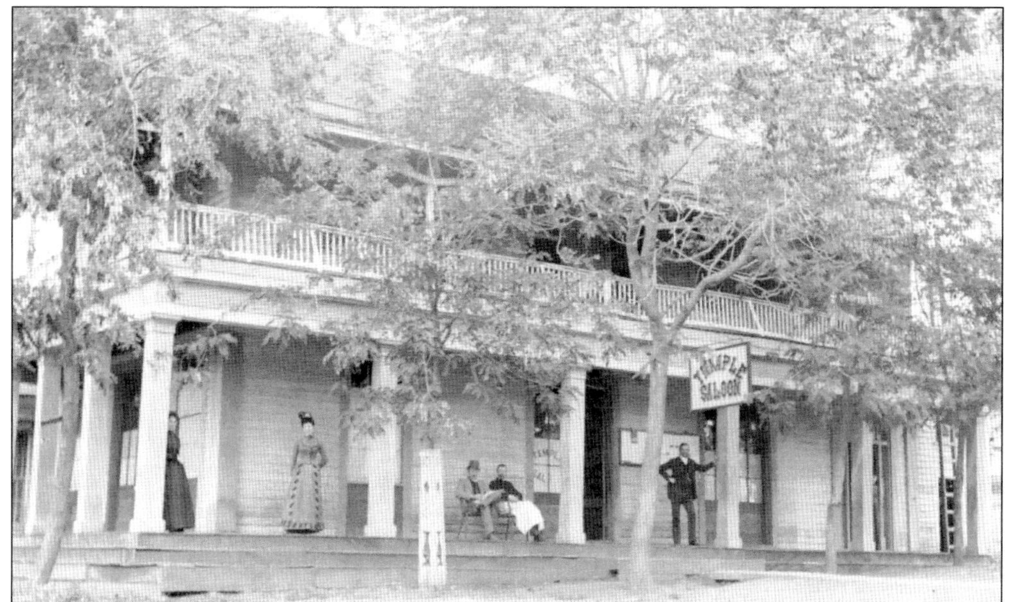

Temple Saloon. Hiram R. Hawkins and Milton Love built their first saloon in 1853. Love was the town constable and a deputy sheriff. Hawkins would later be appointed US consul to Peru. The two sold the first Temple Saloon just months before the great fire of 1855. After the fire, William Duncan purchased the land and rebuilt the saloon. The second story, used for professional offices, was added in 1869. It was located near the present-day Maple Street overpass. (PCM.)

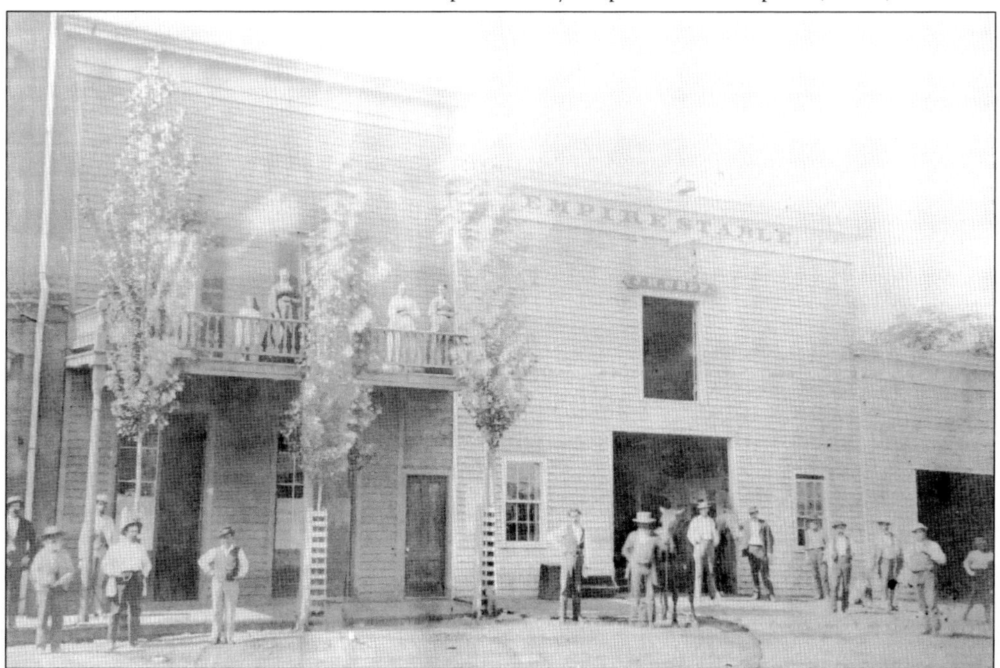

Livery Stable. The Empire Livery Stable was established in Old Town before 1852. It burned in 1855 but was rebuilt by George Stevens in 1856. Jacob Neff, a successful miner, owned the stable from 1871 to 1873. After 1875, the Crosby family ran the livery stable. They would rebuild again after the 1905 fire. This building currently houses an artists' cooperative gallery in Old Town. (AJS.)

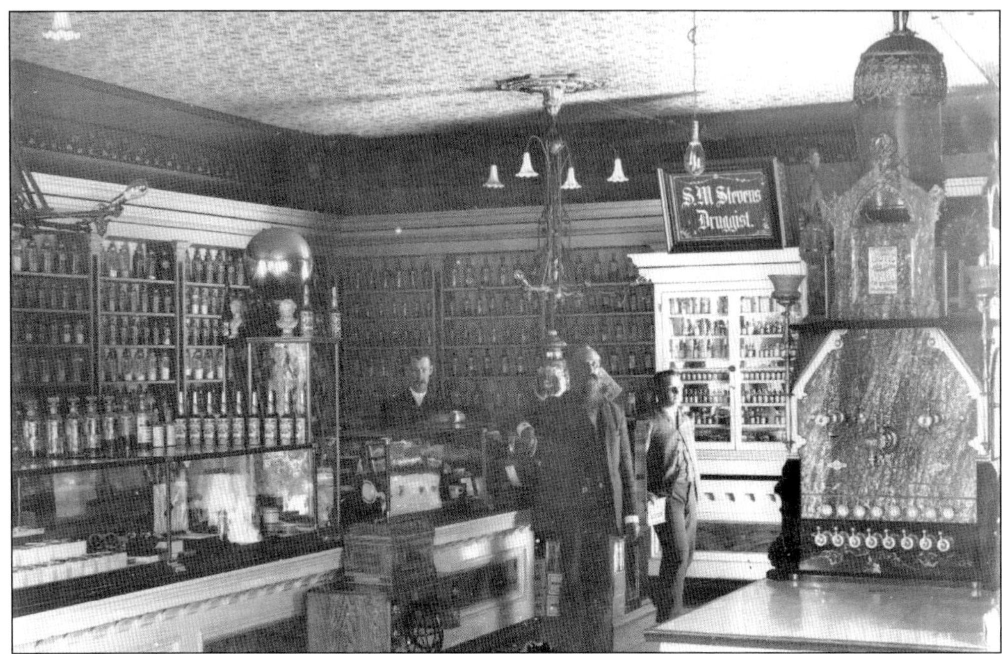

Drugstore. Solon Stevens, pictured at center, came to California in 1855. He opened his first store in 1870. His drugstore offered a myriad of items in addition to the Western Union Telegraph office that he managed for 30 years. The elaborate machine at right is an Arctic Soda Apparatus. His son Fred took over the drugstore, which stayed in business until 1939. (PCM.)

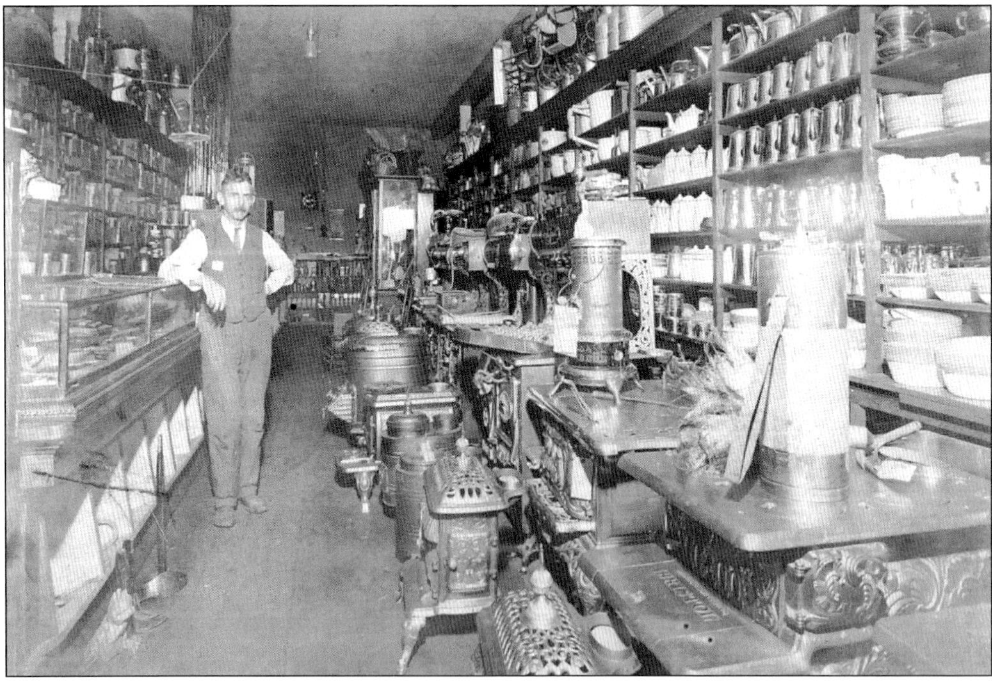

Hancock's Hardware Store. A typical hardware store of this era carried a huge variety of everyday necessities. Looking for a place to bring his family and start a business, Robert Hancock toured a good part of Northern California on his bicycle before opening his first store in Auburn in 1897. (HF.)

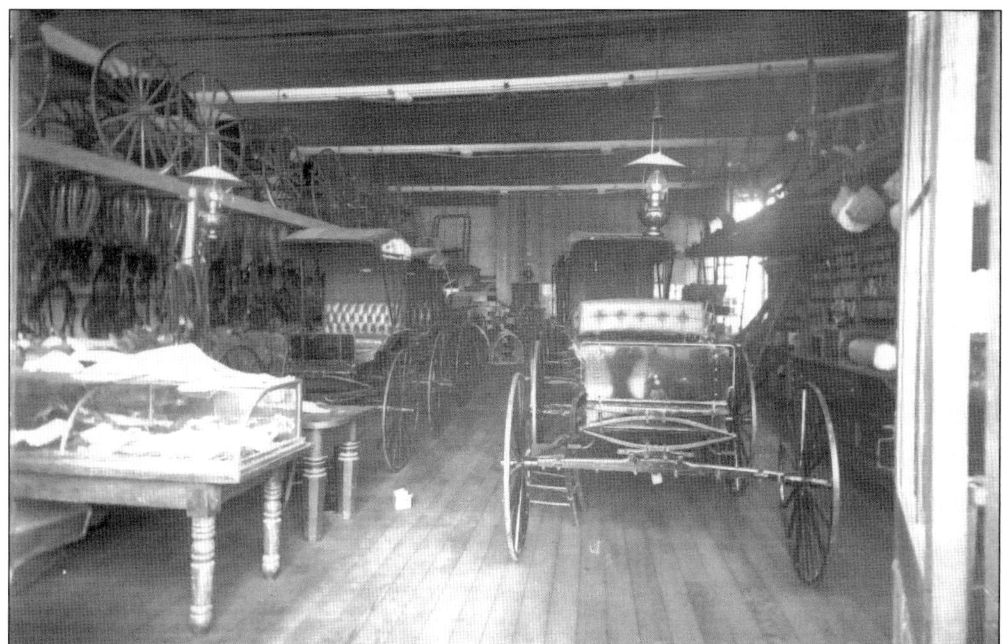

ALLEN'S CARRIAGE SHOP. Auburn boasted many fine carriage makers. Robert Mellon was in business in 1859, and Moses Predom was active in the 1870s and 1880s. Other carriage makers included White and Hinkle in the 1880s and George Bisbee and Allen & Sandhofer in the 1890s. In 1881, White and Hinkle built a stylish phaeton for Frederick Birdsall at a cost of $600, which would be about $15,000 in today's dollars. (AJS.)

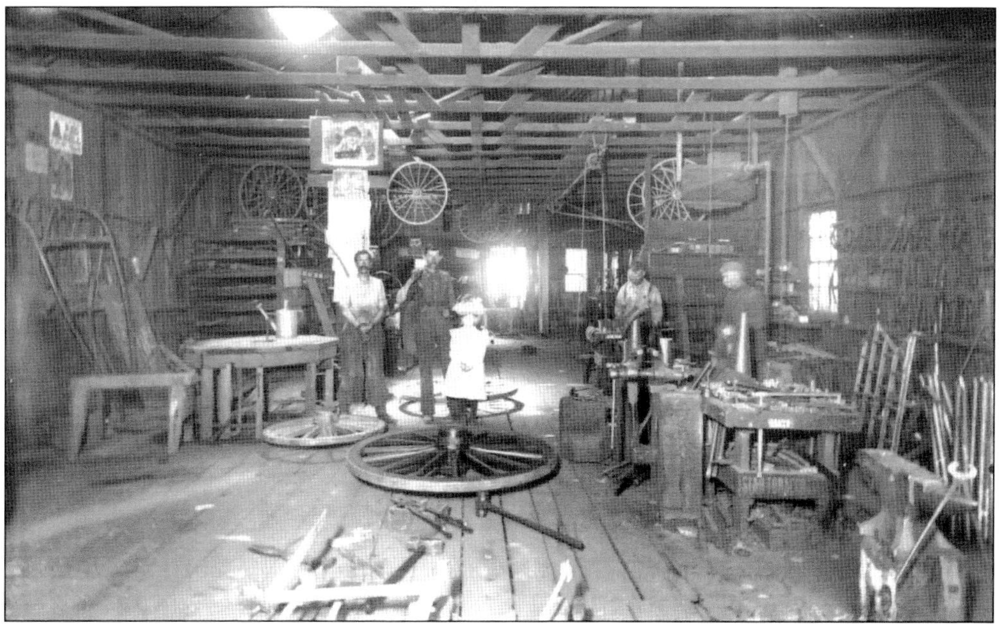

WHEELWRIGHT SHOP. Wheelwrights were critical to the function of the transportation system. Carriages, freight wagons, and farm wagons were all dependent on the skill of the wheelwright to stay up and running. An early wheelwright in town was Joseph Stocking, who conducted his business from a "round tent" in 1854. (AJS.)

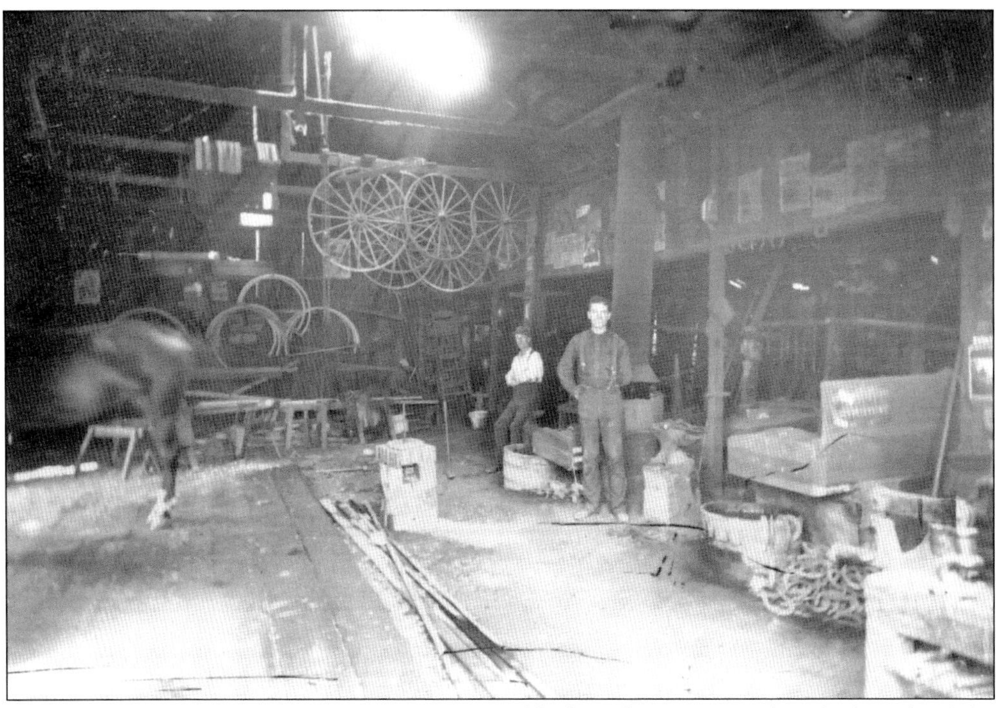

Merrow's Blacksmith Shop. Today, the term *blacksmith* is associated with the job of the farrier, or horseshoer. In the early days, though, a blacksmith was essential to the community for building and repairing most types of metalwork. Here, Herb Merrow is shown seated; the other man pictured with him is unidentified. Merrow's business was located on the corner of Main and Placer Streets. (AJS.)

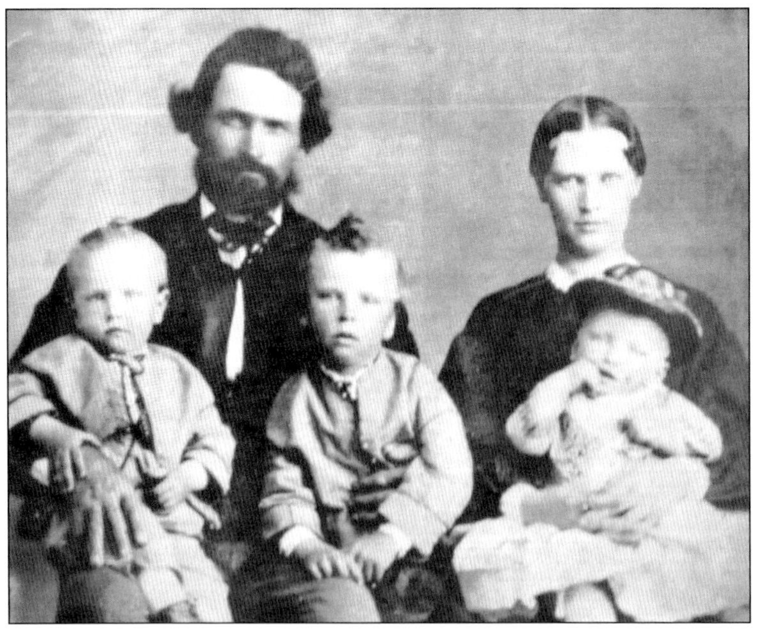

John Bisbee Family. Like many before him, John Bisbee first tried his hand at mining, but he returned to his trade as a blacksmith and carriage maker. Vernon McCann, in whose honor the prestigious McCann award is presented yearly for service to the community, was the grandson of John Bisbee. (PCM.)

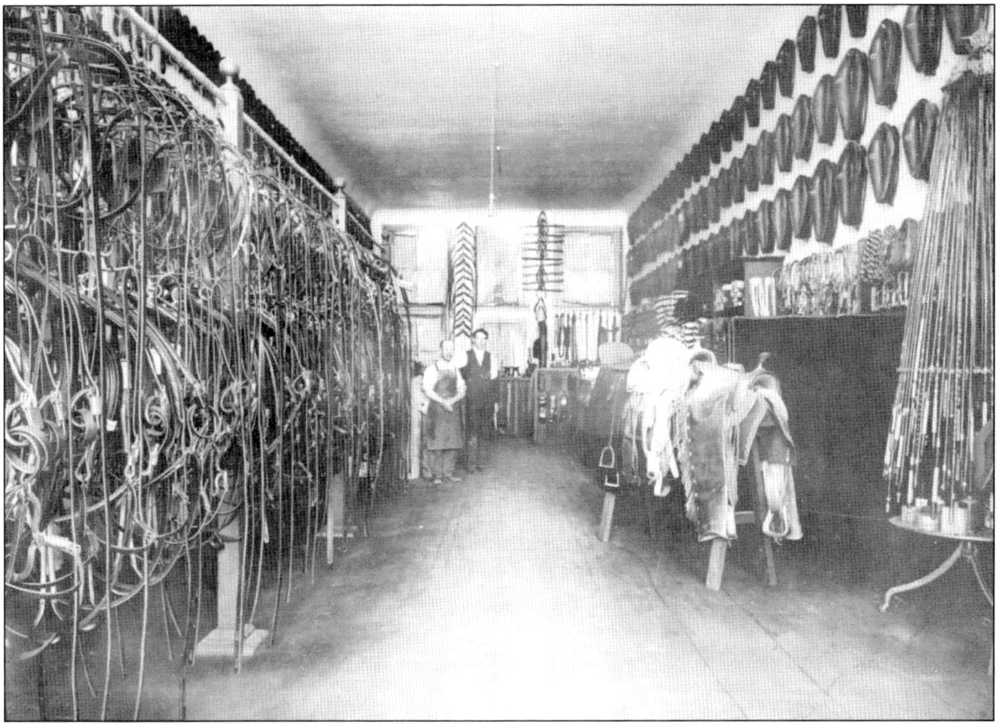

HARNESS AND SADDLE SHOP. The aroma of leather goods is almost perceptible in this image of Ogden Mallory's shop, which he ran during the 1880s and 1890s. Ogden Mallory is on the right, and Carroll Whitten is on the left. (PCM.)

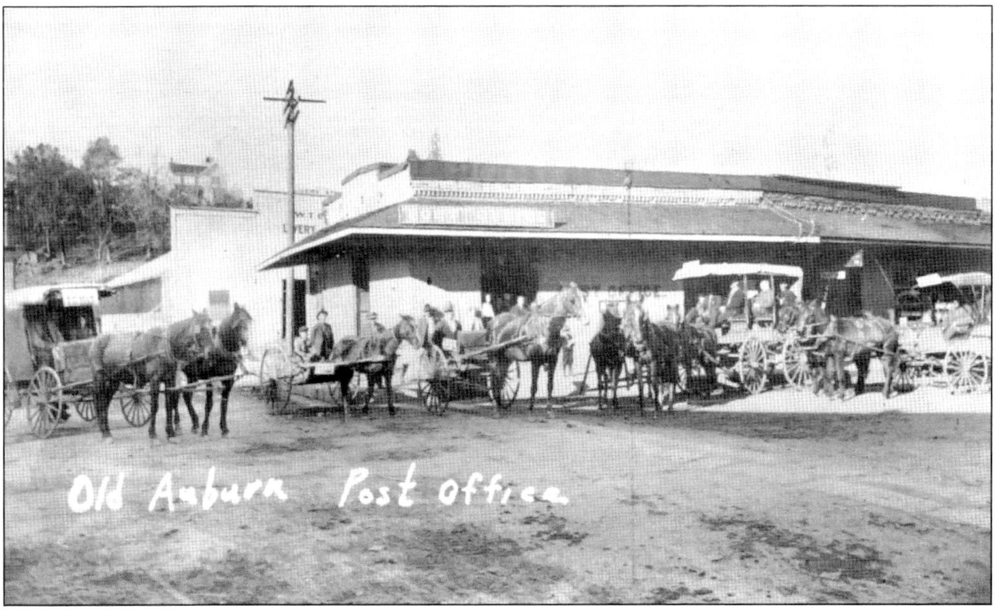

POST OFFICE. Sending and receiving mail was the primary means of communication for the miners. In 1849, miner Isaac Annis reported waiting four hours with more than 500 men to pick up mail in Sacramento. Regularly scheduled mail service came to Auburn in 1851. The post office opened at this location in 1878 and has remained in the same building ever since. (AJS.)

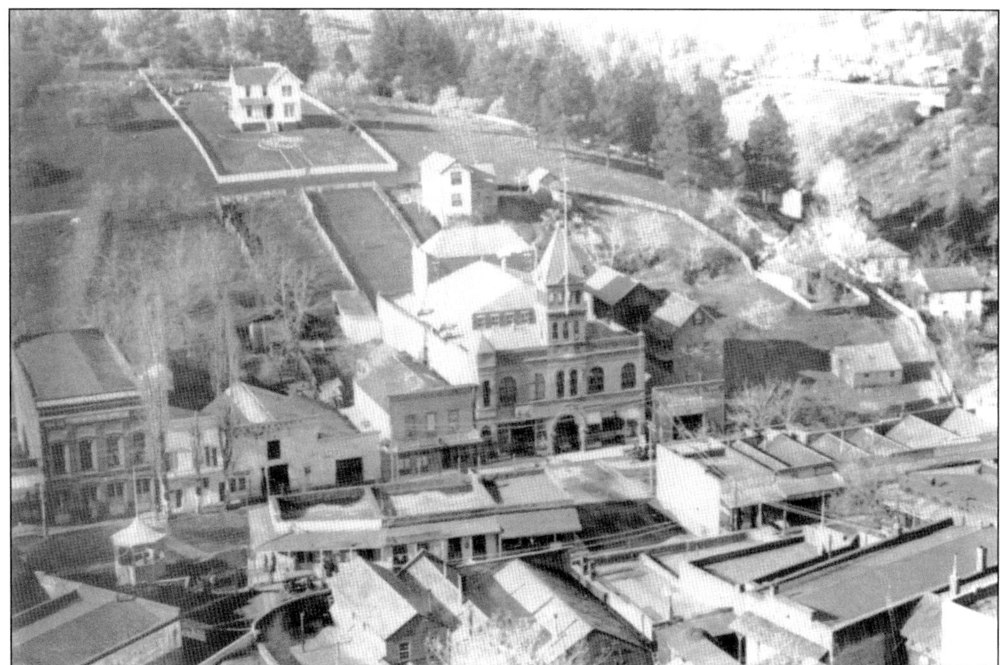

City Hall. The large building at center was referred to as city hall, although it was never used for official purposes. Rather, it housed a large hall on the upper floors used for dances, along with an undertaker and hardware store on the ground floor. The large home seen at the top of the hill in both of these images is the Edmund C. Snowden residence that overlooks Old Town. (PCM.)

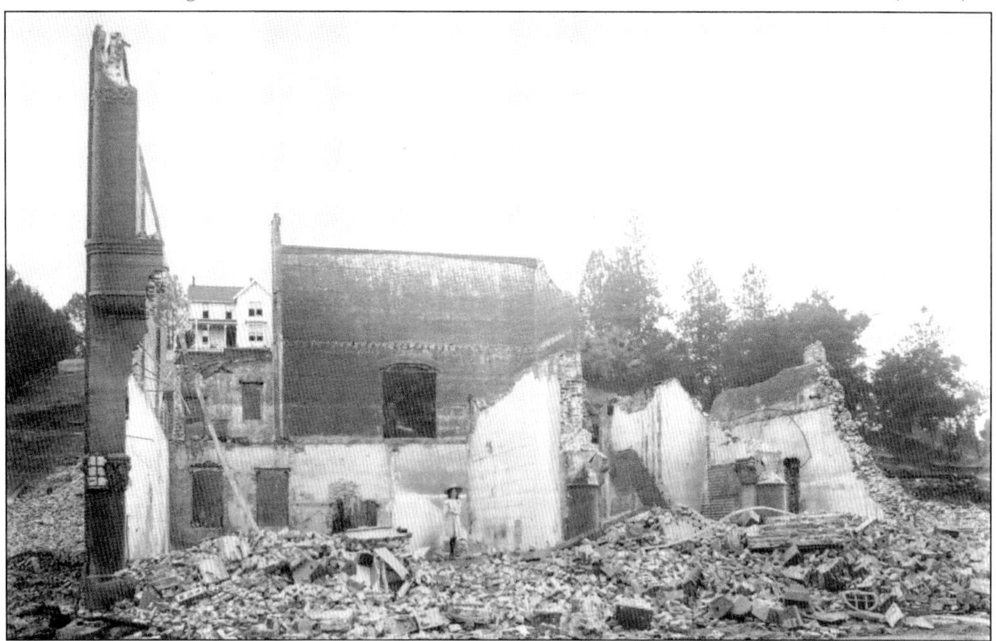

Fires. Many destructive fires swept through Old Town Auburn over the years. The one in 1855 took out most of the town. Major fires occurred again in 1859, 1864, 1870, 1872, and 1877. Each time, the citizens rebuilt using more substantial materials. This is the burned-out city hall after a fire in 1905. (PCM.)

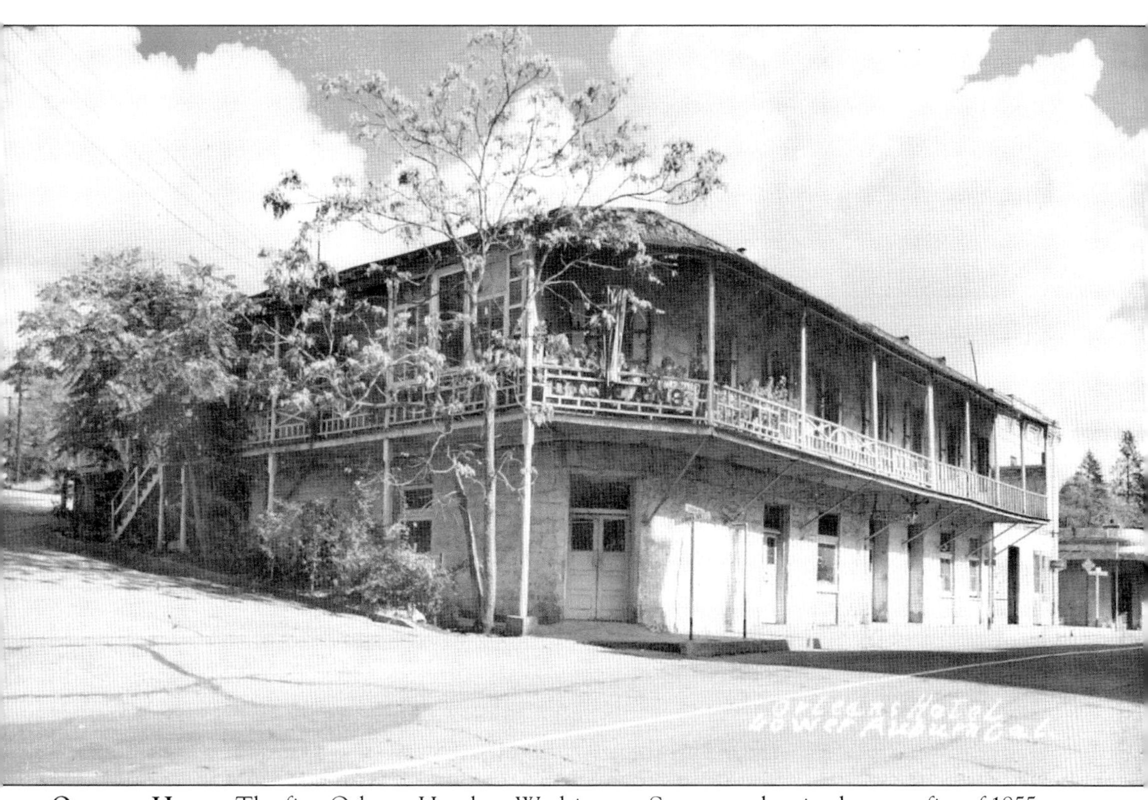

Orleans Hotel. The first Orleans Hotel on Washington Street was lost in the great fire of 1855, and the second, in the fire of 1863. By 1870, the building pictured here at Lincoln Way and Maple Street had been erected. The demolition of the Orleans in 1957 ignited community efforts to resurrect and revitalize Old Town. A footnote in the history of the Orleans is the fact that Jean Baptiste Charbonneau was a clerk at the second hotel in 1861. He was the son of Sacajawea and Toussaint Charbonneau, guides and interpreters for the Lewis and Clark Expedition from 1804 to 1806. After 1806, Jean Baptiste Charbonneau lived with Captain Clark for many years as a youth and later traveled in Europe with Duke Friedrich Paul Wilhelm of Wurttemberg. At the age of 43, he came to the Auburn area with famed trailblazer Jim Beckwourth in 1848. Charbonneau joined William Bickham at Murderer's Bar in 1850. Bickham wrote home, "Old Charbonneau is now with us on the bar and is as full of life and fun as any boy of 18. He can be heard laughing and making merry at any hour between breakfast and midnight." In 1851, he ran a ferry at Manhattan Bar; in 1852, he was assistant county surveyor; and later, he mined in Secret Ravine outside Auburn before taking a job at the Orleans. Charbonneau left Auburn in 1866. (AJS.)

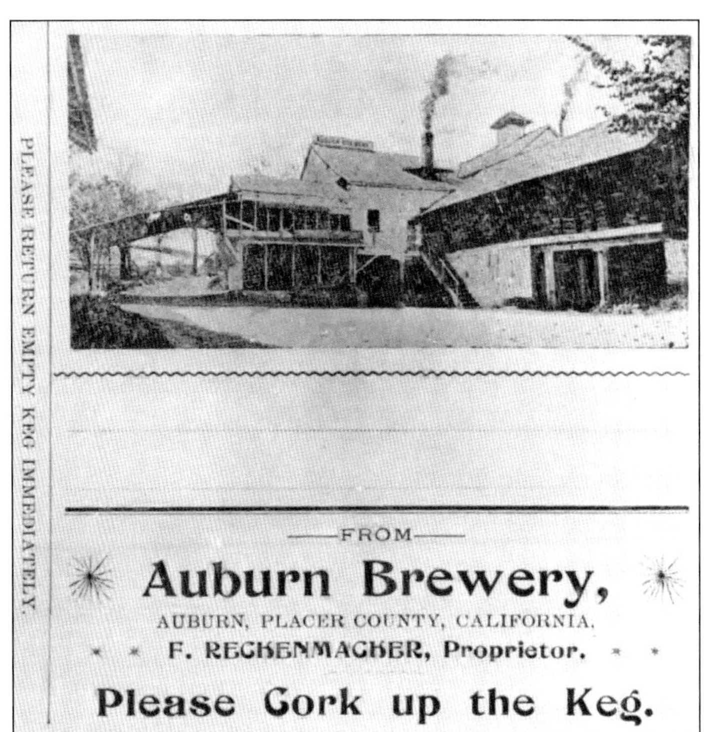

AUBURN BREWERY. Jacob and Samuel Kaiser, brothers from Switzerland, utilized their skills as coopers to establish this brewery in 1856. It opened to an enthusiastic audience who "darkened the very air with bottles, tumblers, tables, and . . . other warlike implements found . . . convenient to the hand." Upon Jacob's sudden death in 1861, the brewery was sold to satisfy creditors. It changed hands several times before the last proprietor, Ferdinand Rechenmacher, finally closed it in 1908. (PCM.)

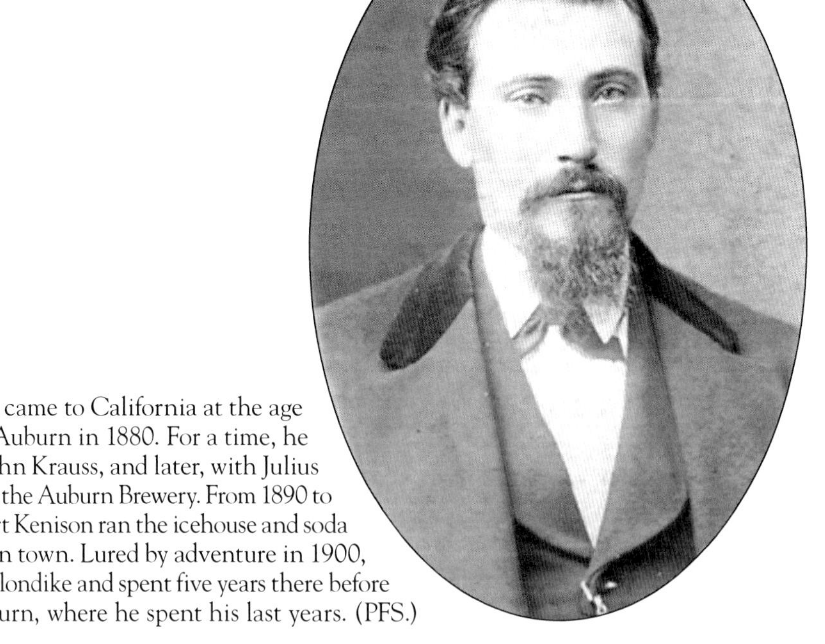

JACOB ROLL. Roll came to California at the age of 14, settling in Auburn in 1880. For a time, he partnered with John Krauss, and later, with Julius Weber, in running the Auburn Brewery. From 1890 to 1893, he and Albert Kenison ran the icehouse and soda water dealership in town. Lured by adventure in 1900, Roll went to the Klondike and spent five years there before returning to Auburn, where he spent his last years. (PFS.)

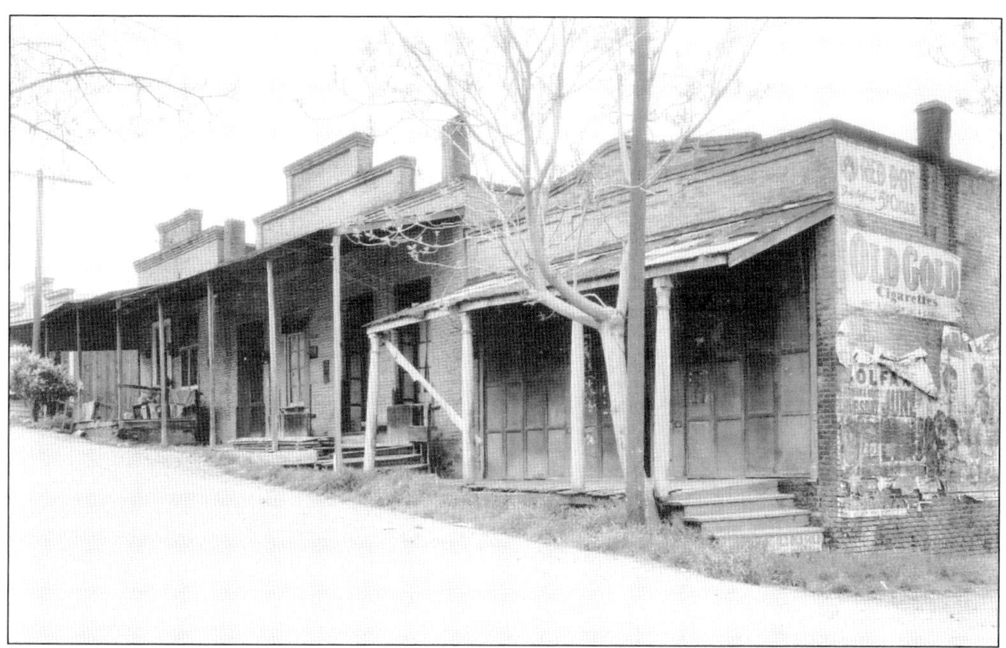

CHINATOWN. With its own shops, doctors, saloons, and theater, Auburn's Chinatown was a vibrant part of town along Sacramento Street, south to the railroad tracks. Unlike other Gold Rush–era Chinatowns, this one was not on the edge of town, nor was it isolated. Rather, it began right in the heart of Old Town and integrated with other businesses. Esteemed merchant Kee Chin constructed the two brick buildings at left. (PCM.)

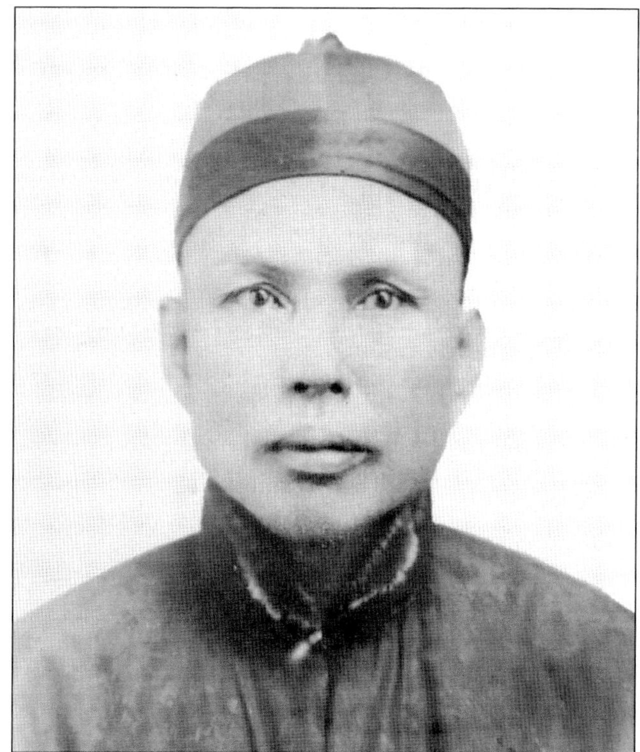

KEE CHINN. Kee Chinn arrived in Auburn before 1860. He made his reputation as a highly respected merchant whose "word was as good as his bond," according to his obituary in the *Placer Herald*. For over 20 years, he leased the area known as China Garden from Bernhard Bernhard. In 1893, he built the brick buildings shown above on Sacramento Street. They were both commercial and residential. He was considered "the Boss Chinaman" of Auburn. (PCM.)

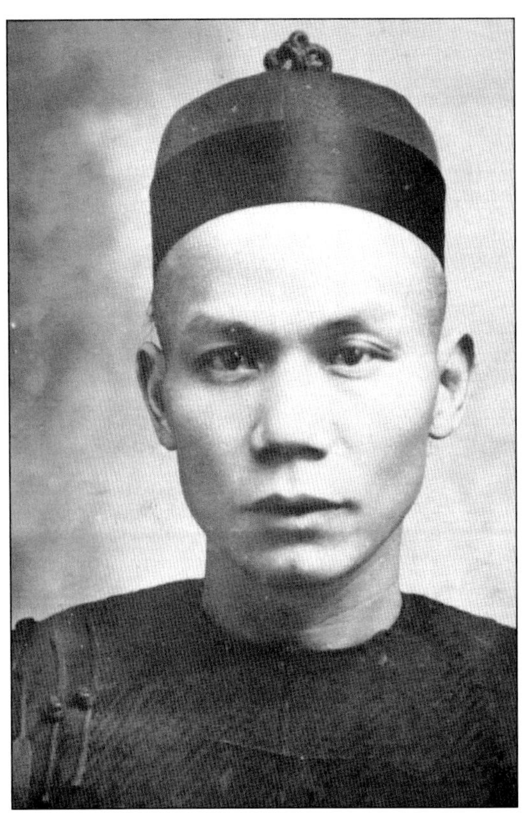

Mar Ying Toy and Leo Gim Moy. Ying Toy was one of the last merchants and grocers to serve the Chinese community in Auburn. His shop, the Quong Hi Company, was on Sacramento Street, and his residence was on Brewery Lane. As a trustee for the Chinese Cemetery, he and Charlie Yue purchased the cemetery land on present-day Highway 49, just north of town, in 1899. The cemetery is still there. Mar Ying Toy and Charlie Yue were instrumental in preparing and shipping bones of deceased Chinese back to China for final burial. Pictured here are Mar Ying Toy and his wife, Leo Gim Moy. (Both, PCM.)

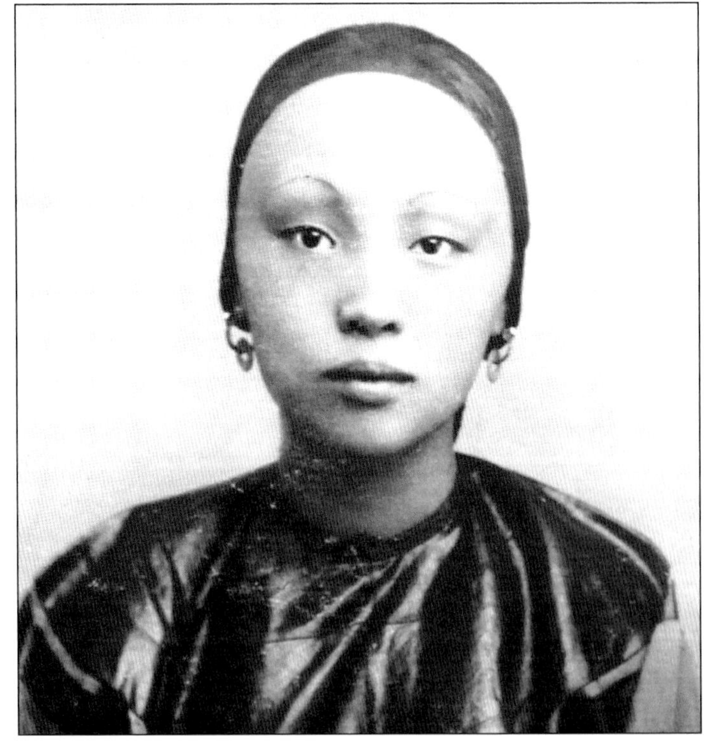

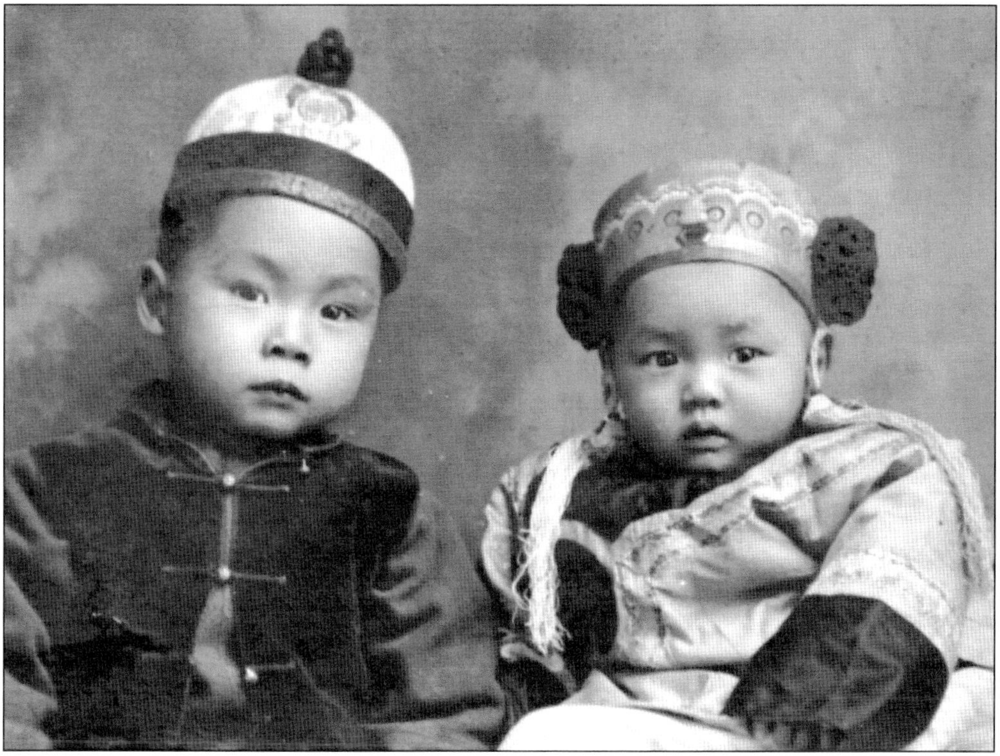

Mar Children. Although faced with pervasive anti-Chinese discrimination in most areas of California, the Chinese generally maintained their traditional clothing, dietary habits, religion, and customs. Above are Mar Gim Toy (left) and Mar Gook Lon. At right is Mar Suey Lon. These photographs were taken before the Mar family embarked on a trip to China; they were part of the documentation needed to assure the family's ability to return to America. (Both, PCM.)

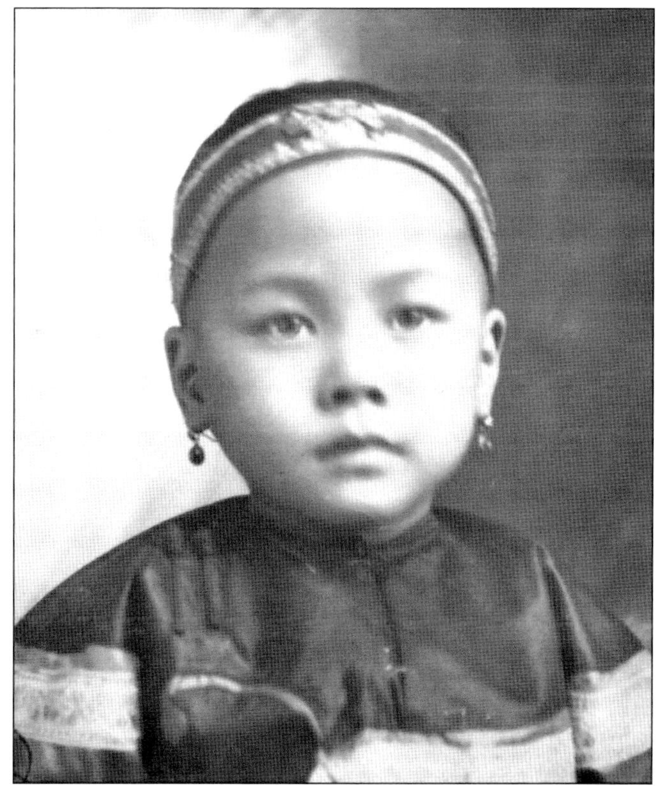

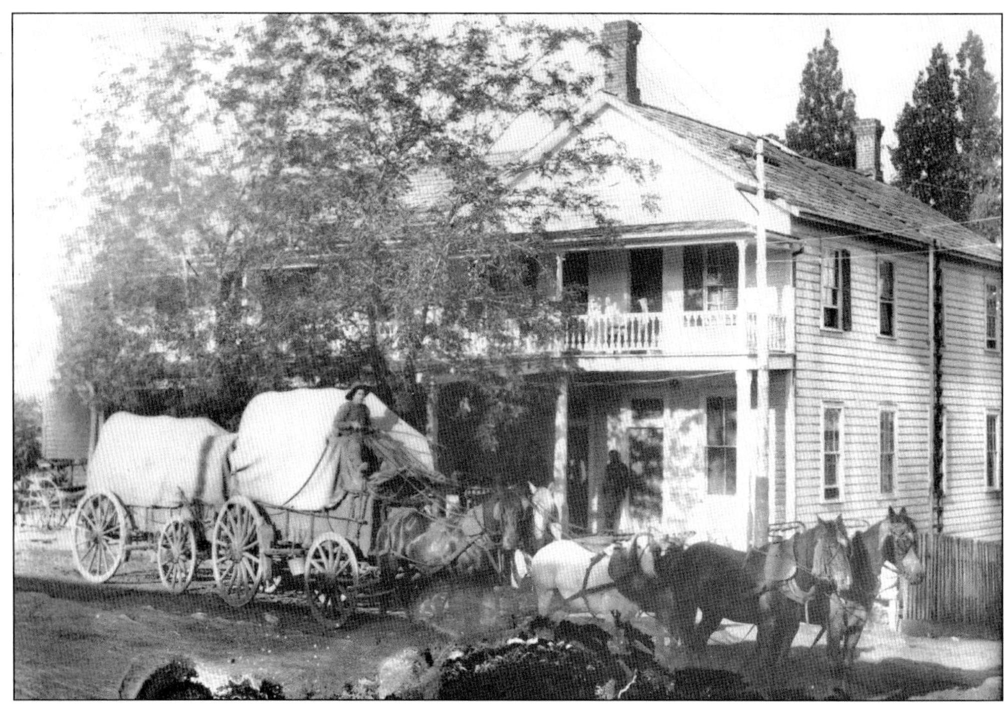

Auburn Hotel. John J. Smith built a hotel across from the depot in April 1870. In October, it burned to the ground. Undaunted, Smith rebuilt this hotel in 1871. Ernest Elfendahl bought it in 1885, and in 1888, Caroline Ludwig, a local moneylender, took ownership. (PCM.)

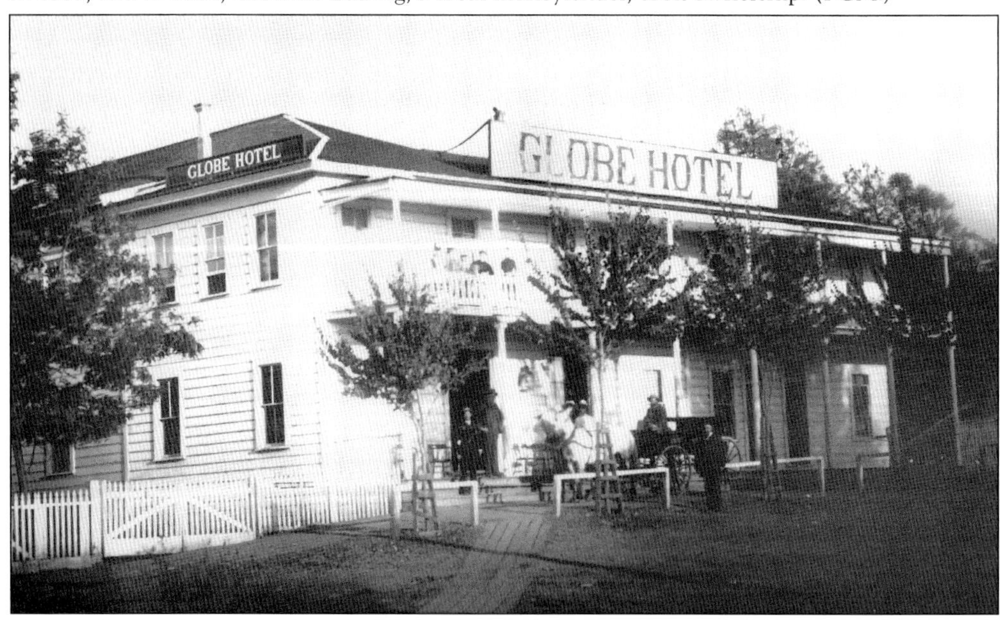

Globe Hotel. Augustine Crawford built the Globe just south of the depot in 1879–1880. For some years, it was known as the Crawford House. In 1887, Crawford sold it to J. Rassette for $8,000. Rassette changed the name to the Arlington and promoted it as a health resort. James Borland bought the establishment in 1893 and renamed it the Borland. The hotel burned down in 1902. (PCM.)

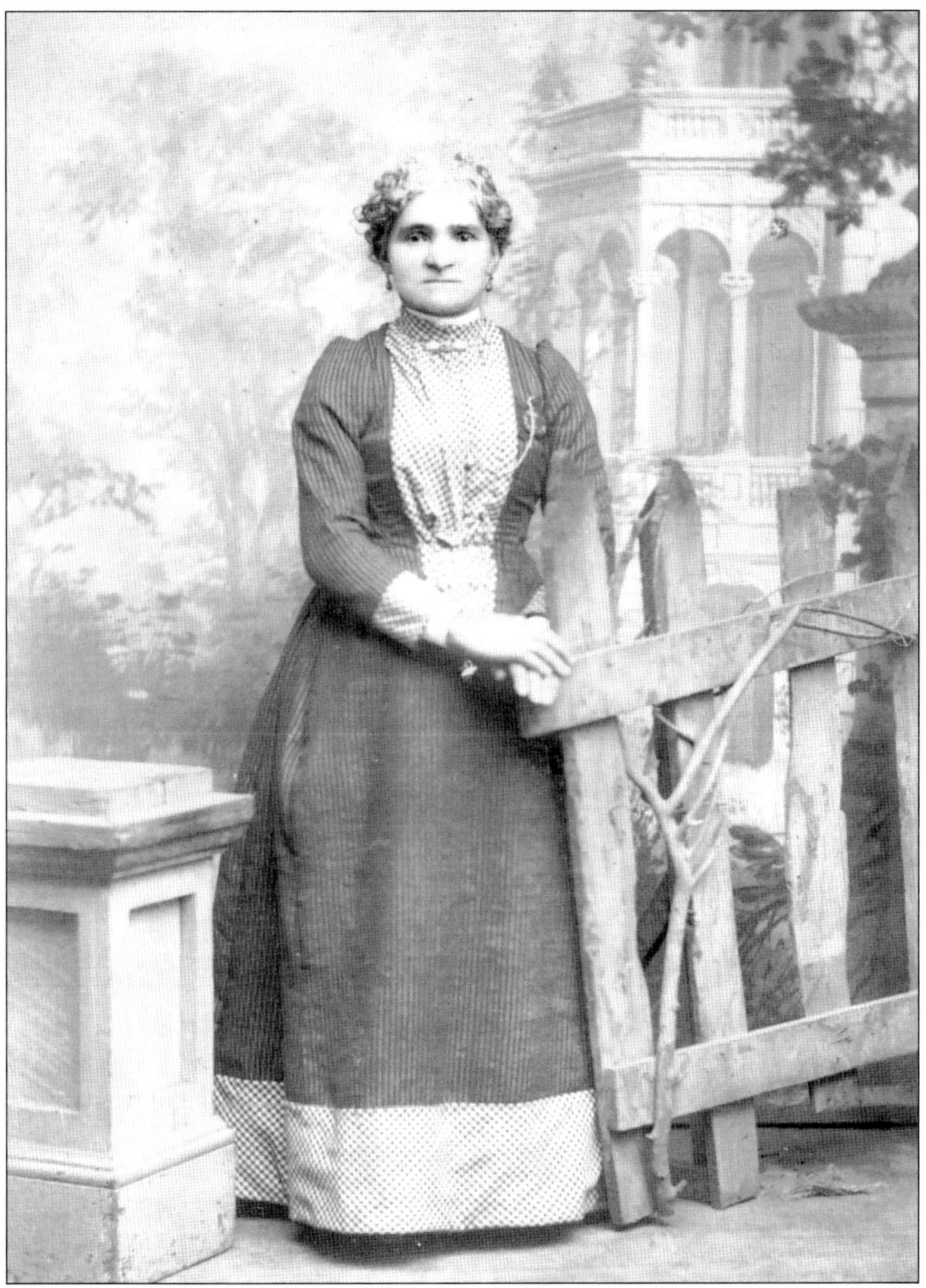

Caroline Ludwig. Caroline came to California from Germany in 1852. She and her husband owned a large ranch in the Lone Star area, a few miles north of Auburn. When she moved to Auburn, she began an extremely lucrative career as a moneylender, boldly listing her occupation as a capitalist in the census. Her obituary noted that she was "an accumulator of property." She owned or held mortgages on a vast number of properties in town. Her estate was valued at $50,000 upon her death in 1921. California offered the unique opportunity for women to step out of their traditional roles with more ease than on the East Coast. Auburn had a large number of women who ran businesses and fended for themselves. (PCM.)

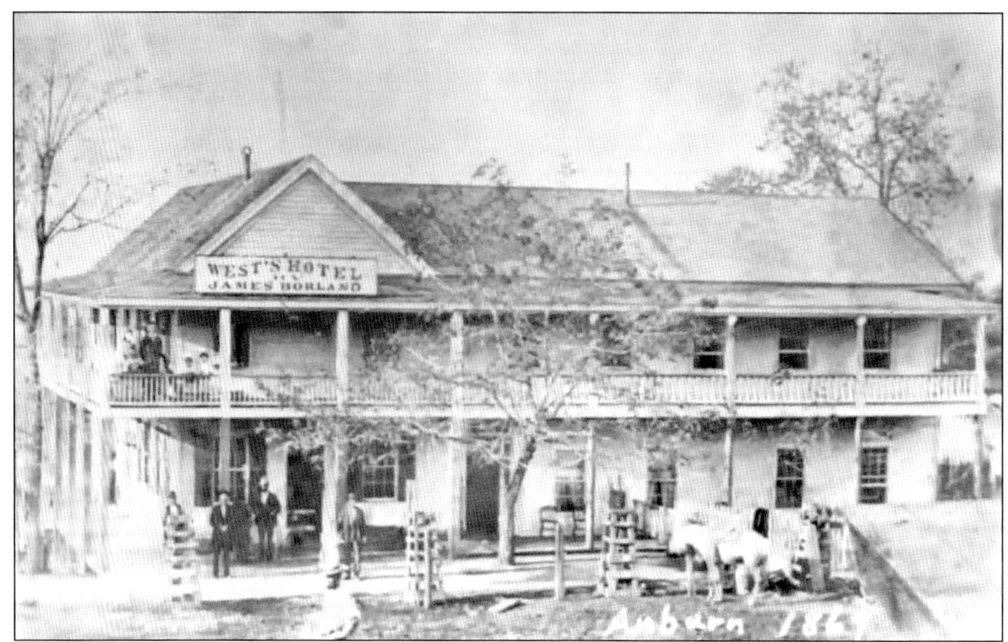

West's Hotel. Elliott West built this hotel near the newly opened railroad station in 1865. To improve traffic to his hotel, West created a more direct route through town, calling it Railroad Street. In 1875, James Borland bought the hotel, and the newspaper reported it "filled with tourists." In 1882, Borland sold the hotel to William A. Freeman. (PCM.)

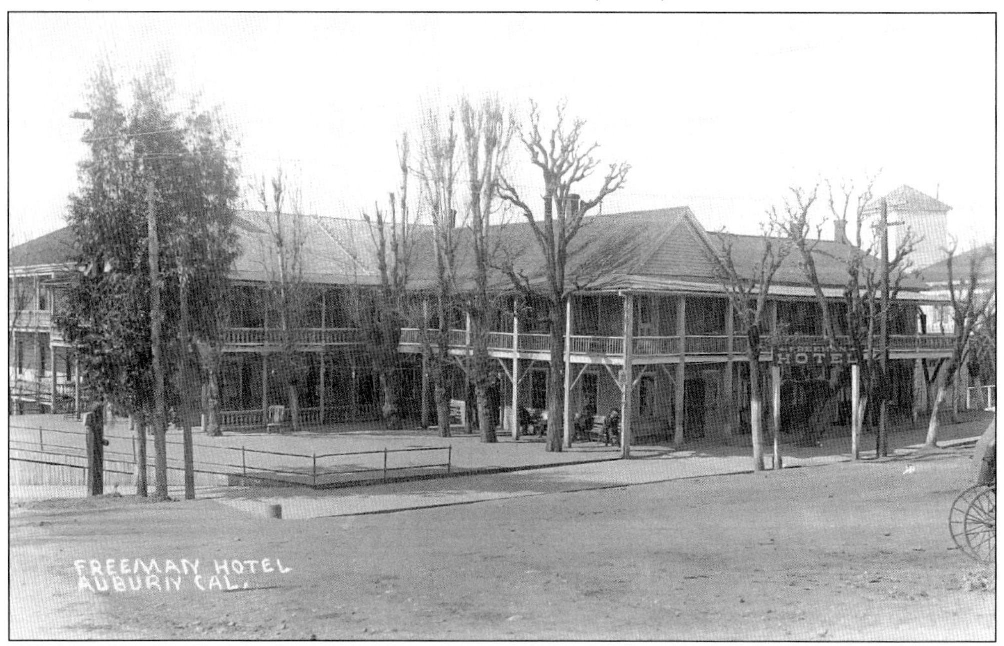

Freeman Hotel. Under William A. Freeman, this hotel became the premier destination for tourists and business travelers. Over the years, modern plumbing and electricity were added. In 1892, a pavilion with a spring dance floor was erected. Spring dance floors were very popular at the time. For years, it was the go-to spot for locals on a Saturday night. This venerable institution, located at the top of Lincoln Way, was torn down in 1970. (AJS.)

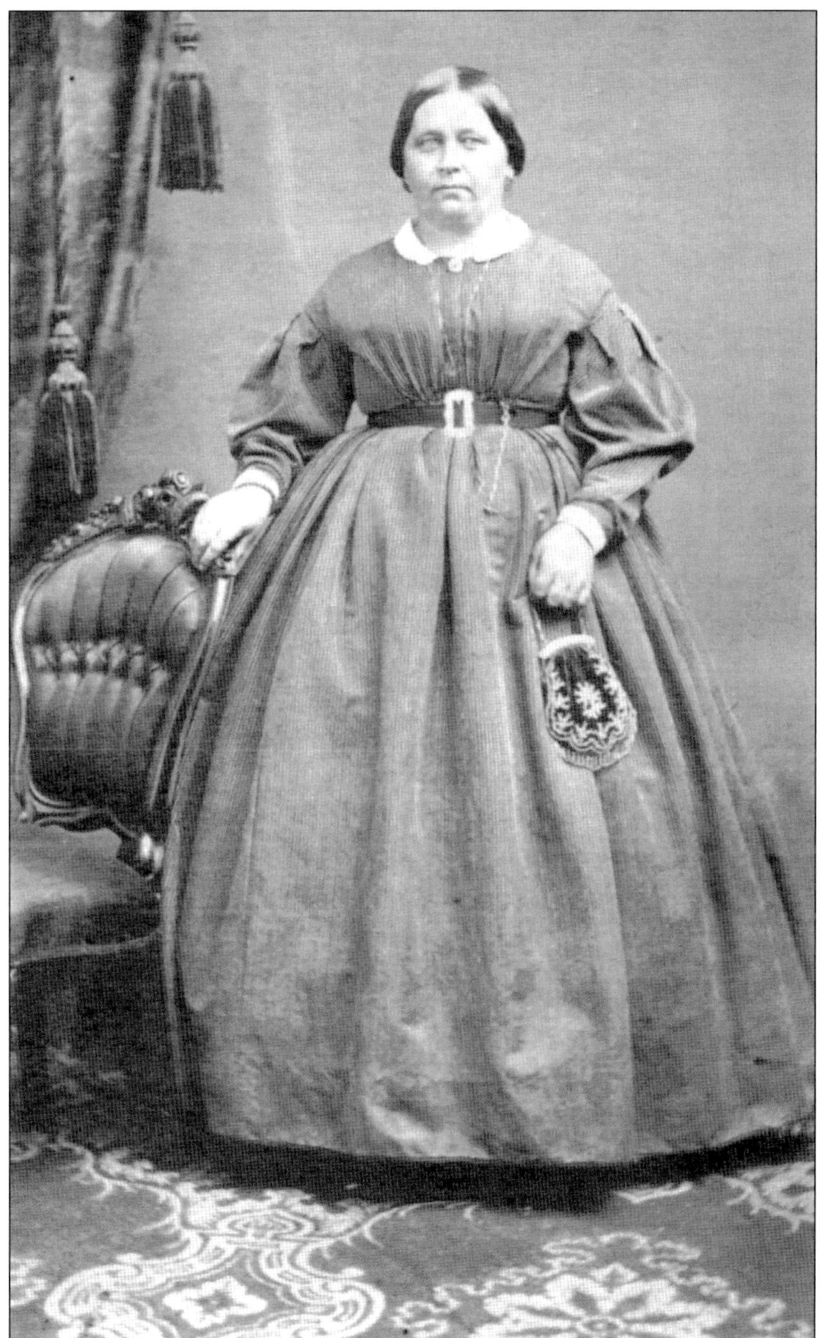

Elizabeth "Carrie" Kittler. Carrie came to California in 1852 when her forty-niner husband, George, returned to Germany to fetch her and their children. She helped him run a hotel near Ophir. When he died in 1858, she took over the hotel and ran it herself. In 1874, she moved to Auburn and bought the Empire Hotel. That same year, she ran an advertisement in the *Placer Herald* boasting "a French cook and no Chinese." Generous to the community, she donated the use of the hotel ballroom for a ball benefitting the Auburn Hose Company No. 2. She owned and operated the Empire until her death in 1894. (PCM.)

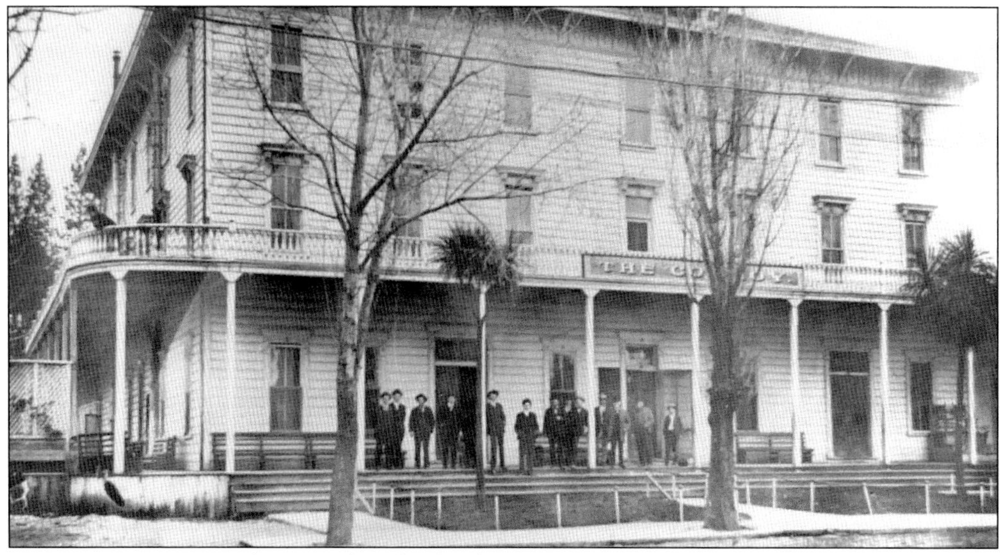

CONROY HOTEL. Samuel Putnam bought the Placer Fruit Drying Company in 1880 and converted it into a hotel called the Putnam House. Rebuilt after burning in 1881, it changed hands a number of times before former sheriff William Conroy bought it in 1899 and renamed it the Conroy. After extensive remodeling, more than 1,000 people attended the grand reopening. It burned again in 1912, then was replaced by the Hotel Auburn. (AJS.)

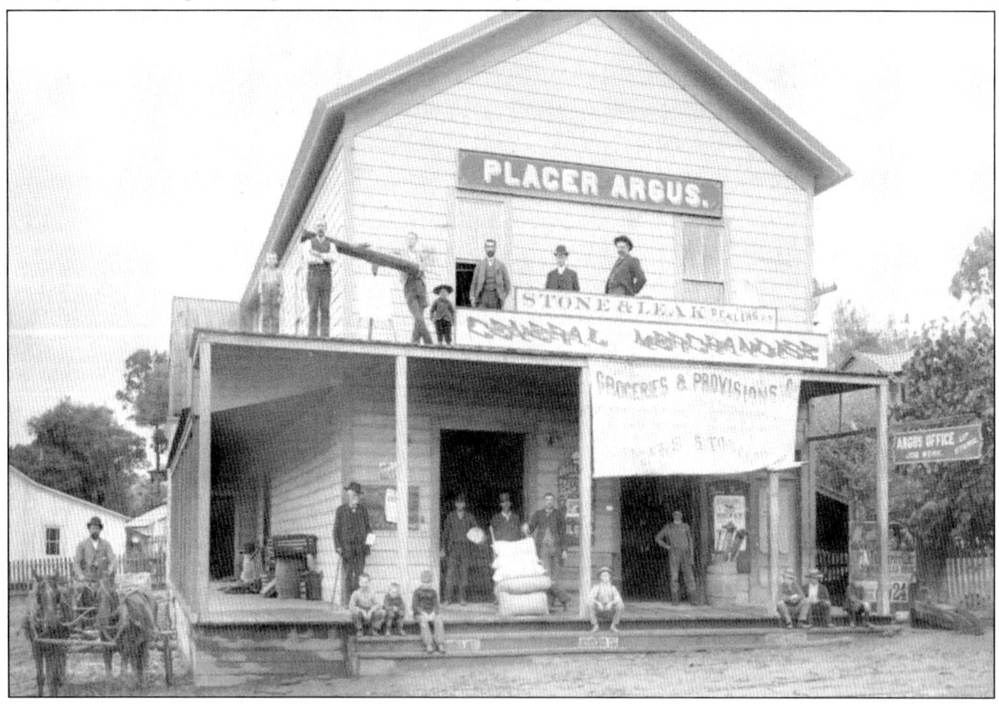

HOHMANN BUILDING. Michael Hohmann built this structure in 1887 on the northeast corner of Cleveland Avenue and Lincoln Way as a general merchandise store. In 1889–1890, his first-floor tenants were Edwin Stone and J. Henry Leak, as seen here. Upstairs was Argus Printing. Moses Andrews, Griffith Griffith, and other men of wealth and political influence first published the *Placer Weekly Argus* in 1872 to present the Republican Party's viewpoint. (BL.)

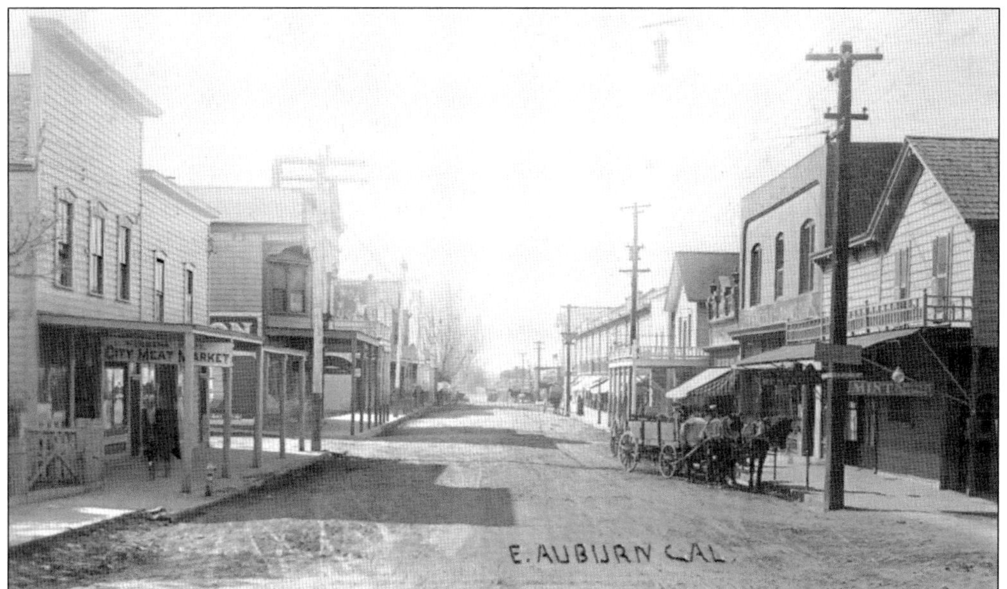

MINT SALOON. Paul Weber built the Mint Saloon, the first structure at right, in 1885. In later years, the building housed a succession of businesses, including a harness shop, a jewelry store, a cigar store, and another saloon. Located on the corner of Lincoln Way and Cleveland Avenue, it is the oldest commercial building still standing in the downtown area. (PCM.)

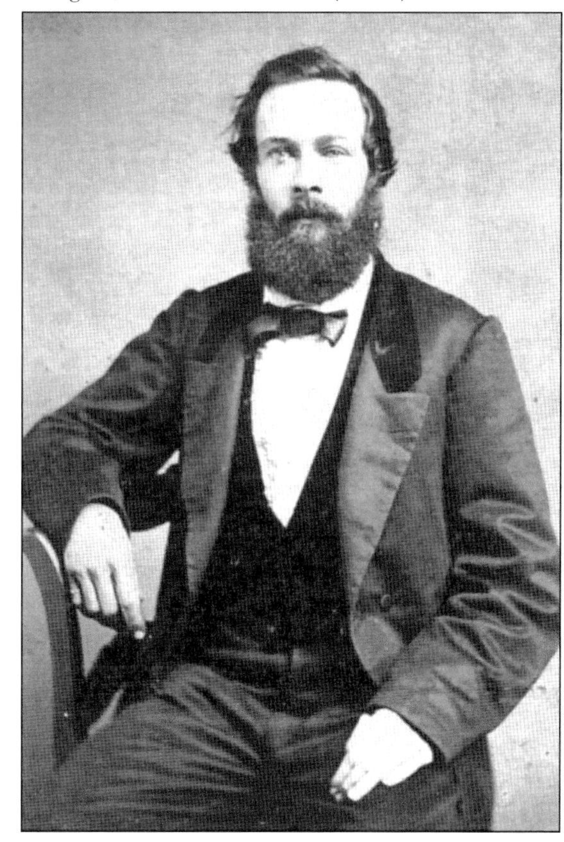

PAUL BERNHART WEBER. Weber is a classic example of an early argonaut who eventually settled in Auburn. Born in Germany, he was a shipbuilder by trade before making his way around the Horn in the early 1850s in a quest for gold. He mined for a few years but later turned to the grocery and saloon business in Auburn. (WF.)

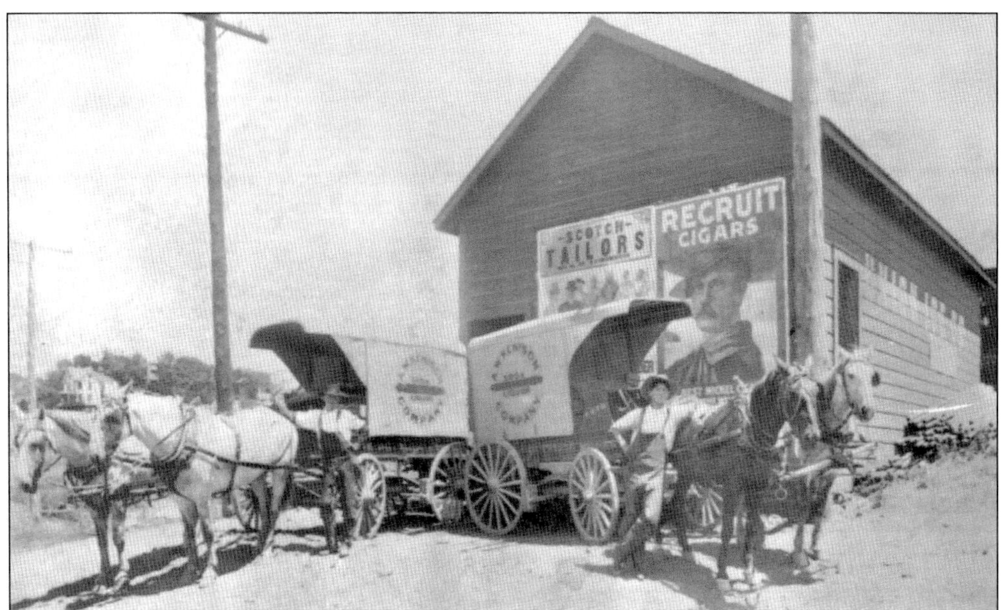

Union Ice Company. Albert W. Kenison and Jacob Roll ran a wholesale and retail liquor and soda business with its own bottling works. Among their many profitable business ventures was the icehouse pictured here near the railroad depot. Ice was produced at three tons per day, then delivered door-to-door. (PCM.)

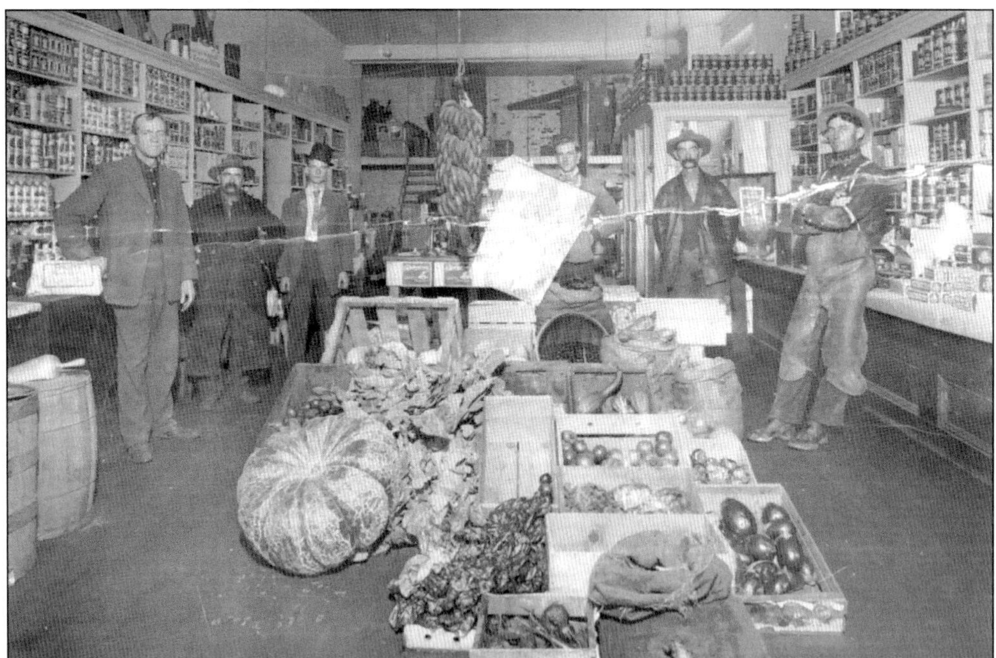

Grocery Store. A display worthy of a modern-day market is featured in this photograph of the Albert F. Ford and Company grocery store. Albert Ford is on the left. This Auburn Ford family was related to Henry Ford, and it created quite a stir in the community when Henry came to town to visit his relatives. This building still stands on the corner of Harrison Avenue and Lincoln Way. (PCM.)

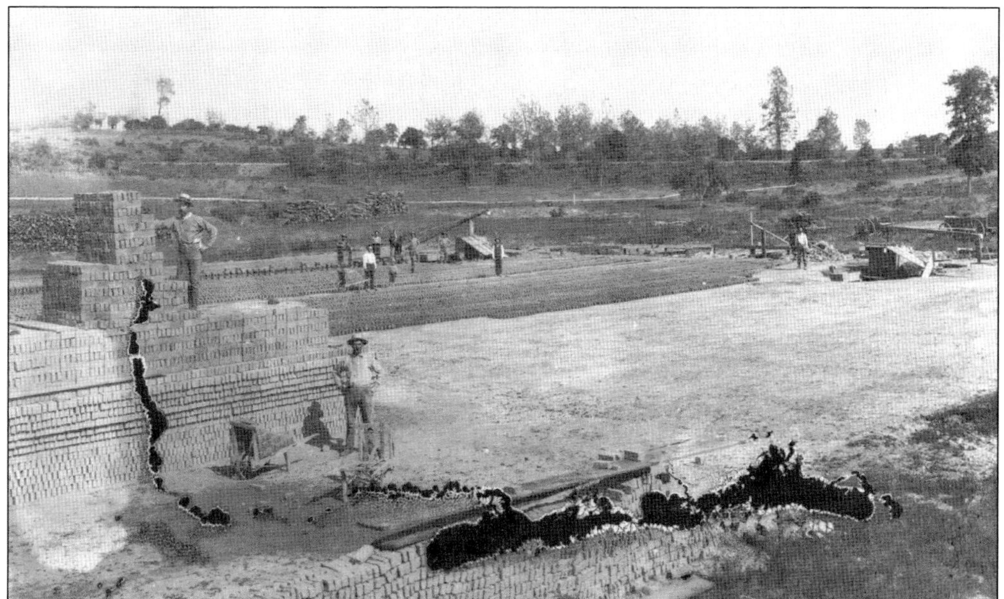

Brickyard. Several devastating fires swept early Auburn. The largest and most devastating occurred in 1855, destroying over 80 buildings. Many of the brick structures still in Old Town were built after this fire, and much of the brick used came from a brickyard at Rich Flat. Other brickyards were located at the racetrack, on Palm Avenue, and near Chamberlain Avenue. (PCM.)

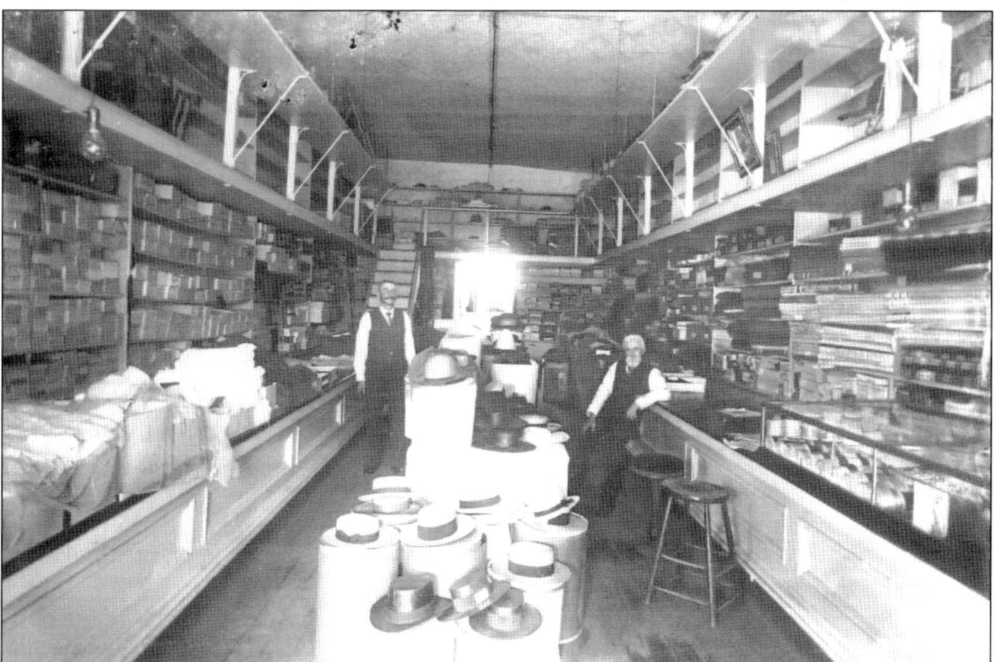

Eastern Bargain Store. Nathan Cohen had this clothing and dry goods store in Old Town Auburn around the turn of the century. For a few years, he ran this store in Old Town as well as one in East Auburn. As new residential areas opened farther uptown, many Old Town merchants opened branch stores in the "new" part of town. Old Town became almost derelict in the 1930s until its renaissance in the 1960s. (PCM.)

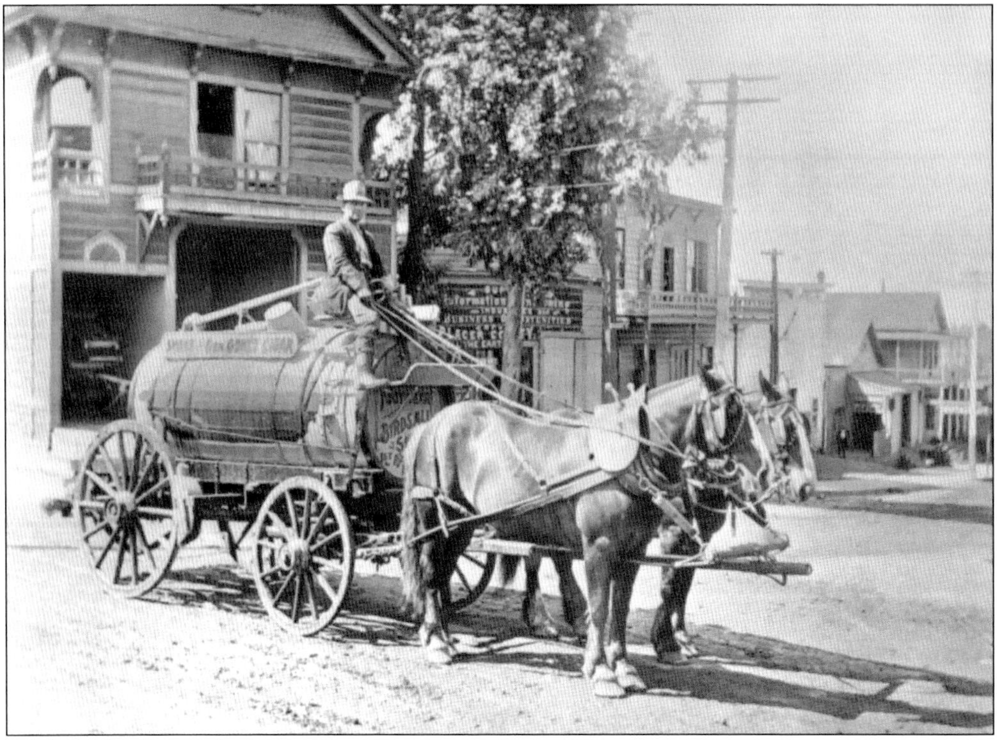

Tamping Down the Dust. The dirt streets in Auburn were a source of aggravation for both travelers and townspeople. Many visitors complained about having to trek from the train depot to the courthouse on streets without sidewalks, fighting the dust in the summer and the mud in the winter. The water wagon above was used to tamp down the dust in the summer. The image below, with the Congregational Church in the background, shows the condition of the streets in Central Square. Auburn's streets were not paved until after the turn of the 20th century. (Both, AJS.)

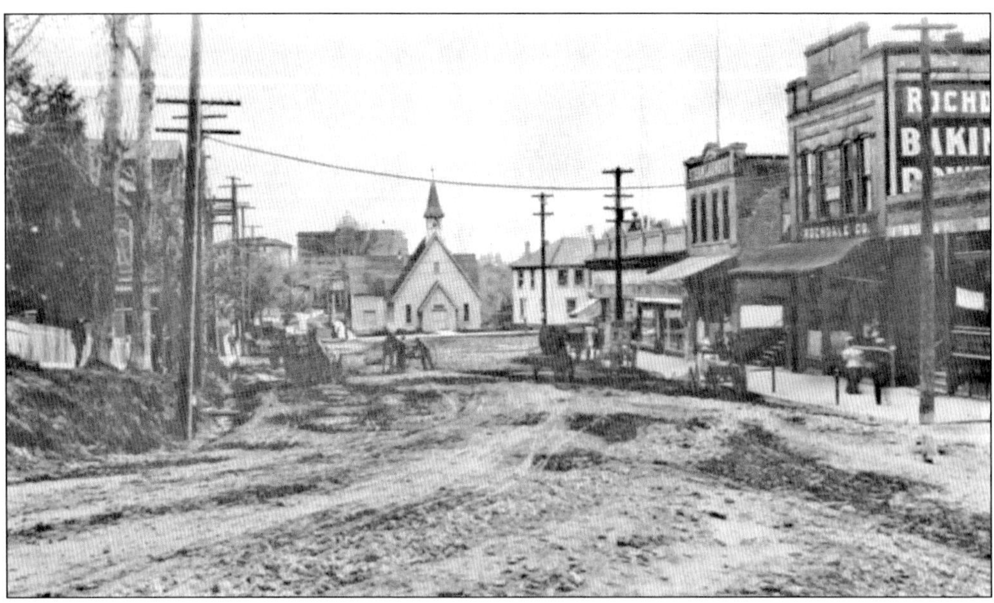

Eight

Making and Breaking the Law

The discovery of gold in 1848 came at a very chaotic period in California's political growth. The Mexican-American War was barely over; the Treaty of Guadalupe Hidalgo had been signed just two weeks before. The new American territory was under military control. Col. Richard Barnes Mason, military governor of California, had a scant 50 men under his command. Recognizing his inability to regulate the massive influx of gold seekers, he wrote, "I am resolved not to interfere but to permit all to work freely."

Having essentially no formal government in place did not imply lawlessness. Miners themselves quickly formed agencies of control, specifically miner's courts and miner's codes based on the principle of "discovery and development" in Mexican mining law. The idea of a claim became standard. Mostly, miner's codes regulated claim size, the number of claims held by an individual, and the work required to retain possession of a claim. An important aspect of the reliance on Mexican law was the selection of an alcalde, or mayor. Almost every mining camp chose, by popular vote, an alcalde who could settle disputes and be judge and jury (or else appoint a jury).

In Auburn, Samuel Wirt Holladay was selected as alcalde by his fellow miners in August 1849 His first job was to deal with a man accused of theft. Holladay appointed a sheriff and organized a jury. The man was found innocent.

Formal government came into existence after California became a state in 1850. Counties were organized in that same year. Auburn was part of Sutter County until demographics caused the formation of Placer County in 1851. Auburn was voted county seat by a large majority. Voting boxes were attached to trees throughout the region. The votes cast for Auburn outnumbered the population of the entire county.

Becoming the county seat influenced the growth of the town. People came to town (and stayed in hotels and ate in restaurants) to attend to official court business. There were property claims to file, real estate and business sales to record, and court sessions to attend. Auburn hosted the county, district, and superior courts.

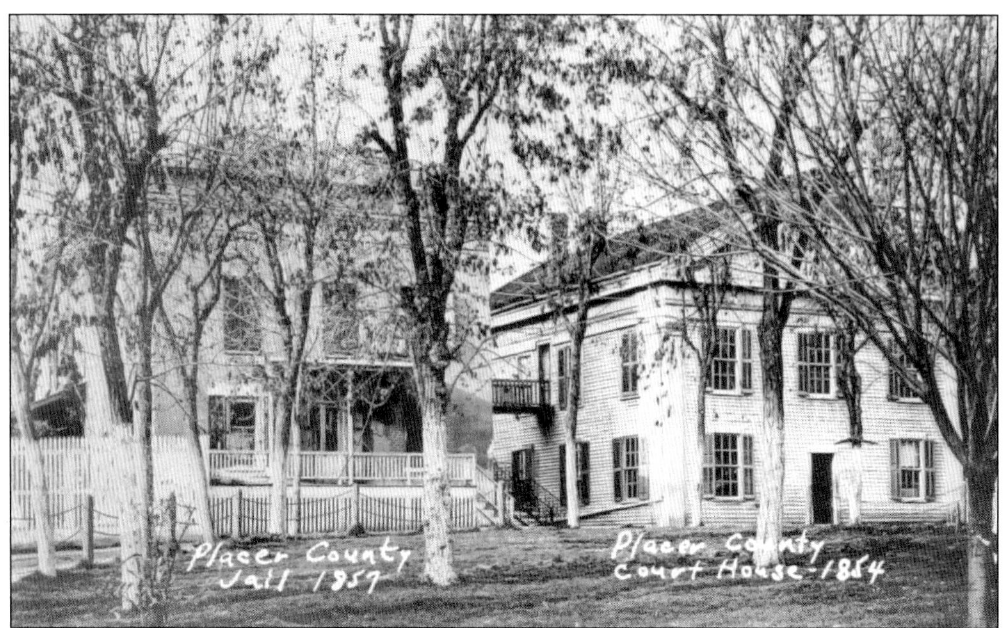

Courthouse and Jail. The very first courts met in a canvas-and-wood structure where the Maple Street off-ramp is located today. A substantial log jailhouse was built next to it. In 1852, the bids were let for the courthouse at right. It was finished in 1853. The jail at left was built in 1855–1856. The present-day courthouse was constructed on the site of these later buildings. (AJS.)

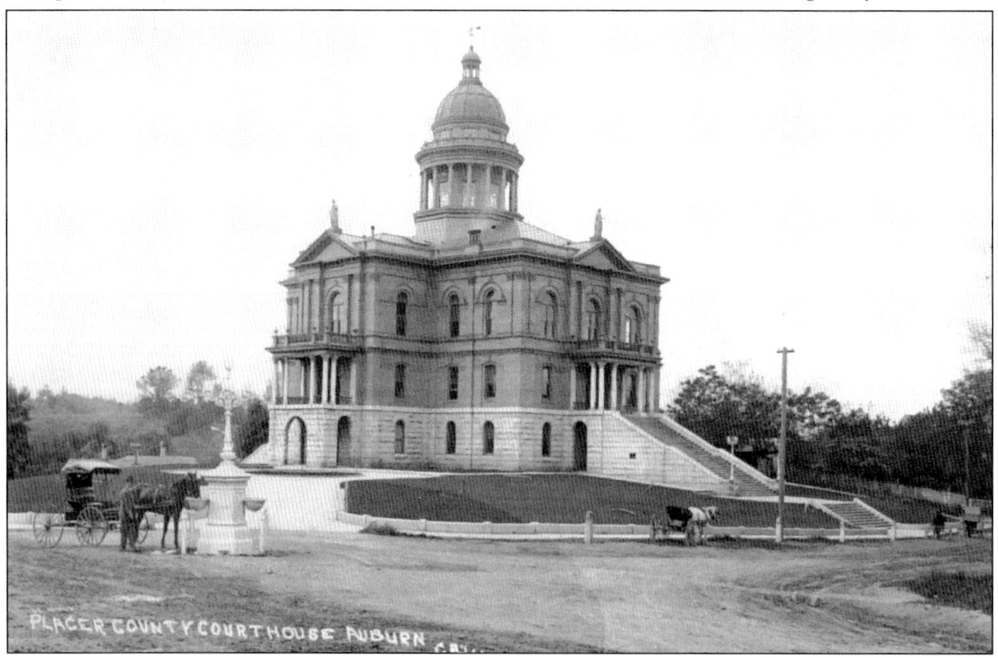

Courthouse. Construction of this grand courthouse, designed by architect John M. Curtis, began in 1894, followed by a dedication in 1898. This very symbol of Auburn came close to being leveled in the 1960s and 1970s for the sake of modernity, but public outcry led to the formation of committees and fundraising efforts to save the building. Restoration and earthquake retrofitting were begun in 1986. Today, the courthouse hosts a museum, as well as court offices. (AJS.)

Charles and Maria Tuttle. Tuttle had already been admitted to the New York State Bar before crossing the Great Plains in 1849. He was mining at Stony Bar in 1850 when he was pressed into service to defend another miner in front of a miner's court. He returned east in 1852 to fetch his wife, Maria. Over the years, he held many public offices while also maintaining his law practice in Auburn, Sacramento, and Oakland. (PCM.)

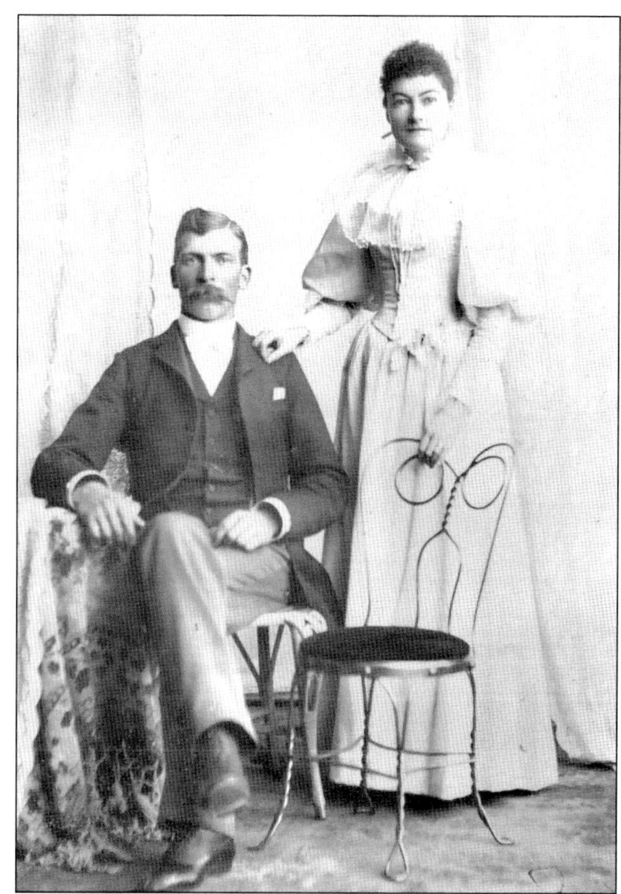

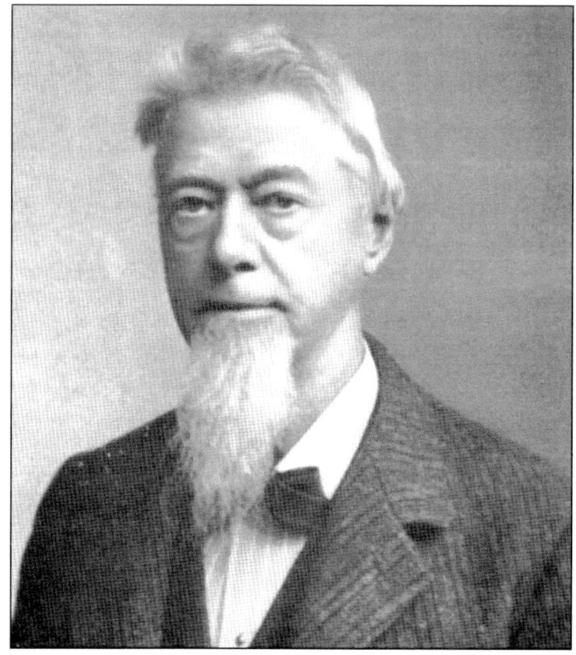

Curtis Justin Hillyer. Hillyer came to Placer County in 1852 and practiced law with Charles Tuttle. Active in Republican politics, he became reporter of decisions for the state supreme court in 1862. He moved to Virginia City and was elected to the Nevada State Assembly in 1867. In 1869, he successfully pushed through a bill for women's suffrage, only to have it defeated two years later. (www.findagrave.com.)

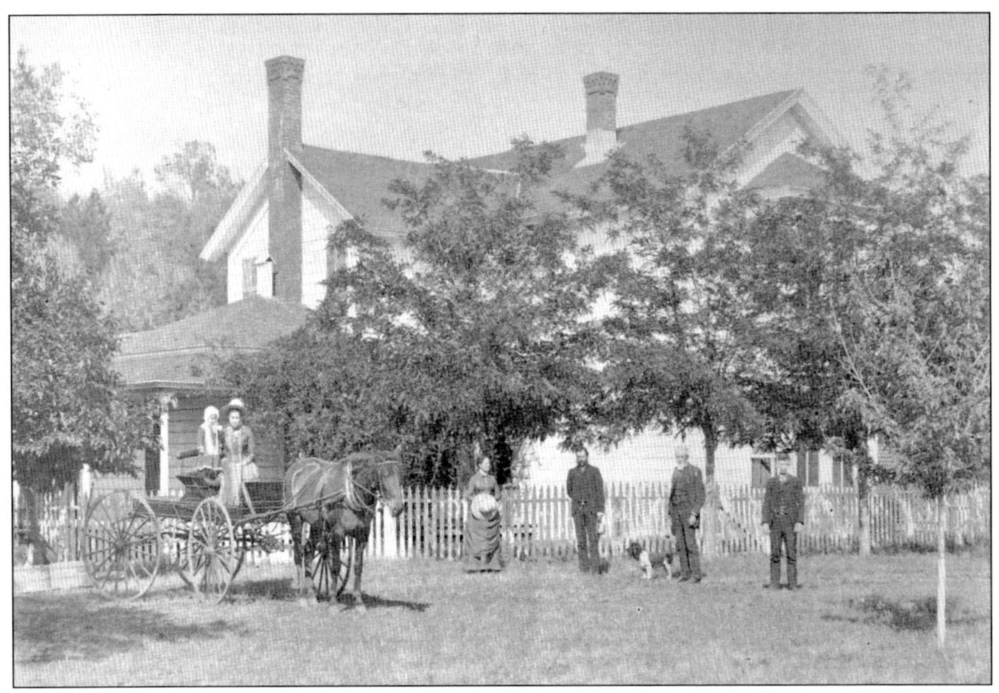

Benjamin Franklin Myres. Myres came to California in 1851. He was a district judge from 1859 to 1864 and a superior court judge from 1880 to 1891. Judge Myres and family are posed in front of his home, Baltimore. This home still stands today and is owned by a descendant of the judge. From left to right are baby Ben Myres, Florence Myres Michael, Elizabeth Myres, unidentified, Judge B.F. Myres, and Warren Sumpter Myres. (PCM.)

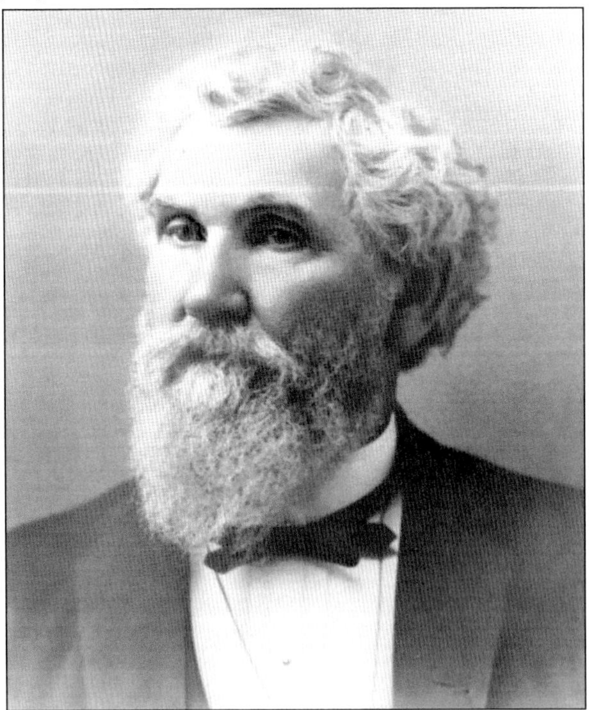

Thomas Bard McFarland. McFarland came to California in 1850 and mined for three years. In 1853, he returned to his legal profession. He was elected to the 14th District Judgeship in Auburn twice, but contrary to both law and public opinion, his decision to permit Chinese testimony against a white man doomed his candidacy for a third term. In 1886, he was elected associate justice of the state supreme court. (CSC.)

William Crutcher. Crutcher was deputy sheriff and a posse member who was wounded at the last shoot-out of outlaw Rattlesnake Dick in 1859. By 1867, he had gotten involved in the Auburn Water Works, acquiring the rights to various springs around town. With four reservoirs, he supplied drinking water to residences and businesses, as well as the water tank at the railroad depot. (PCM.)

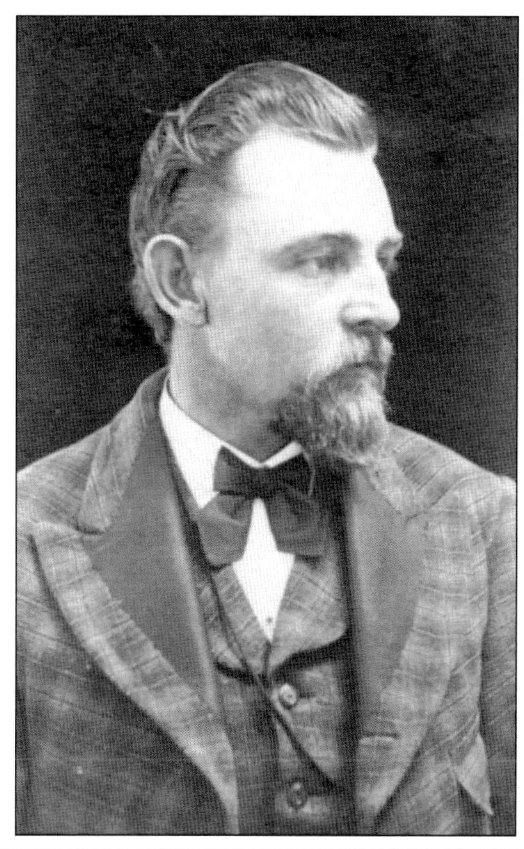

Crutcher Home. On this 10-acre farm in town, William and Mary Elizabeth Crutcher grew persimmons, grapes, walnuts, Italian chestnuts, and almonds, along with 60 orange trees. In 1877, 1880, and 1881, they found significant amounts of gold in their large garden. This site on High Street has been covered over with cement to accommodate the *Auburn Journal* building. Mary was a talented musician who gave lessons to many in the community. (TW.)

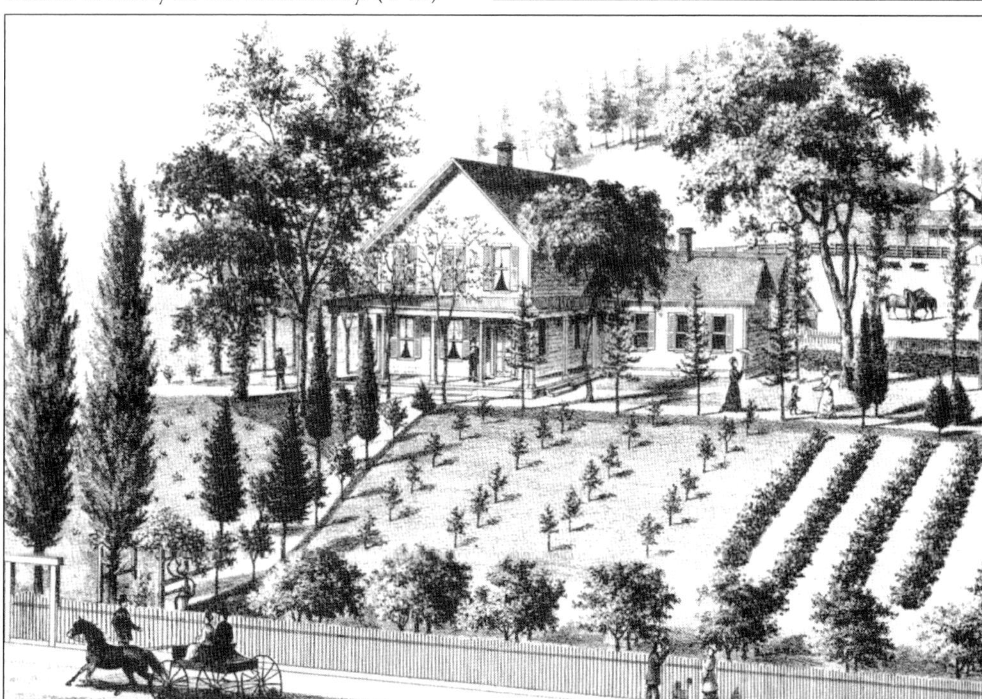

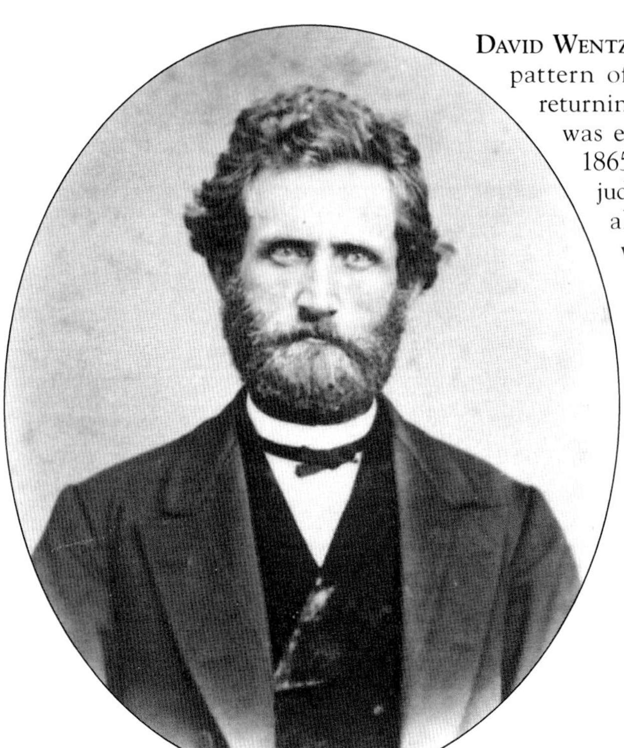

David Wentz Spear. Spear followed the typical pattern of mining for a few years before returning to his profession as a lawyer. He was elected county clerk in 1863 and 1865. In 1867, he was elected county judge. In 1870, under his supervision, all the unclaimed land in the city was put up for auction and sold from the steps of the courthouse. (DH.)

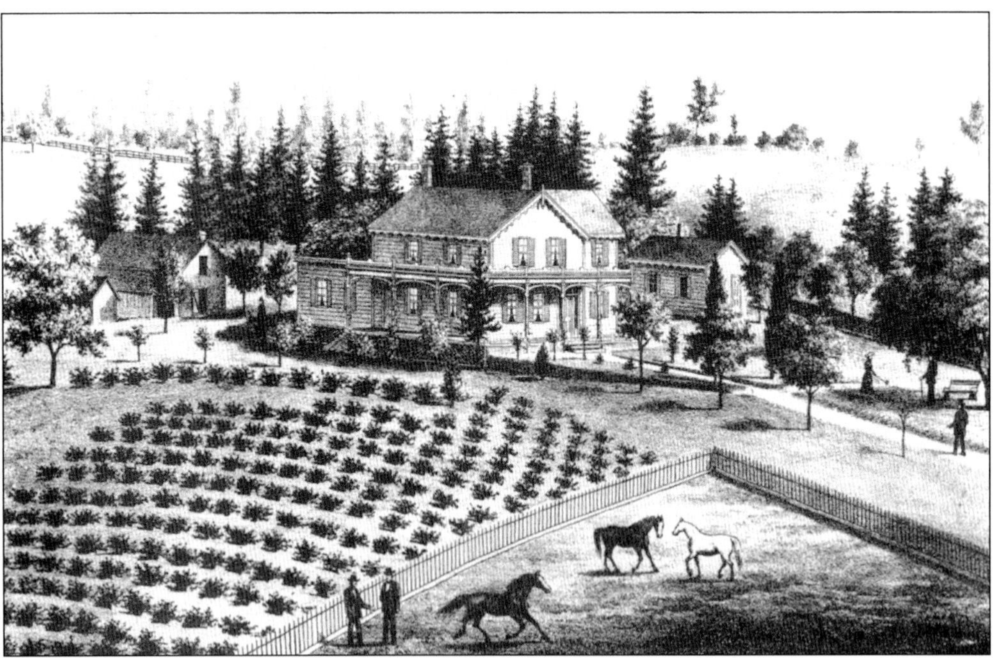

Spear Home. David and Mabel Spear lived in this Sacramento Street house on three acres of property right in the middle of Auburn's Chinatown. Its location was directly across the street from Auburn's present-day Joss House. After the fire of 1877 that originated in Chinatown, Spear was included in a group of men that tried, unsuccessfully, to buy out the Chinese in Auburn. (TW.)

Edward Lewis Craig. Craig came to California in 1852 and mined for several years before studying law in Nevada City. After moving to Auburn in the early 1860s, Craig became a two-term district attorney. He eventually became the general solicitor for the Central Pacific Railroad and was known for clarifying local railroad land ownership issues. He was also known as a great hunter, always having the best-trained hunting dogs and the best shotguns. (DH.)

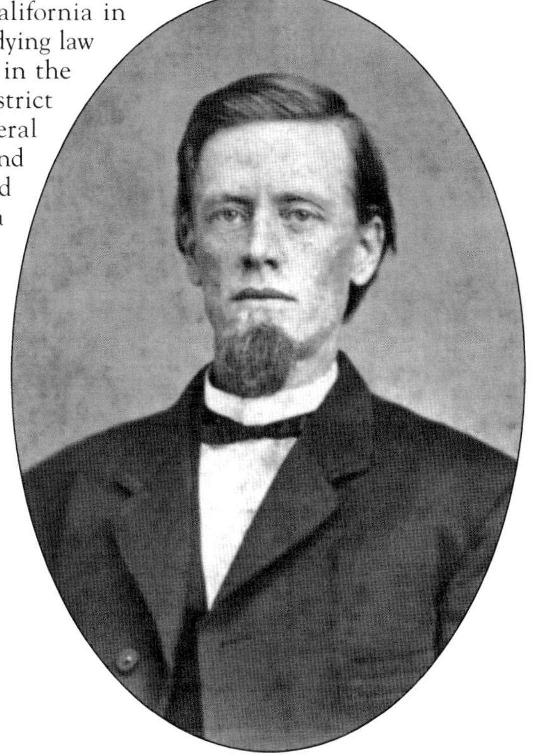

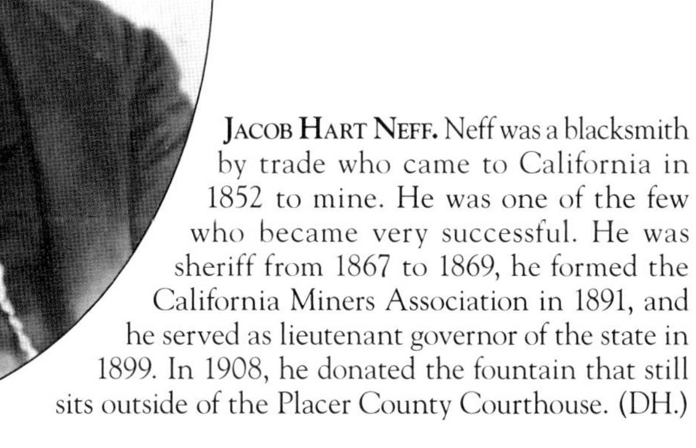

Jacob Hart Neff. Neff was a blacksmith by trade who came to California in 1852 to mine. He was one of the few who became very successful. He was sheriff from 1867 to 1869, he formed the California Miners Association in 1891, and he served as lieutenant governor of the state in 1899. In 1908, he donated the fountain that still sits outside of the Placer County Courthouse. (DH.)

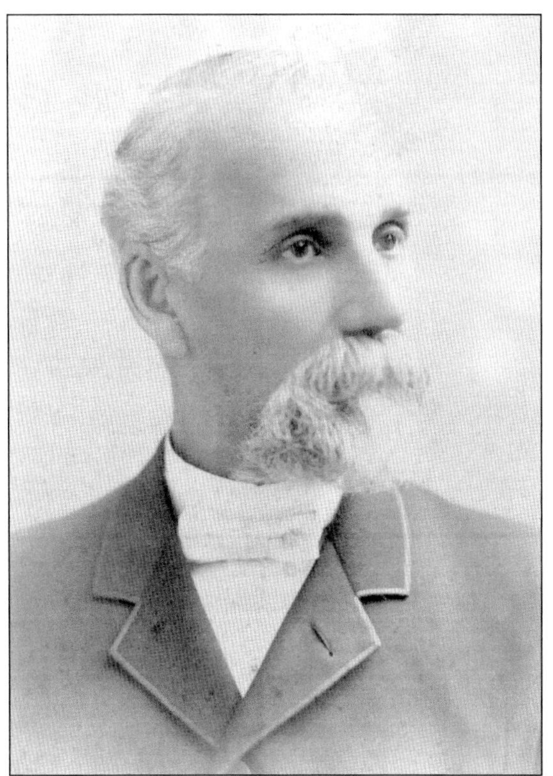

John M. Fulweiler. Fulweiler crossed the plains with his father in 1850. He mined in several counties for the next 15 years but turned to the law after an injury. He was elected district attorney for Placer County in 1871. He was easily reelected to a second term, after which he returned to private practice, specializing in mining law. He was considered one of the finest practicing attorneys in Auburn. (PCM.)

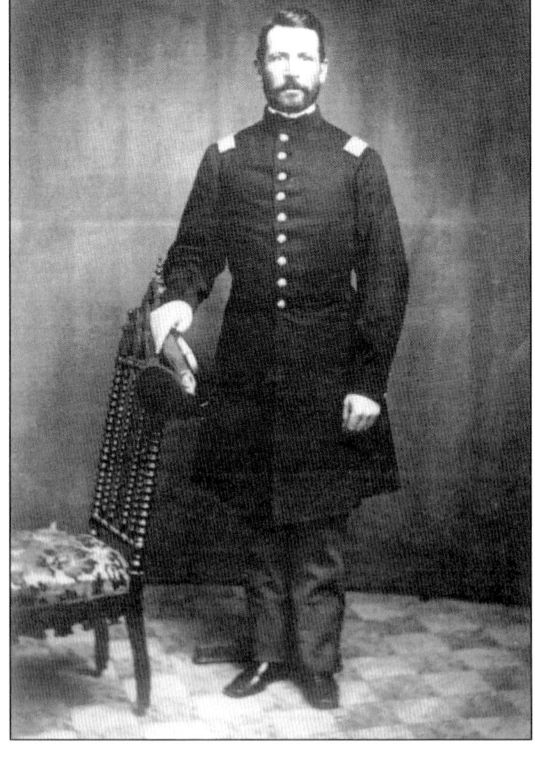

Capt. Jesse Ives Fitch. At the outbreak of the Civil War, Fitch, who was active in Republican politics, raised a company of volunteers from the Foresthill Divide that served the duration of the war. Later, he was active in the Grand Army of the Republic, as well as community affairs involving the planning and construction of the Auburn racetrack. He was county judge from 1872 to 1880. (PCM.)

Charles Chase Crosby. Crosby was elected sheriff in 1877. He held the post of county recorder for three terms and served on the school board as well. Before the fire stations were built, his Empire Livery Stable in Old Town housed 40–50 buckets and several ladders for the volunteer fire department. (DH.)

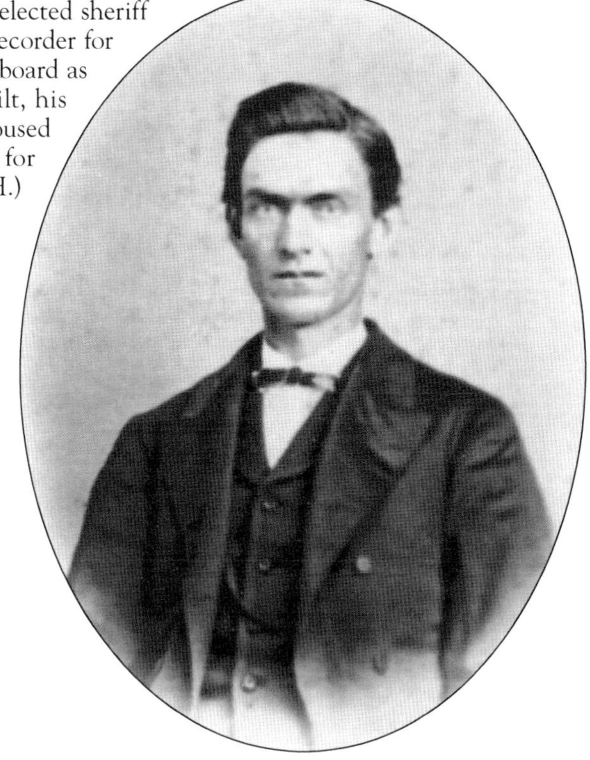

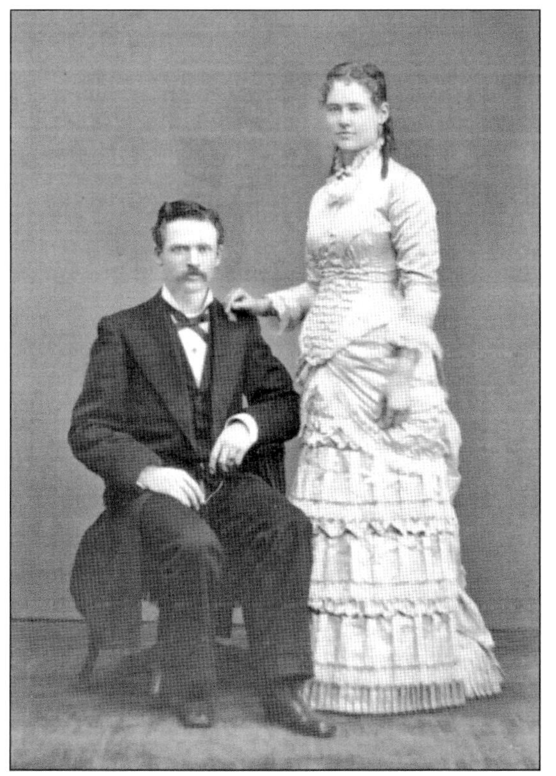

William and Jennie Lardner. Deprived of early schooling, Lardner doggedly pursued his education, receiving his law degree in 1877. He was elected district attorney and was known as an excellent trial lawyer. He prosecuted the men who derailed the train near Colfax in 1881. In 1924, he and Michael J. Brock wrote the voluminous *History of Placer and Nevada Counties*. (PCM.)

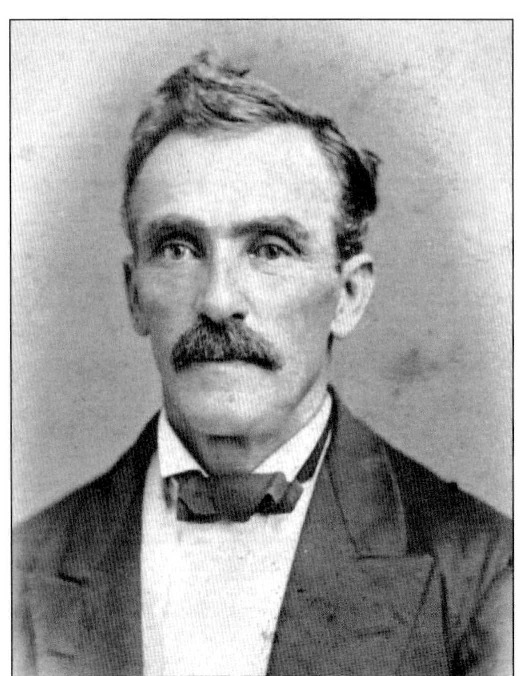

Asahel Huntley. Huntley was a merchant seaman before coming to California in the early 1850s. He served as undersheriff for several years before being elected sheriff in 1882 and again in 1884. He was noted for his courage and coolness in hours of physical danger. He built the impressive mansion in downtown Auburn that is now known as the Power's Mansion Inn. (PCM.)

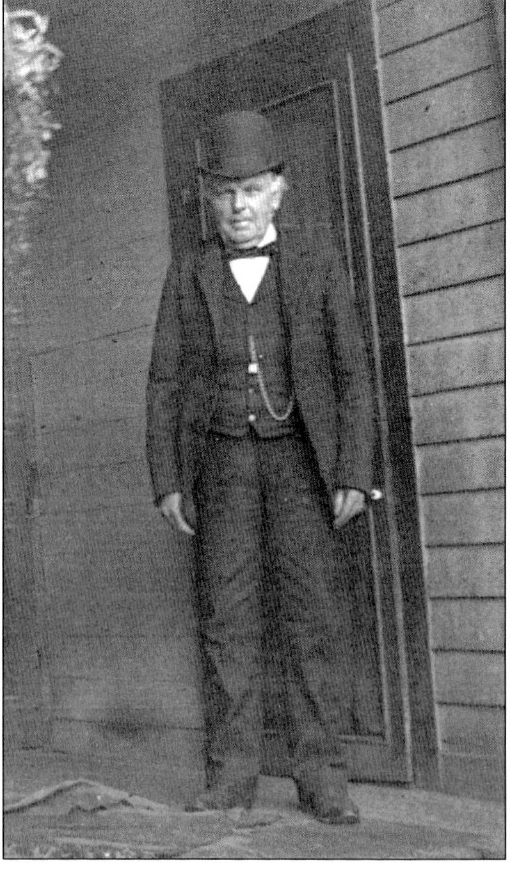

Edward Walsh. Edward and his brother James came to California in 1851. As Irish Catholics, the Walshes donated land for the local Catholic church. Though there was much anti-Catholic sentiment in Auburn, Edward was elected the town's first mayor in 1888 when the city was incorporated for the second time. The Walsh family was known for the festive celebrations they held each St. Patrick's Day. (PCM.)

Judge James E. Prewett. It was fitting that Judge Prewett was one of the orators at the dedication of the new county courthouse in 1898, as he had already served in Auburn as a lawyer, district attorney, and superior court judge for over 20 years. He was a multilingual chemist, historian, land developer, and motorcyclist, as well as president of the local literary society. He was also the first to have an automobile in Auburn. (PCM.)

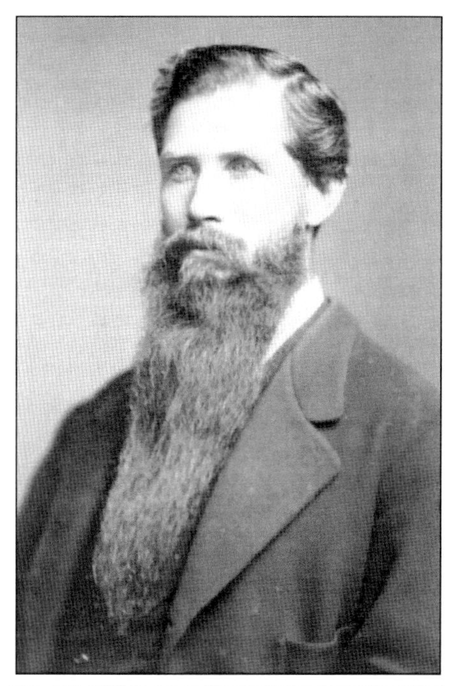

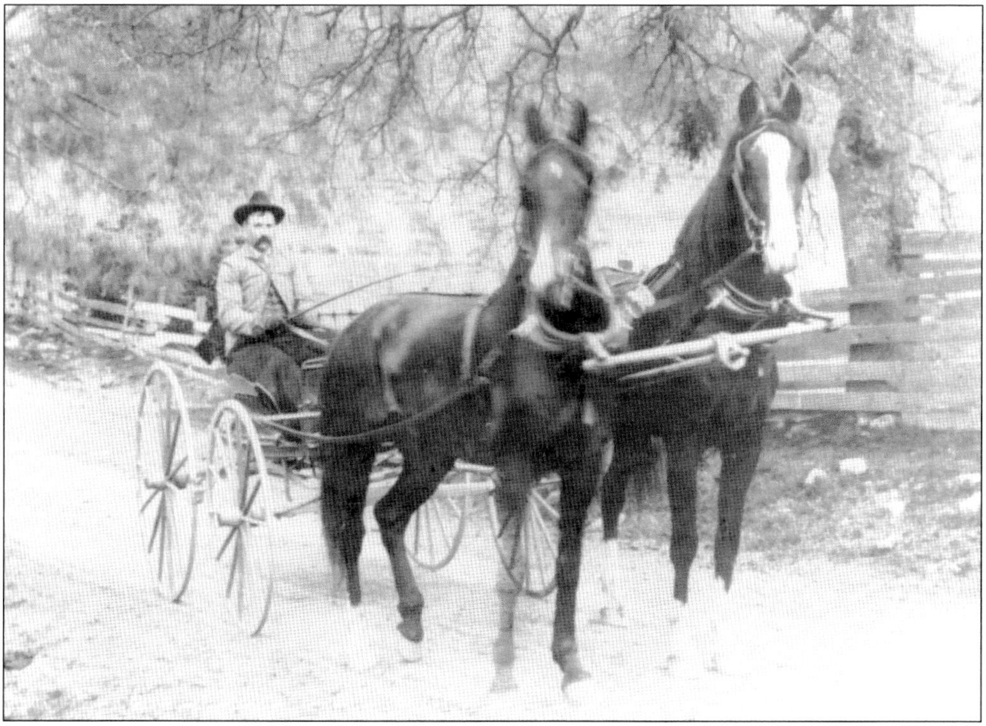

Charles Keena. Keena served two terms as sheriff. He was also a county supervisor and the county assessor. It was during his term as sheriff that 19-year-old Adolf Weber of Auburn killed his father, mother, sister, and brother in 1904. Keena served the warrant to arrest Weber and later escorted Weber to Folsom Prison to be executed. Keena owned and raced very fine thoroughbred horses; he is shown here with Michy and Free. (PCM.)

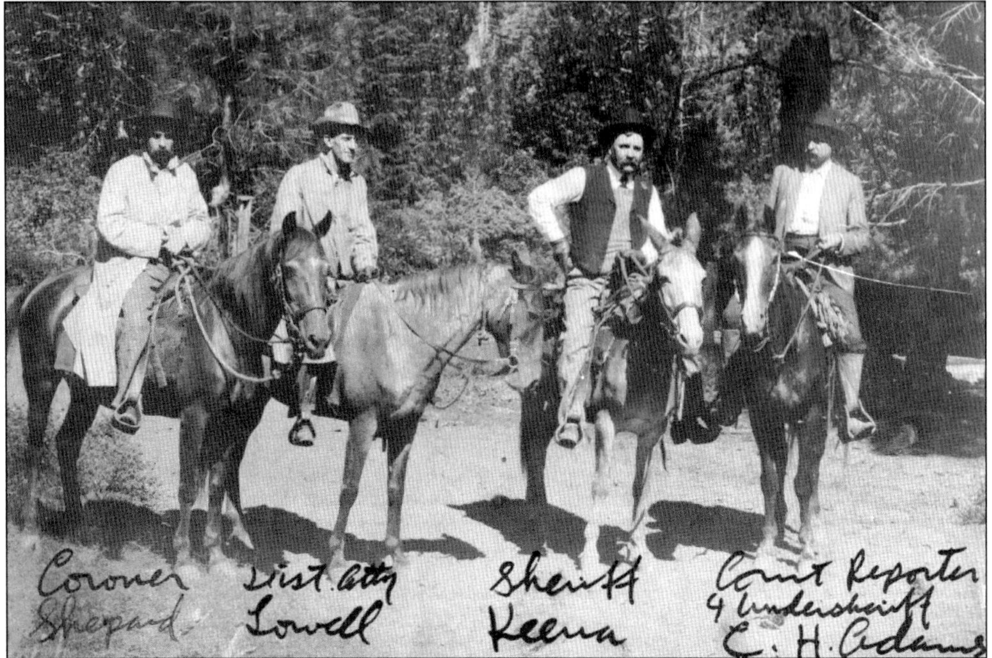

POSSE ON HORSEBACK. This posse is headed out in pursuit of the criminals involved in a Michigan Bluff murder. From left to right are Will Shepard, coroner; Marshall Lowell, district attorney; Charles Keena, sheriff; and Charles H. Adams, court reporter and undersheriff. Even by 1905, horseback was still the easiest way to traverse the rough territory. (PCM.)

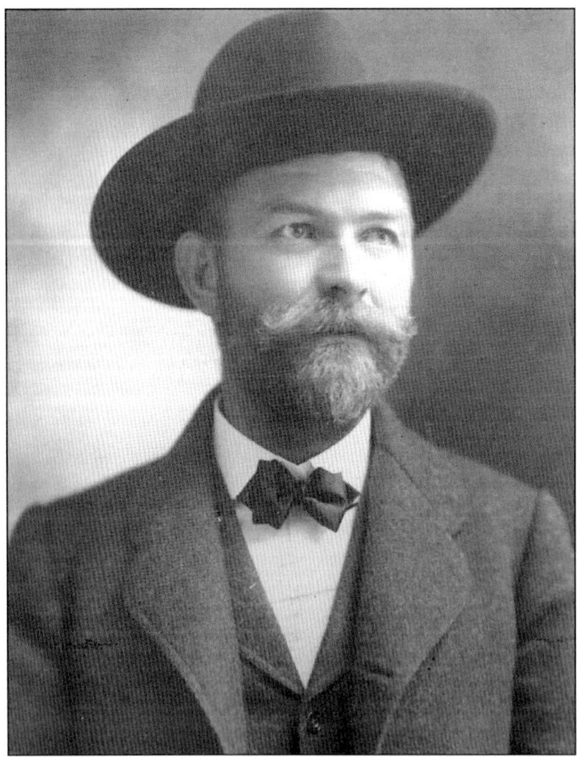

FRANK HENRY DEPENDENER. Nicknamed "Big Dip" because of his six-foot-seven height, Dependener was considered "the most feared man in public service," according to his obituary in the *Placer Herald*. As deputy sheriff for 37 years, he was said to have 7 bullet wounds and more than 30 marks inflicted by criminals with weapons of various kinds. He was killed in an automobile accident after a raid on a bootlegging operation in 1928. (PCM.)

William Henry McDaniel Jr. McDaniel was a miner, merchant, and landowner. He owned many of the houses in Chinatown, where he had his store and home. McDaniel was known to be a great friend to the Chinese community. When an out-of-town Chinese man murdered him in 1867, Auburn's Chinese community raised $1,000 for a reward. The local Chinese added the Chinese characters for "Here Lies a Good Man" to his tombstone. (CS.)

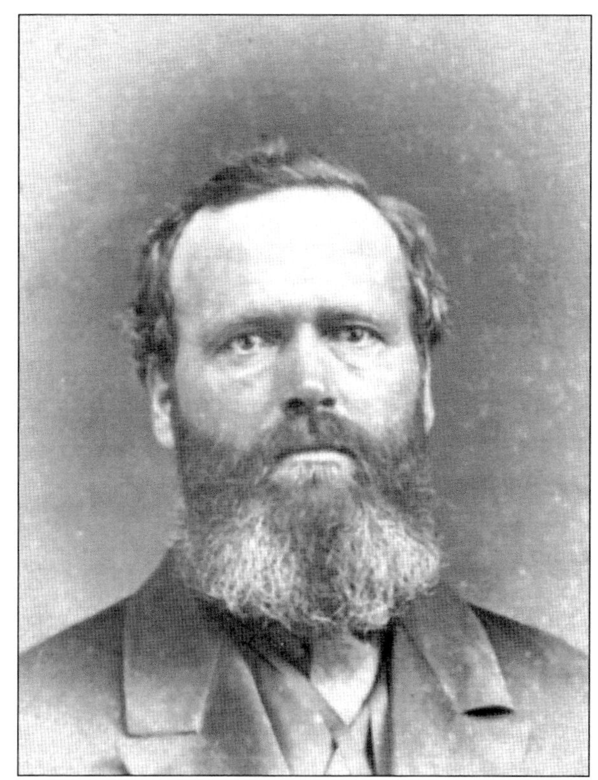

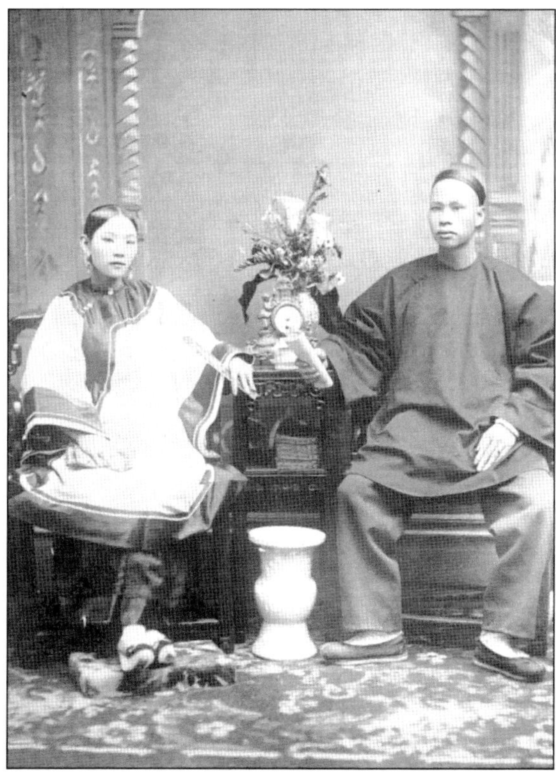

Chuey Fong and Go Sam. This handsome couple was involved in one of the most intriguing and bewildering court cases held in Auburn in the 1890s. The Anglo court had a difficult time sorting out fact from fiction. Entwined in the case were China Mollie, who ran a Chinese whorehouse in Auburn; representatives of the San Francisco tongs; and an overweight "hag" as a false stand-in for the lovely Chuey Fong. (PCM.)

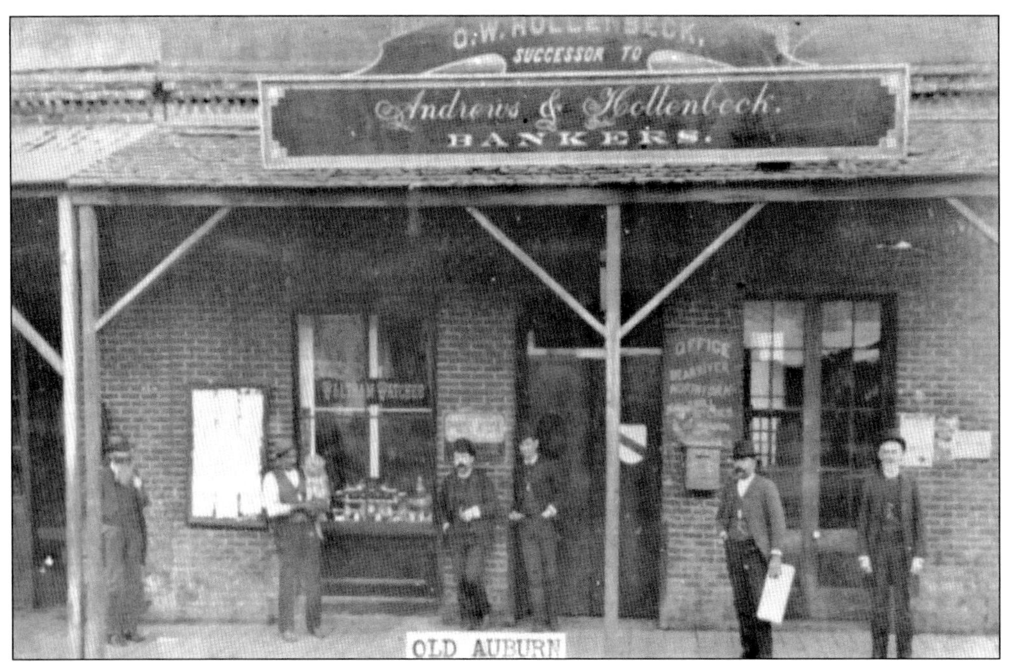

HOLLENBECK'S BANK. Orrin Whitcomb Hollenbeck, whose portrait is seen here, founded the mining town of Gold Run and was at one time elected both county treasurer and Auburn city treasurer. He became the sole banker and Wells Fargo agent in 1883 after his partner Moses Andrews died. He still kept Andrews's jewelry business and enjoyed the fine reputation that he and his partner had built up over the years, but on a Black Monday in 1892, his bank was found short of funds. His poor management had led to insolvency, scandal, and prosecution. Although there were several trials, his many friends raised money to help him repay public funds so he could evade criminal charges; he was a destroyed man nonetheless. (Above, AJS; left, DH.)

Nine

The Social Fabric

The transformation of Auburn from a mining camp and distribution center into a town was in large part due to the arrival and influence of women. There were very few women in the village in the early days. Sheriff John Boggs recalled only two ladies in attendance at a dance in 1849: Nancy McCormick and Eliza Elliott, who both ran hotels. One miner later wrote, "Wherever women is not there reigns vice and immorality."

As more women arrived, the rough-and-tumble atmosphere of the early camp began to change. As historian Joanne Levy wrote of the Gold Rush era, "Women, literally and figuratively, rolled up their sleeves and went to work to tidy up society."

While there were ministers among the fortune hunters, they gave only occasional sermons. Sundays were observed by the miners, but mostly as a day of rest and relaxation and a time to catch up on onerous household chores.

The organization of formal churches was paramount to many women. They believed that churches would bring stability and civility to the camp. One can only imagine the prim and proper Harriett Crandall, Belle Love, and Mary Loving marching in corsets and bonnets through the streets of the camp, entering each saloon and gambling house to solicit money for the construction of the Methodist Episcopal Church.

The first school in Auburn was run by a Mrs. Horton in 1851. Initially, classes were held on the lower floors of the Masonic Hall near the courthouse. By 1854, there were 39 boys and 29 girls of school age.

The all-volunteer fire department was organized in 1853. The county established a hospital for the benefit of the sick and indigent in 1855. The Sons of Temperance (ladies welcome) held weekly meetings as early as 1859. A lending library was organized in 1887.

The arrival of women had little influence on the fraternal societies, as many of the miners simply reestablished the traditional male-dominated organizations upon arriving in California. Eureka Lodge No. 16 of the Masons was established in 1851, and the Odd Fellows followed in 1852.

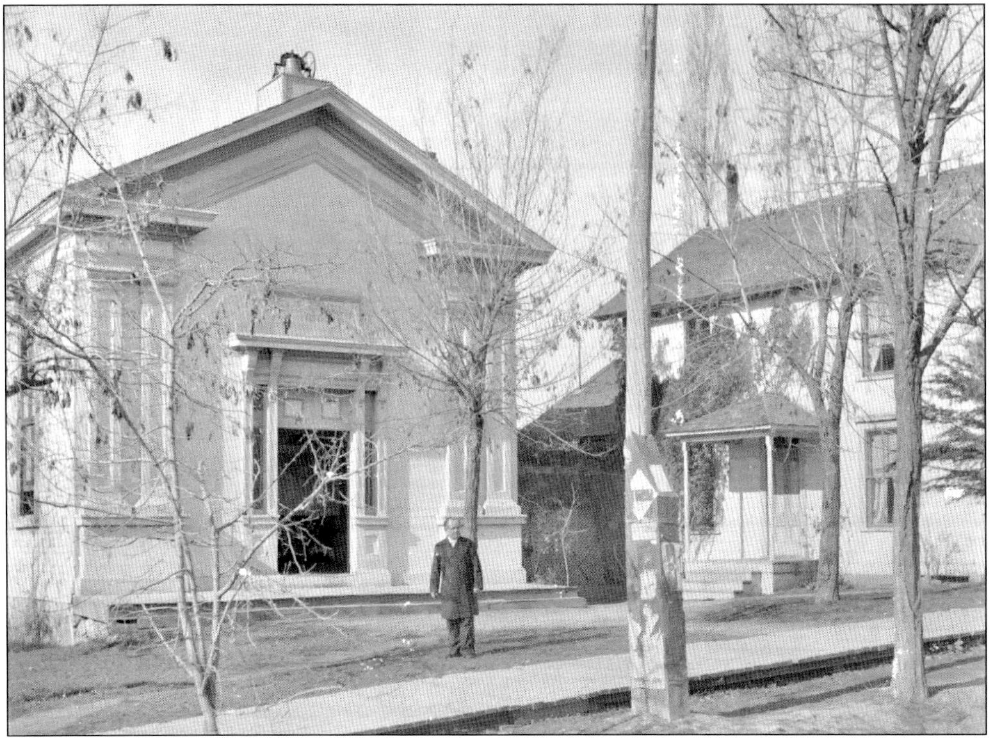

METHODIST EPISCOPAL CHURCH. This church was built in 1858. It was the second Methodist Episcopal Church in town. The first, built in 1853, was located on Sacramento Street. This church, with modifications and additions, still stands today as the Pioneer Methodist Church. A bequest from Harriett Crandall's estate built the tower and new wing for the church in 1905. (AJS.)

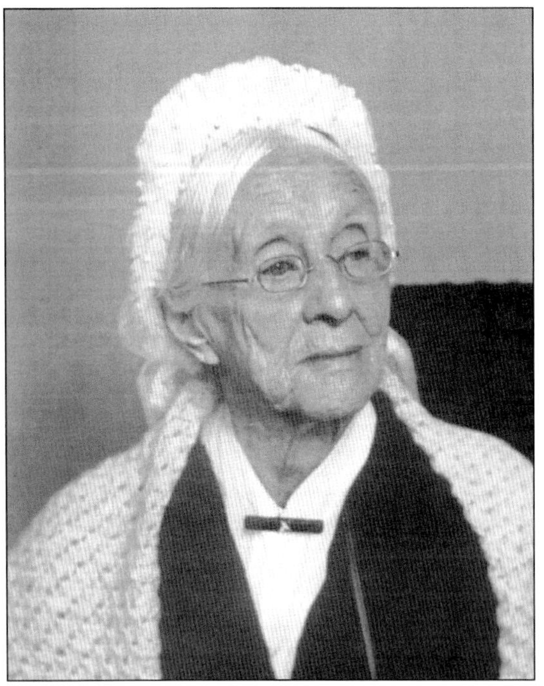

HARRIETT J. (RUSSELL) CRANDALL. Harriett married John Crandall in 1835. John came to California in 1849, and Harriett joined him in 1851 via the Isthmus of Panama route. The Crandalls owned about 20 acres on High Street, between Old Town and Downtown Auburn. They held the land intact until the 1880s. The Crandalls were influential in founding and supporting the Methodist congregation. Harriett is credited with planting the first orange tree in Auburn. (PCM.)

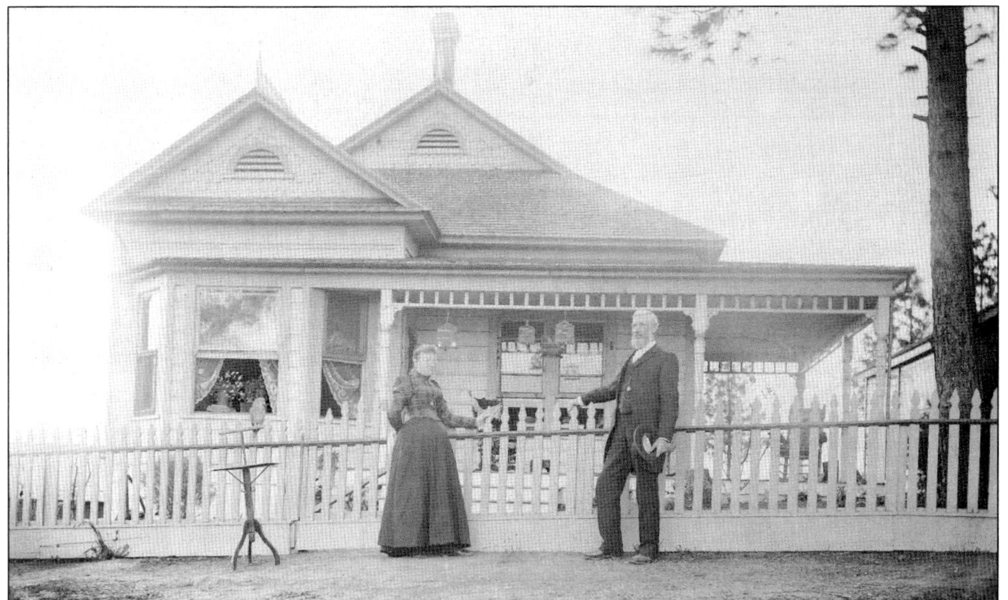

Rev. John and Johanna Chisholm. John was the minister at the Methodist Episcopal Church for many years. He and his brother James had a fruit packinghouse near the East Auburn railroad station. This house still stands at the top of California Street. Note the parrot perched on the table at left. (PCM.)

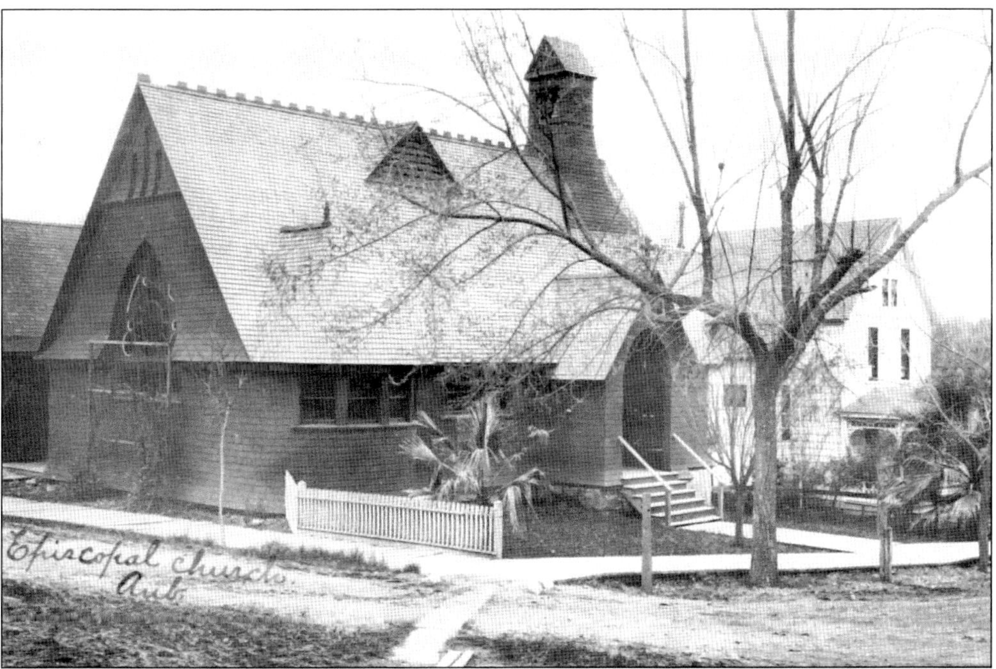

St. Luke's Episcopal Church. The congregation of St. Luke's organized in 1887 and built this church a few years later in 1890. The distinctive and unusual design was featured in the *California Architect and Building News* that same year. This church still stands on Lewis Street and houses a vibrant congregation. (AJS.)

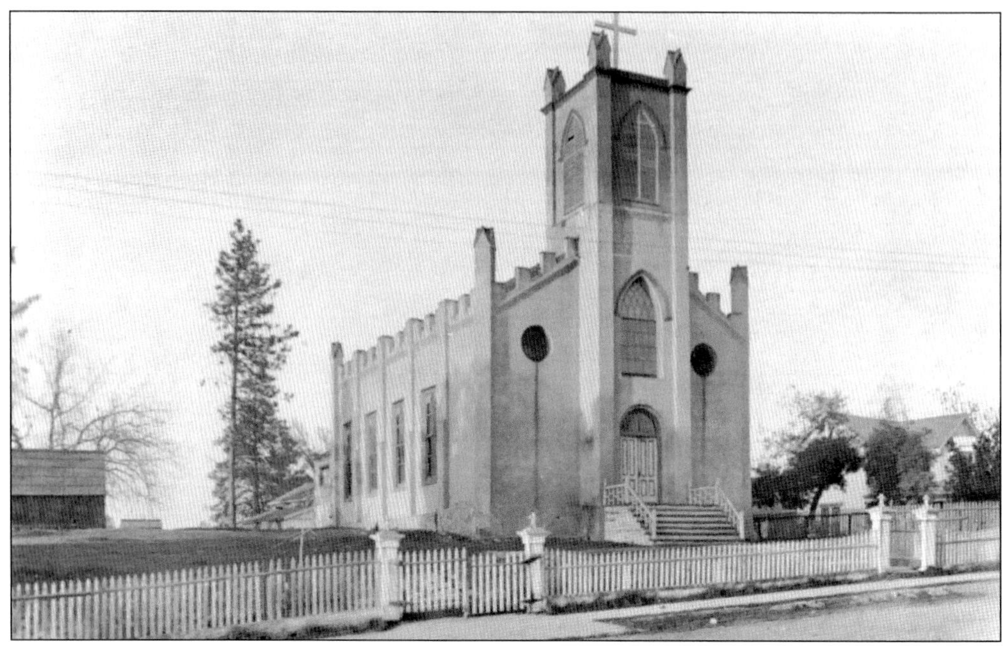

St. Theresa's Catholic Church. Auburn's large number of Irish and German Catholic immigrants first held church services in the county courthouse in the 1850s. Dedicated in 1859, this large brick church was built in just four months to serve the local Catholic community. The present St. Joseph's Church was constructed on an adjoining lot in 1911 in response to the needs of a growing congregation. (AJS.)

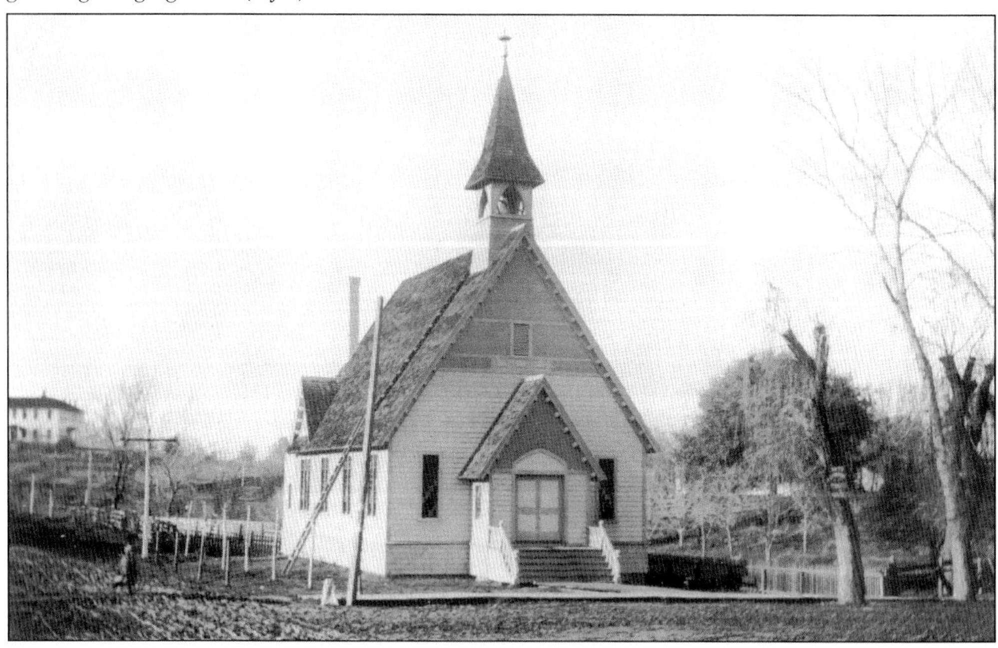

Congregational Church. In 1875 a Congregational Church of nine members was formed in Auburn. Benefit concerts were held at the music hall in 1880 to raise funds for its construction. The church was dedicated in February 1883 with Annie Reamer at the organ. A major addition to the church was made in 1897. It was replaced by a service station in the 1940s. (AJS.)

First Baptist Church. The Auburn First Baptist Church was organized in 1892 and, for the first few years, held services in the Good Templars Hall. In 1898, this church was built on the corner of East Placer and High Streets. Visible is the plank bridge that crossed the South Fork of the Auburn Ravine. At one time, the ravine ran right through town, but it is now mostly underground. (PCM.)

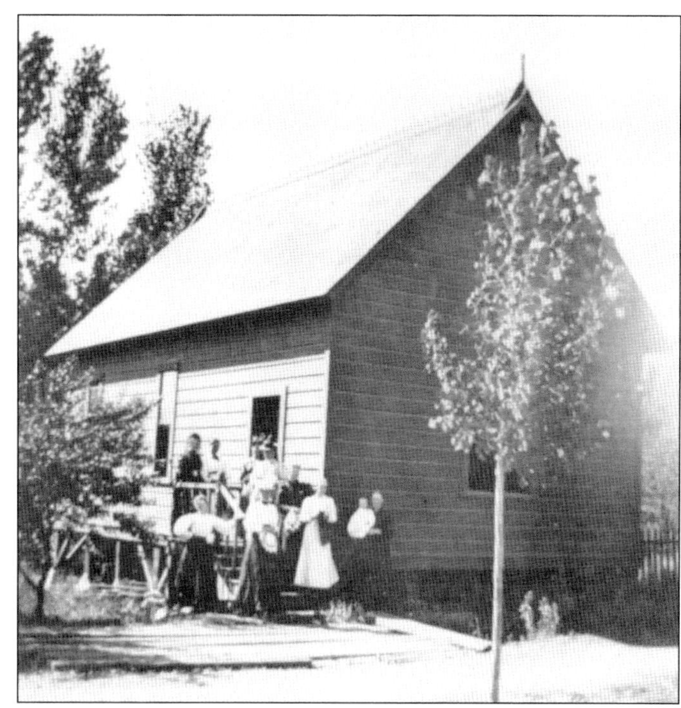

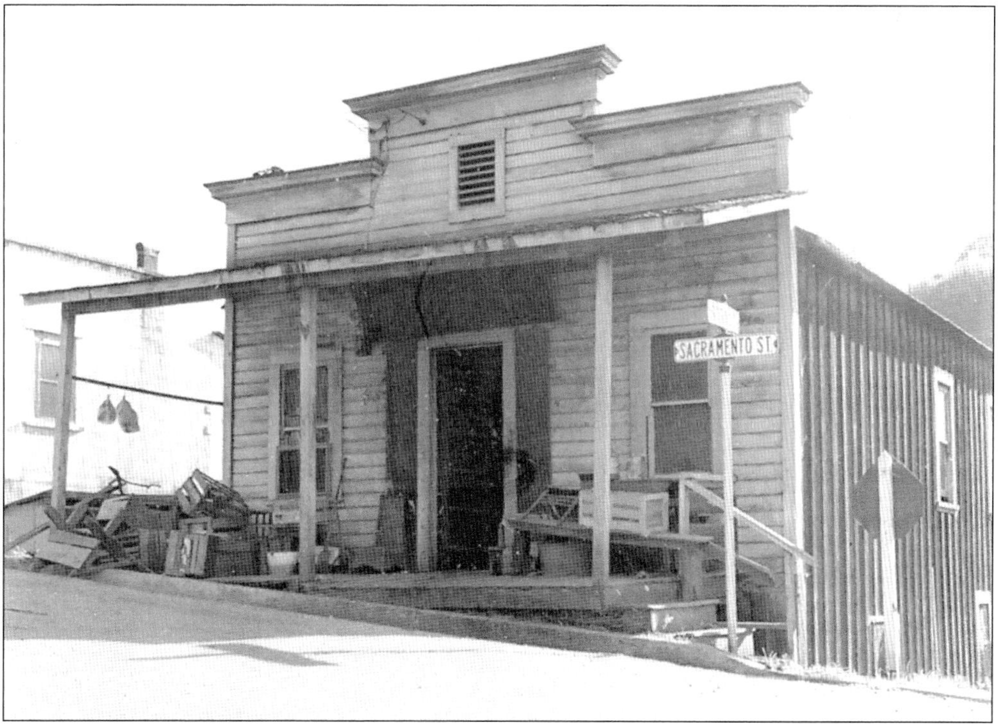

Joss House. This is the fourth Joss House built in Auburn. It was the meeting place of the Ling Ying Association and, like its predecessors, fulfilled the needs of the Chinese community as a place of worship, a social center, and even a boardinghouse. The plain exterior is juxtaposed with the colorful and ornate 1860s altar within. (PCM.)

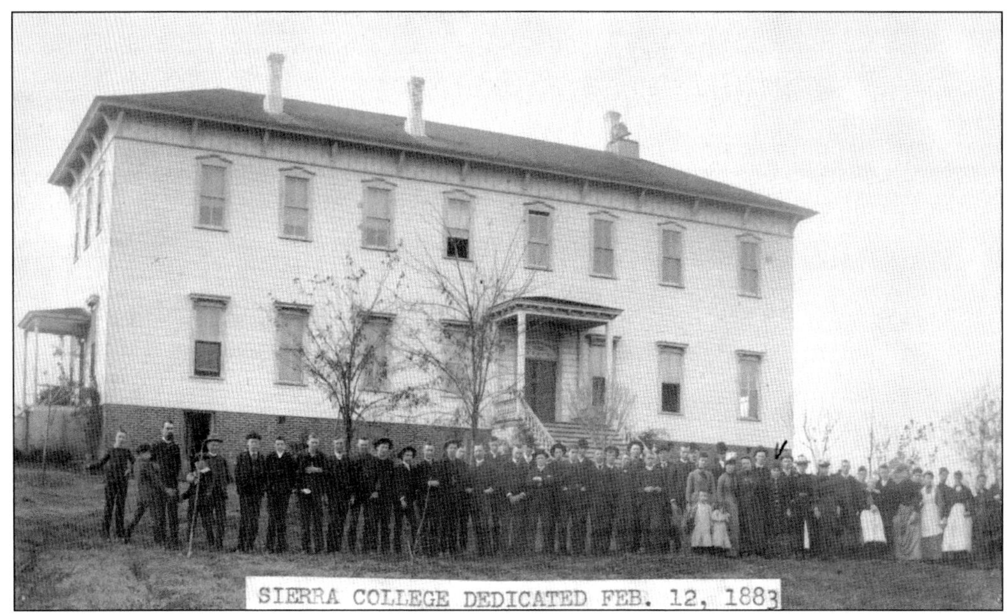

SIERRA NORMAL COLLEGE. Built in 1883, this school was organized by three teachers who promised to match funds raised by the community. The school offered business, collegiate, and musical courses. In 1893, the name was changed to Auburn College. The site, originally called Chaparral Hill, then College Hill, is now the home of the present-day high school. (PCM.)

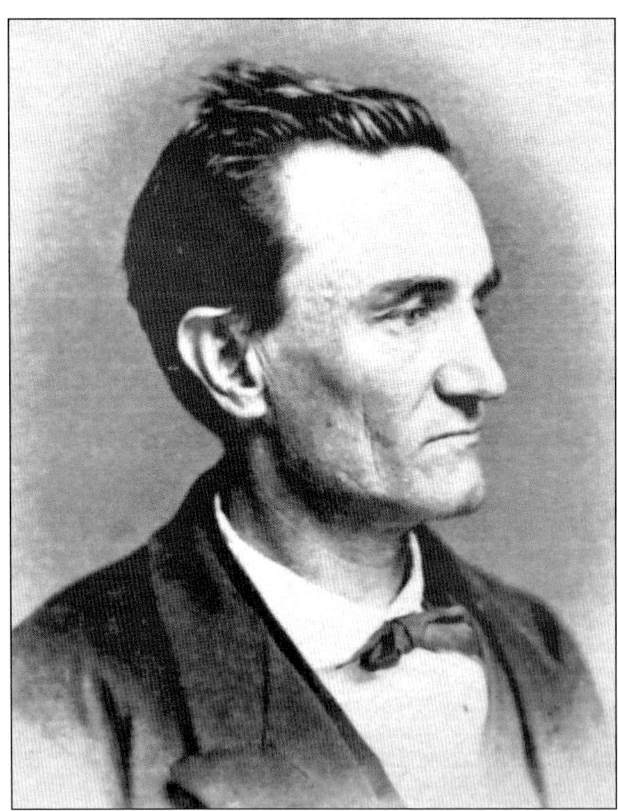

"GENERAL" JO HAMILTON. Hamilton was a successful and wealthy lawyer. Contemporaries noted his foghorn-like voice and said that his "gift for oratory made him feared by opposing counsel." He owned an interest in the Hidden Treasure mine. Generous to the community, he contributed cash and land for the Sierra Normal College. He received the moniker "General" for his two terms as state attorney general in 1871 and 1874. (CS.)

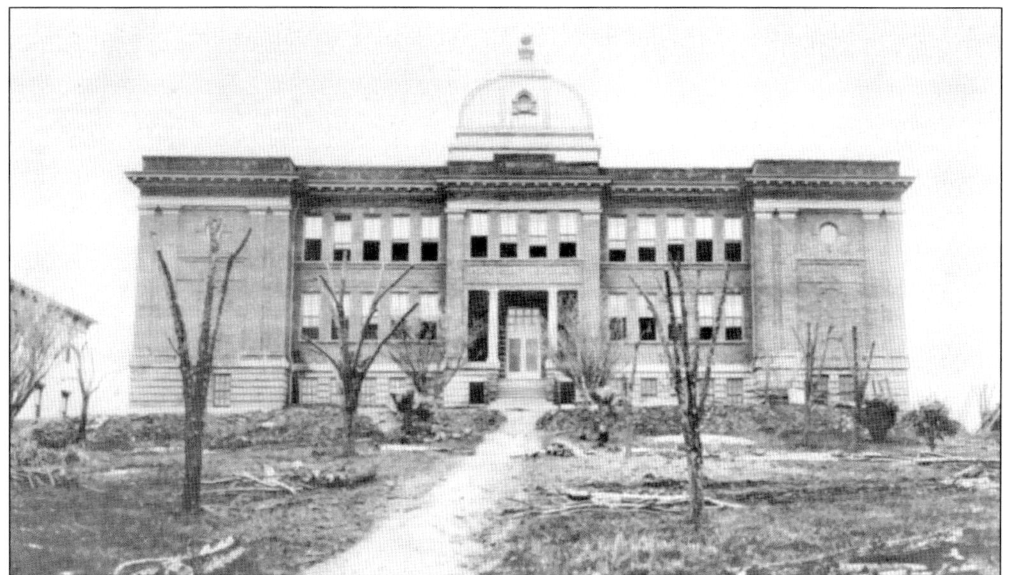

Placer County High School. This ornate tin-domed building was constructed in 1906–1907. The dome was removed in 1916 to permit structural changes to the rooms below. The school's mascot, the Hillmen, was suggested by alumnus Wendell Robie in 1936. The Hillmen athletic teams have remained a source of community pride for many years. The Sierra Normal College is barely visible at left. (PCM.)

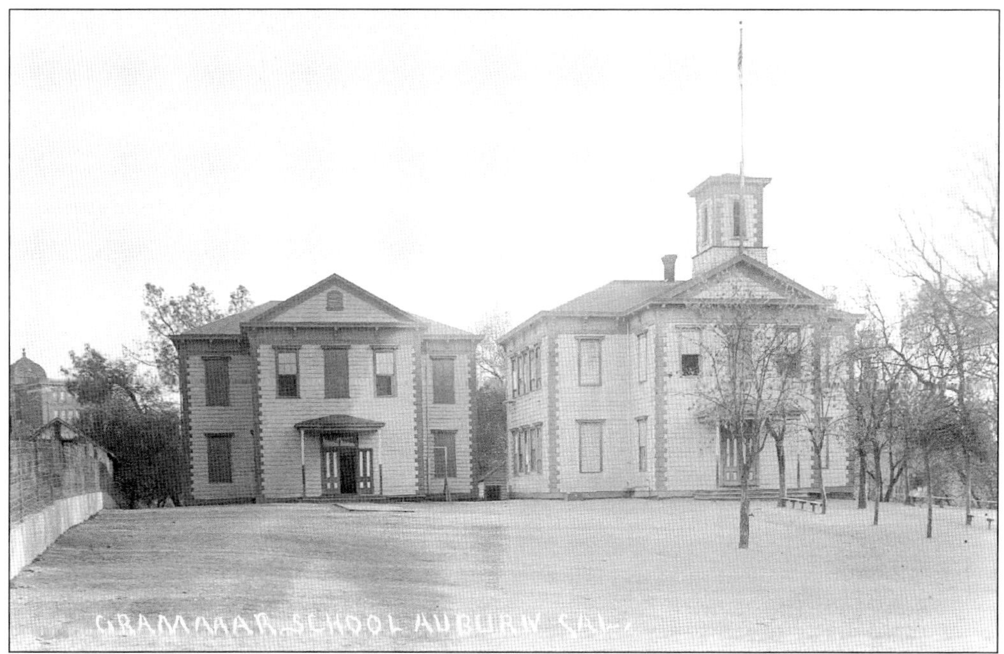

Grammar School. Capt. Alden Radcliff built the schoolhouse at left in 1866, and C.H. Hicks built the one at right in 1874. Edward M. Hall, Auburn forty-niner turned San Francisco banker, donated the 200-pound bell. Although the second grammar school was built as a two-story structure, the upper rooms were not finished until 1879. The high school is seen in the left background. (PCM.)

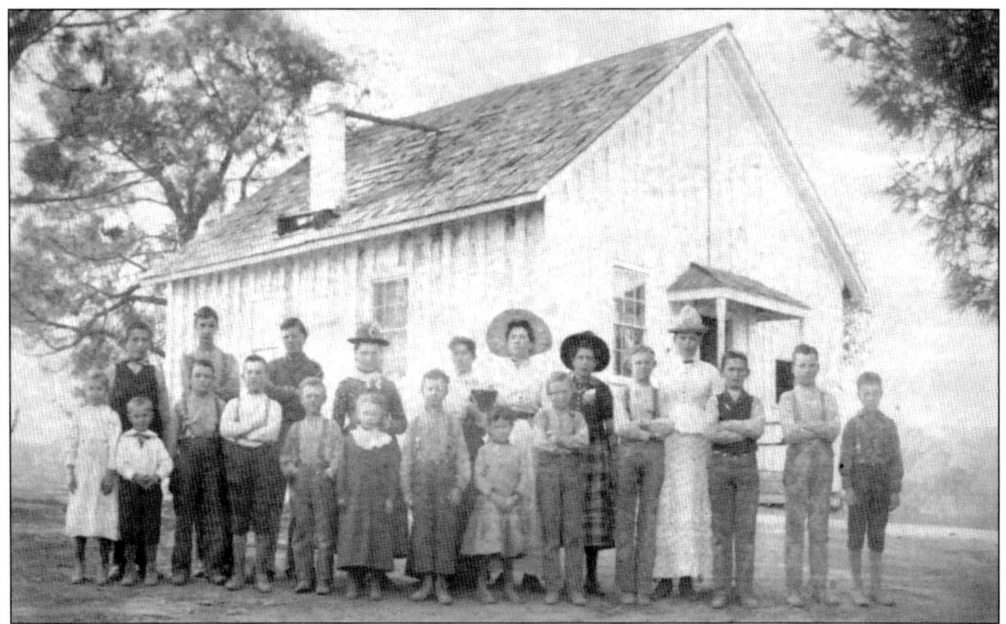

Outlying Schools. The one-room schoolhouse at Rattlesnake featured here is an example of the many rural schoolhouses essential to the educational system in the county. Edgewood, Lone Star, Foresthill, Christian Valley, Ophir, Long Valley, Alta, and Rock Creek were just a few of the outlying communities that all fed into the district-wide high school in Auburn. (PCM.)

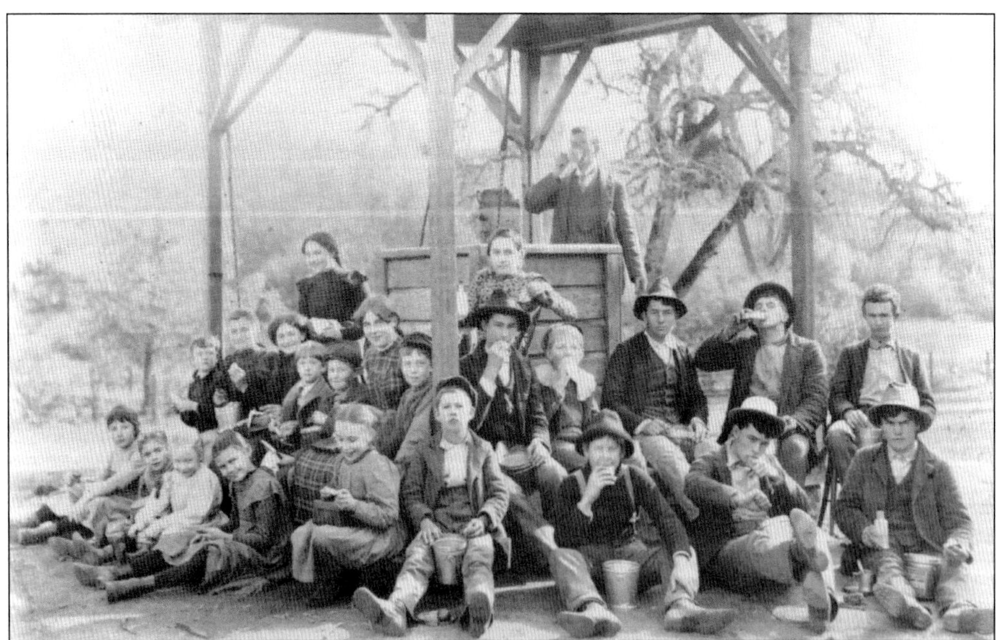

Long Valley School. The age range of the pupils at this typical one-room schoolhouse is shown in this photograph. The schoolmaster taught first grade through eighth grade. Long Valley is just south of the Auburn city limits. (PCM.)

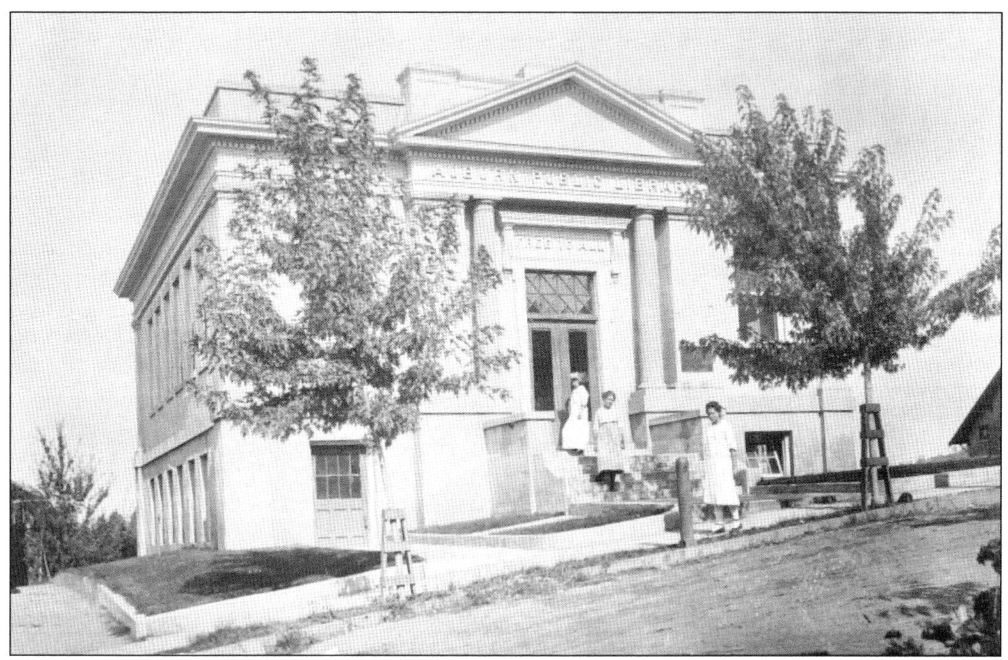

Carnegie Library. This is one of the 1,689 libraries built across America with funds from the Carnegie Foundation. Andrew Carnegie was a Scottish American businessman and philanthropist. This library opened in 1909. Although citizens offered more than a dozen sites for the library, it is still a mystery why this particular location was chosen. The building is now home to the Old Library Art Studios. (AJS.)

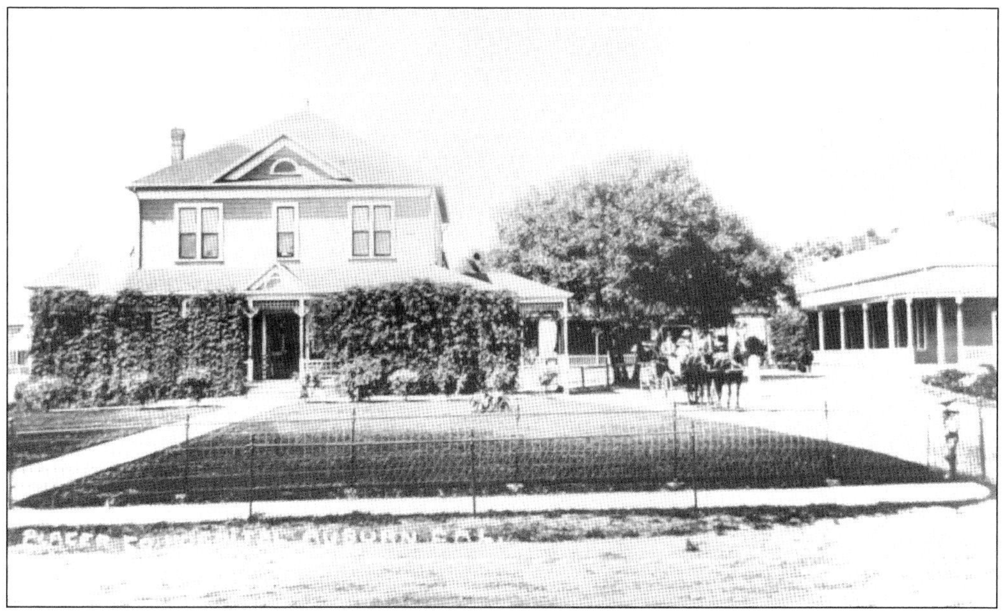

County Hospital. The growing problem of sick and indigent men, a majority of them former miners, had forced the county to establish a hospital by 1855. Pictured here is the third hospital run by the county. This large complex, built in 1900, covered 52 acres and included an orchard and a large vegetable garden. All labor on the grounds was performed entirely by the patients. (AJS.)

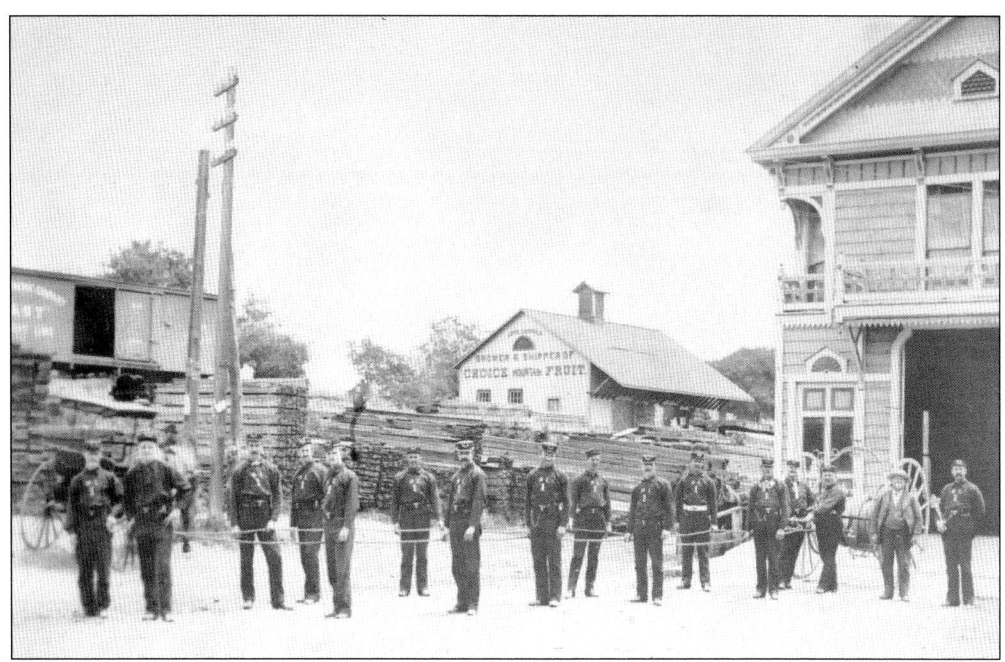

Firehouse. Although the town organized a volunteer fire department in 1852, there was no firehouse until this one was built in 1888. The downtown volunteers were first called the Central Hose Company, followed by Auburn Hose Company No. 1, then Hook and Ladder No. 1, and finally, "the Rattlers." This station is known locally as Firehouse No. 1. In 1973, it was moved to its present location on El Dorado Street. (PCM.)

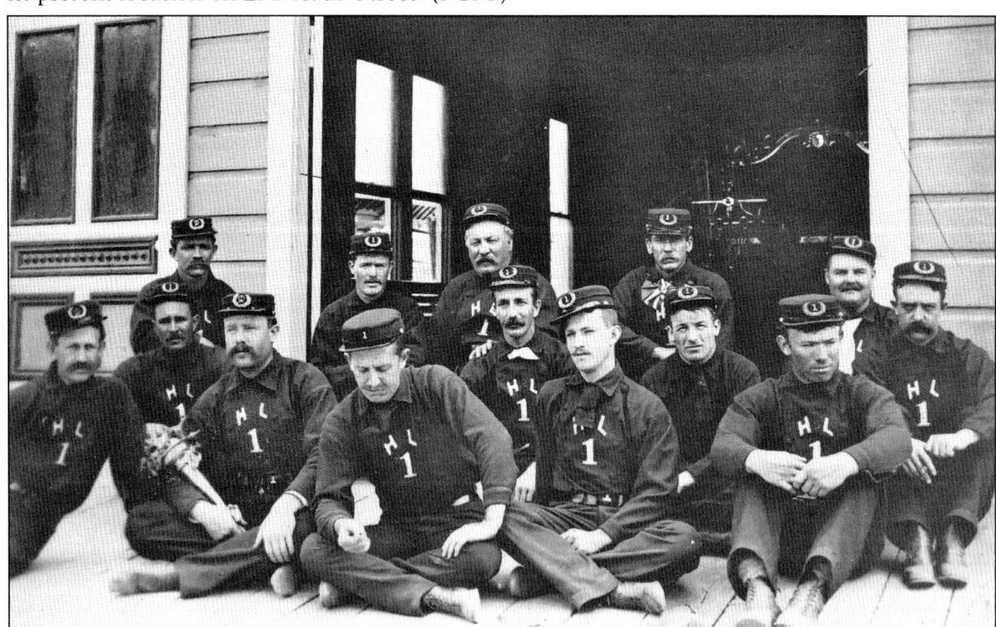

The Rattlers. Here, members of the volunteer fire department are seated in front of Firehouse No. 1. Their shirts were a distinctive red with "H.L. 1" printed on the front to signify Hook and Ladder No. 1. Some of the funds for building Firehouse No. 1 were received from Frederick Birdsall, who ran the Bear River Water and Mining Company from the upstairs part of the building. (PCM.)

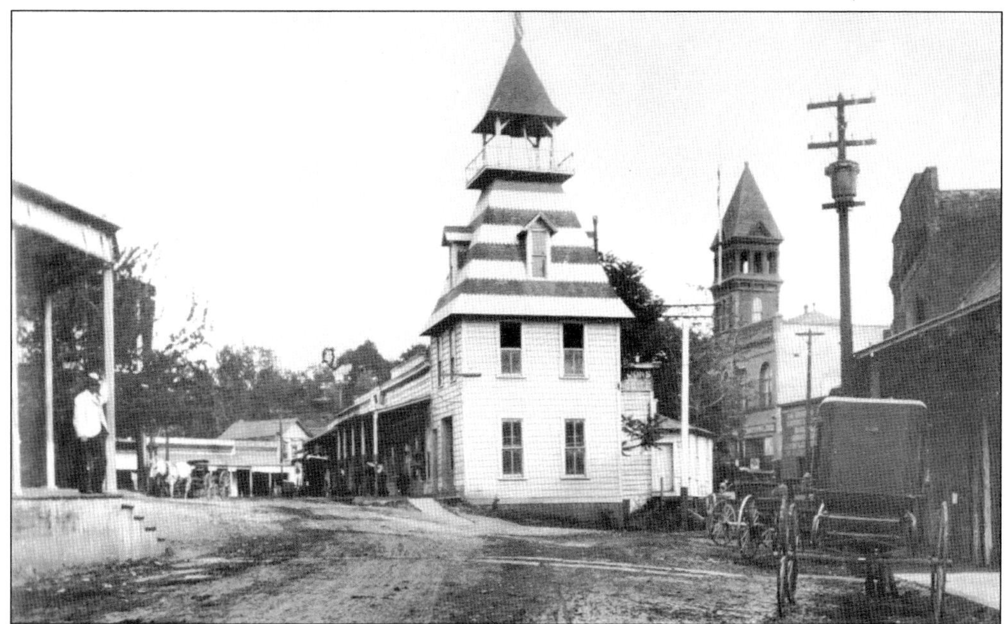

Old Town Firehouse. Firehouse No. 2 was built in 1891 and dedicated in 1892. This firehouse was moved a short distance in 1957 when the new freeway took out a significant section of Old Town. The tower at right was part of the privately built city hall that burned in 1905. (PCM.)

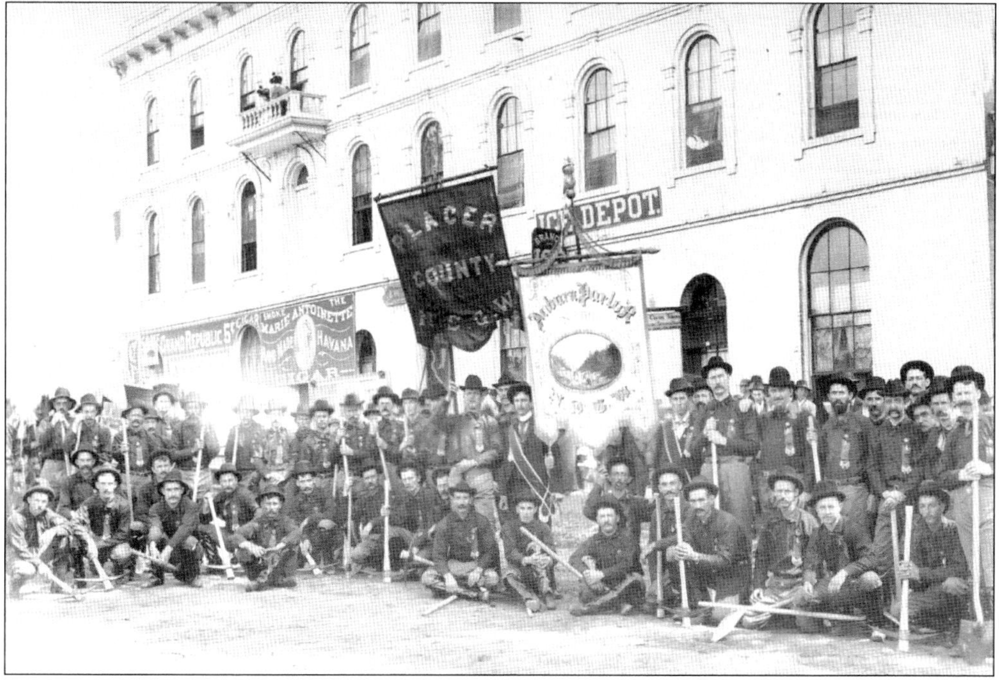

Native Sons of the Golden West. The Auburn and Placer County parlors joined together in Sacramento to celebrate Admission Day in 1895. The Native Sons of the Golden West (NSGW) were founded in 1875 with the goal of preserving and protecting California history. Today, the Auburn Parlor is noted for their participation in historical activities and the many plaques they have placed at historic sites throughout the area. (PCM.)

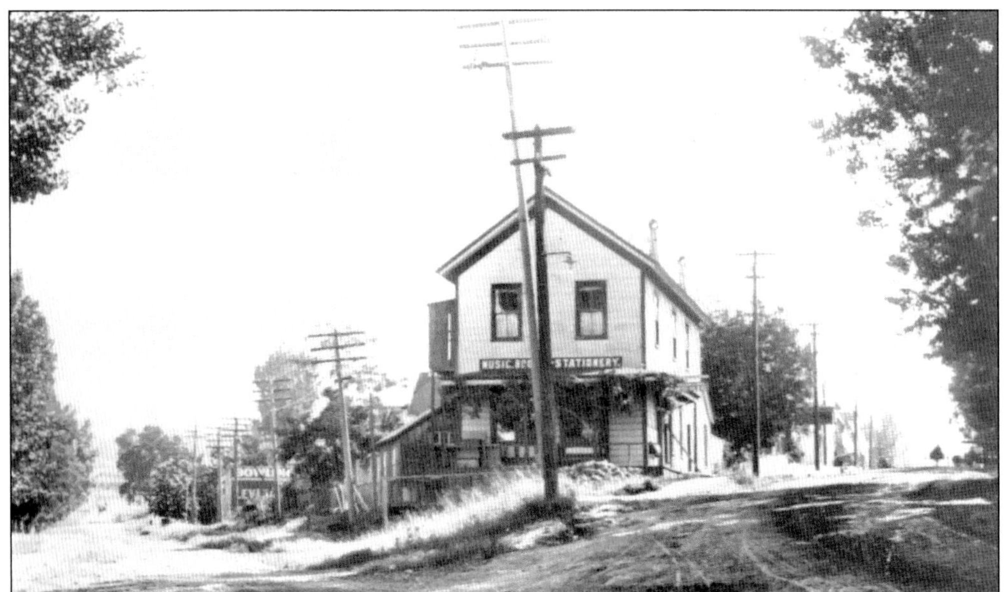

Good Templars Hall. Built on this triangular lot at the convergence of High Street and Lincoln Way in 1883, the Good Templars Hall had various uses over the years. In 1908, it was moved to its current location at 812 Lincoln Way. Temperance organizations, advocating abstinence from the use of alcohol, were unusual for the time; not only did they encourage women as members, but many women also held official positions. (AJS.)

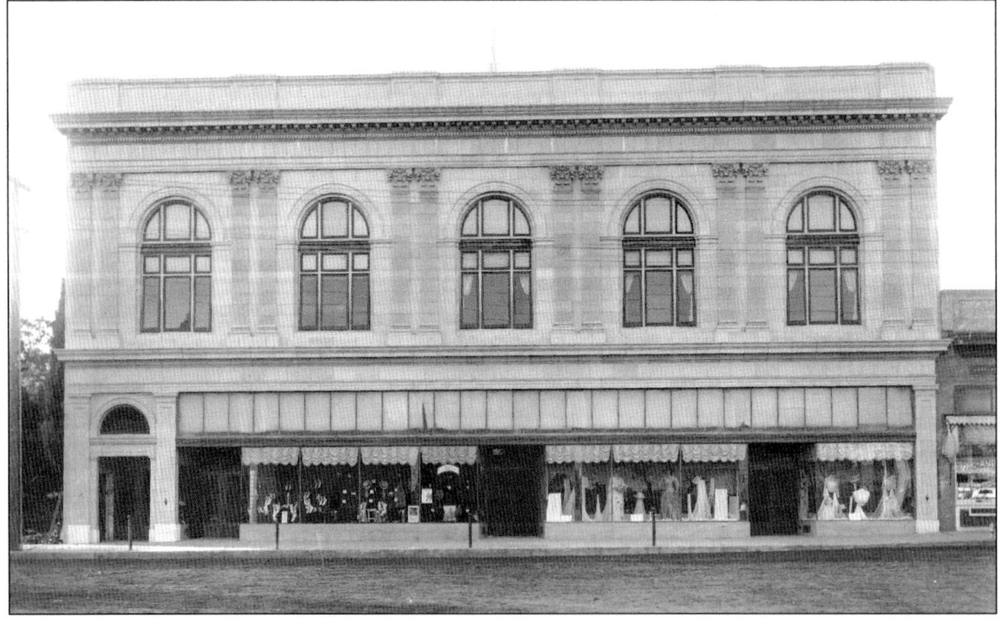

Masonic Order. The Masons are one of the world's first and largest fraternal organizations. Masonic miners founded the Eureka Lodge near Eureka Bar in early 1851. As the gold in that region waned, the lodge's headquarters was moved to Auburn in November 1851. In 1913, the organization bought what was a one-story building; the two additional stories were completed in 1916. Allen D. Fellows was the architect for the project, with the Herdal brothers as the contractors. (PCM.)

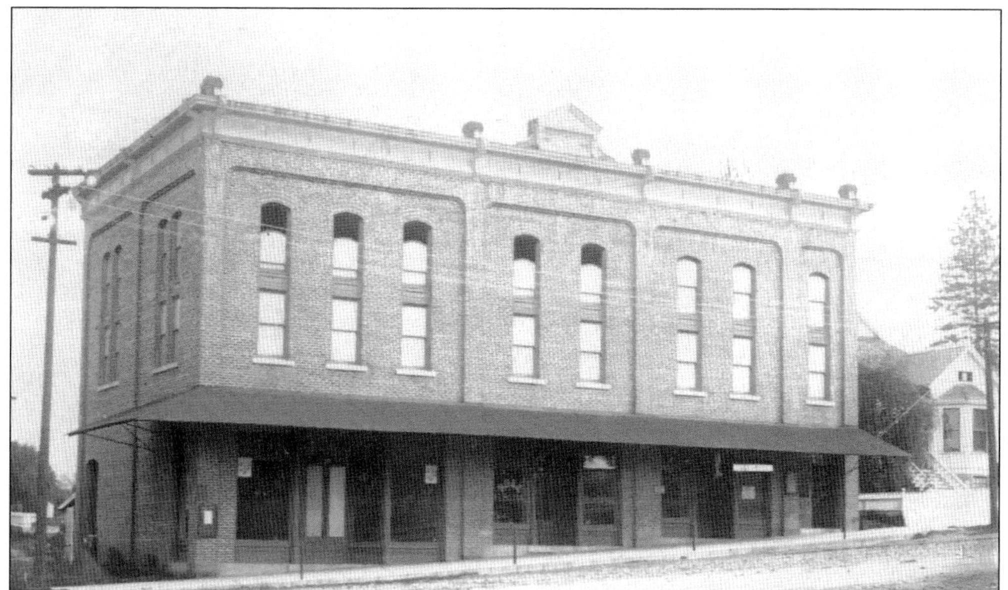

Odd Fellows. The local chapter of the Independent Order of Odd Fellows (IOOF) was formed in 1852. This building, one of many different IOOF halls over the years, was erected in 1894. The mission of the Odd Fellows was to "visit the sick, relieve the distressed, bury the dead and educate the orphans." The Odd Fellows were influential in establishing the public cemetery in Auburn. (AJS.)

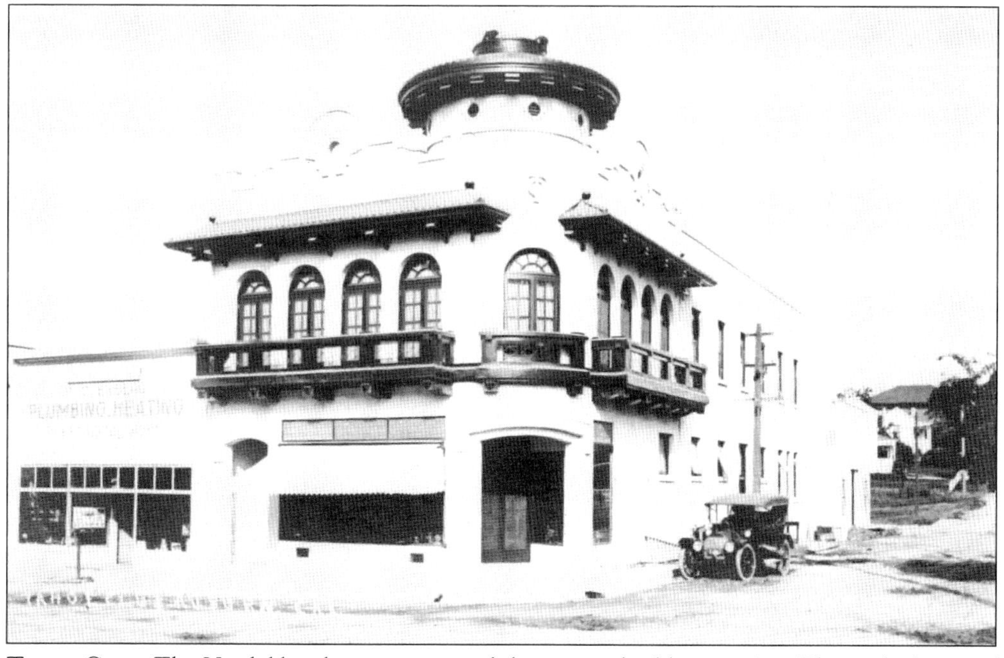

Tahoe Club. The Herdal brothers constructed this ornate building in 1914. This is the home of one of the many social clubs formed in Auburn and one of the few to have their own building. Auburn also boasted a debate club, a dance club, an athletic club, an improvement club, a literary club, and the Monday Night Club, among others. (AJS.)

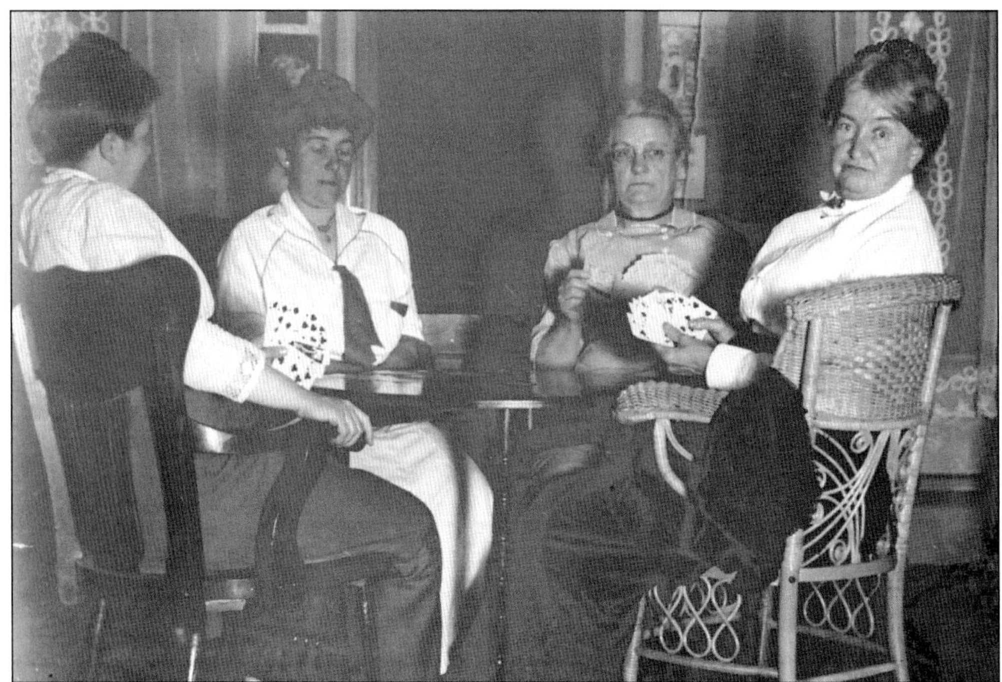

Town and Country Club. This innocent game of cards masks the power and influence held by these ladies and other women of the town. Along with organizing the Women's Improvement Club, local women were involved with the establishment and improvement of parks, libraries, and schools. From left to right are Mattie Shepard, Elizabeth Roumage, Amy Rooney, and Sarah Jane Dunlap. (PCM.)

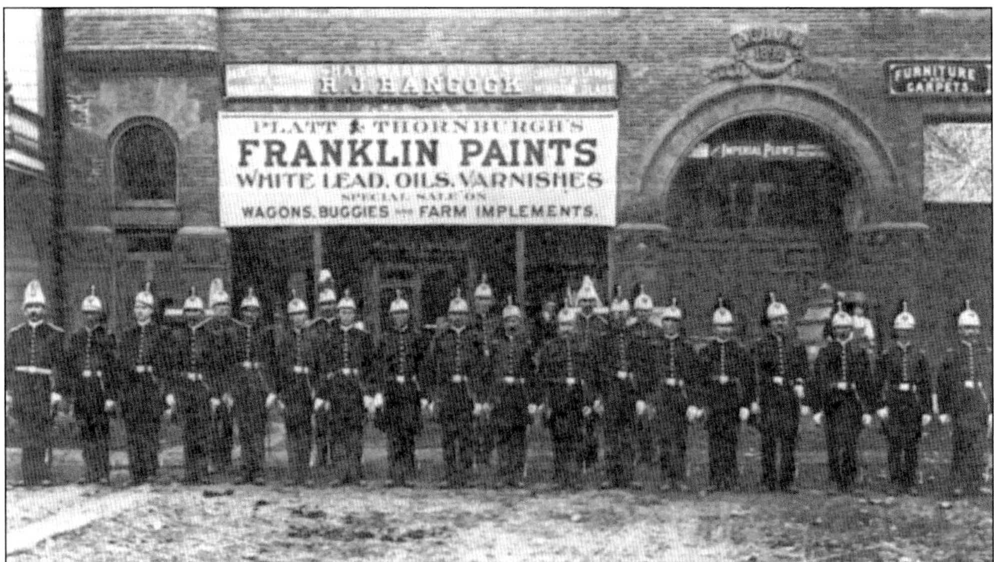

Knights of Pythias. This fraternal order is an international nonsectarian organization founded in 1864. Dedicated to the cause of universal peace, the Knights of Pythias stress the fundamental principles are friendship, charity, and benevolence. The Auburn Lodge was established by district attorney Alexander Kelly Robinson in 1891. Robinson held the district attorney position in 1904 and prosecuted the infamous Adolph Weber murder case. (PCM.)

Ten

Entertainment

Numerous gold-mining claims and its location on a supply route led to the founding of Auburn. The very early years were turbulent. Hoards of mostly young men passed through on their way to the latest strike or stayed in town to ride out the winter. The saloons and gambling halls flourished. It must have been a heady experience for these men—an adventure of the highest order. One miner described it as a "gaudy freedom." As James Maxfield wrote home in 1850, "I feel bad sometimes when I think of home and the comfort I am deprived of being away. Then again, come to think of how dull it is at home, I do not want to be there."

Along with the saloons and gambling halls, the mother lode was awash with many forms of entertainment, even from the earliest days. Traveling show groups quickly began touring, and many reaped the riches from an area saturated with generous miners who had few entertainment options on which to spend their gold dust.

Early on, drinking, smoking, playing, betting, swearing, lying, cheating, and swindling might have been the order of day, but not for long. Changes in population brought changes in both entertainment and amusements. Gold levels were declining from a record high of $80 million in 1852 (some $971 million in today's dollars), falling year by year to less than $18 million in 1865. By 1860, fewer than one in 10 men still mined for gold, but the biggest change was the significant increase in women and children.

Entertainment became more subdued and family oriented. During the 1860s, minstrel shows, touring concert groups, musicians, public speakers, and circuses all visited Auburn. Regular public dances were introduced, along with celebrations for the Fourth of July, Christmas, New Year's Eve, and St. Patrick's Day.

By 1870, all forms of athletics, including baseball, cycling, football, racing, shooting, and skating, as well as a community brass band and picnics, had become more popular. Many of these amusements continue—in one form or another—to the present day.

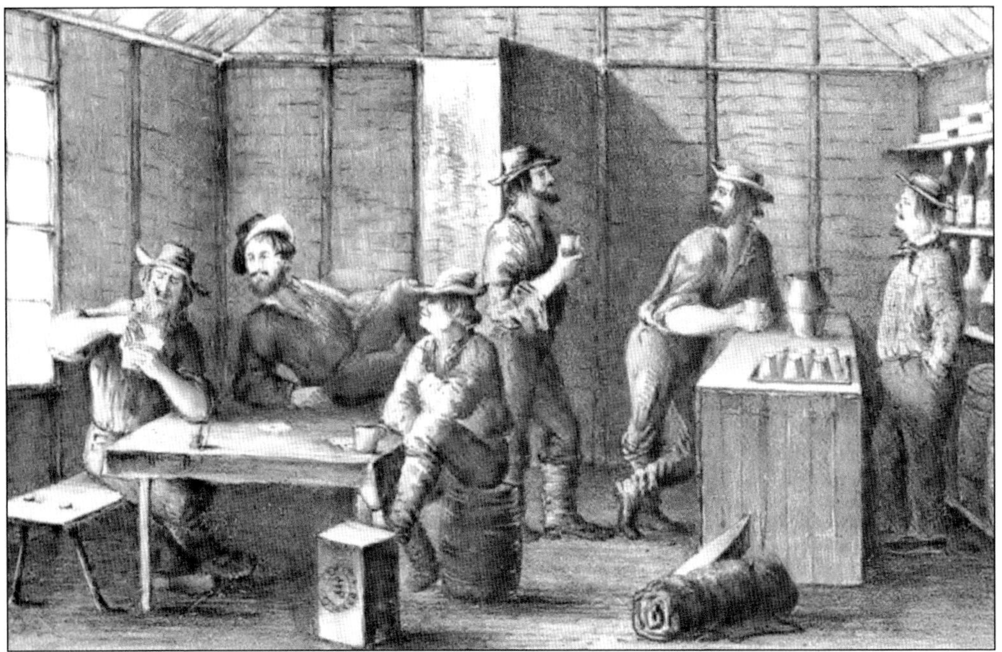

Drinking. As stated in a forty-niner diary, "Almost everybody drinks here—boarding houses and provision stores do all the business." In 1851, nearly every Auburn business held a liquor license. At $1 a drink or one ounce of gold per bottle, the 40 licensees (including Nancy McCormick and Eliza Elliott) thrived, with their clientele primarily consisting of miners, teamsters, and visitors on county business. (LOC.)

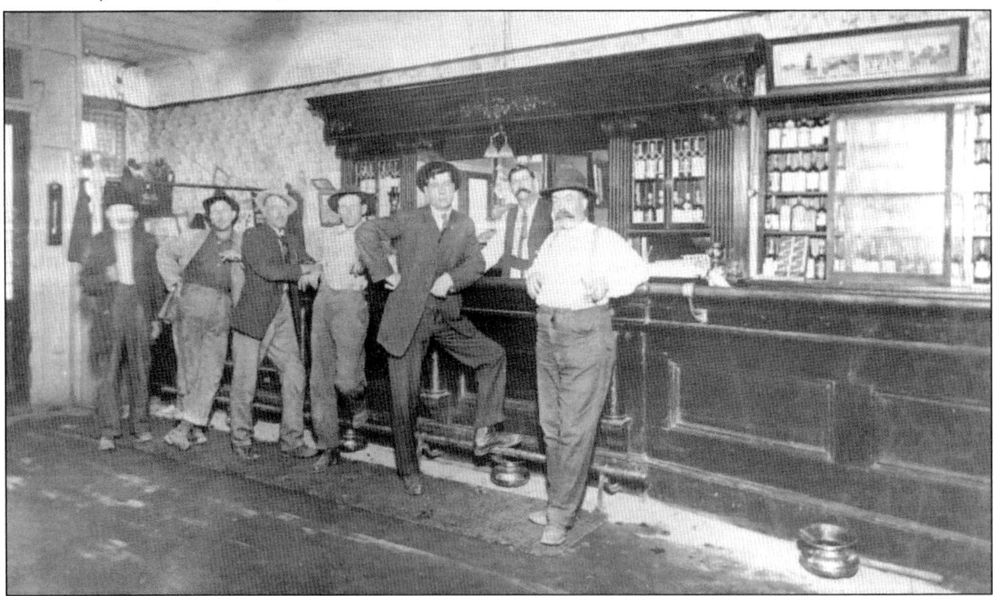

Union Saloon. First opened in 1866 by Thomas Hollis and E.L. Gardiner, the Union held sway in Old Town for years. Note the two tall men, second and third from right; they are most likely the Dependener brothers. Sam owned a partial interest in the bar, and Frank was the deputy sheriff. Both were noted for their extreme height. Today, this site is a charming upscale eatery and wine shop. (PCM.)

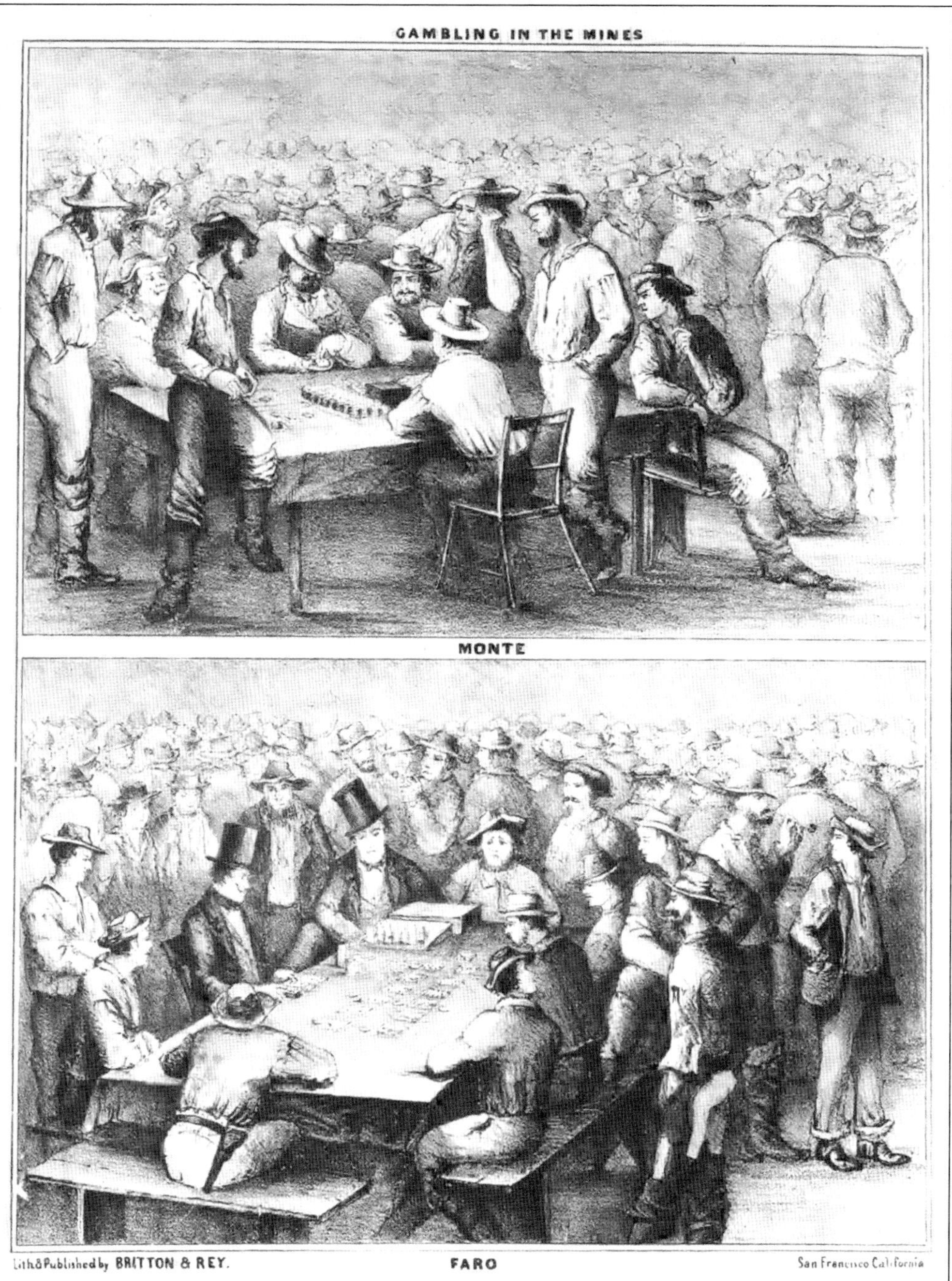

GAMBLING. Most observers generally agreed almost everybody in this country gambled. The two most popular games were Faro and Monte. An attractive diversion from the monotony of prospecting and wishful thinking about letters from home, the local gaming tables at the Round Tent, Robinson Crusoe, El Dorado, and other saloons and hotels provided a steady source of exciting entertainment. As William Bickham wrote home in 1850, "I entered not a public house on the route which had not its Monte table." Pounds of gold were wagered at the gambling tables, and many miners lost hard-won earnings in a few turns of the cards or rolls of the dice. (JK.)

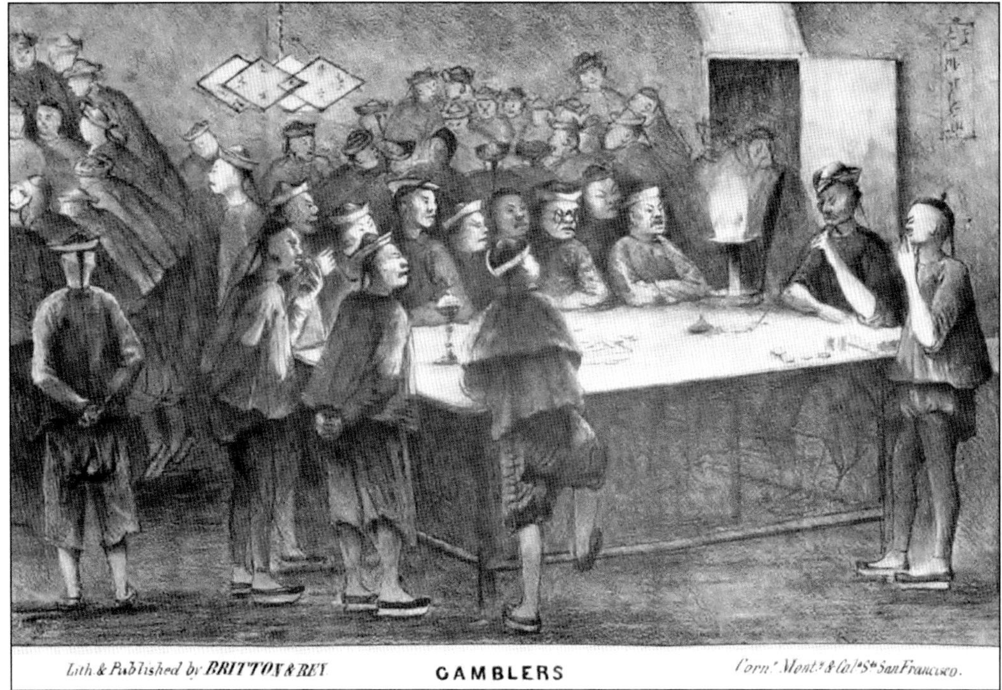

Chinese Gambling. Shortly after vast numbers of Chinese arrived in 1852, gambling halls appeared among the businesses they established on Sacramento Street. In no time, they had eight gaming table licenses and a steady stream of customers. In later years, several of these halls were joined by houses of prostitution and opium dens. The photograph below shows the site of one of the last Chinese gambling halls in Auburn's Chinatown. Now an alley, it was located between the two brick structures. (Above, LOC; below, AJS.)

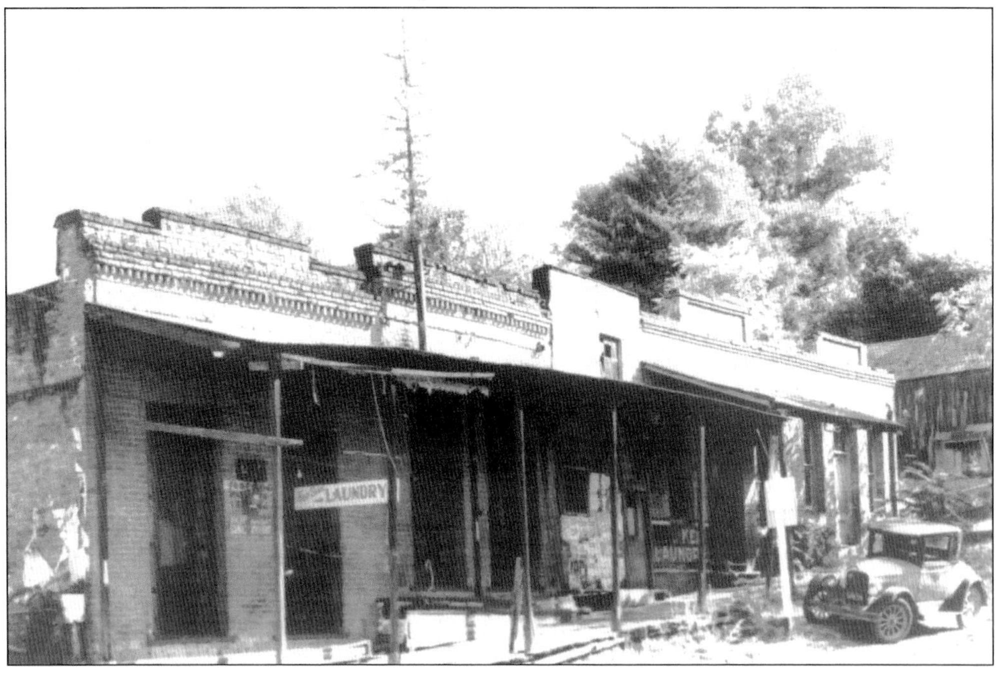

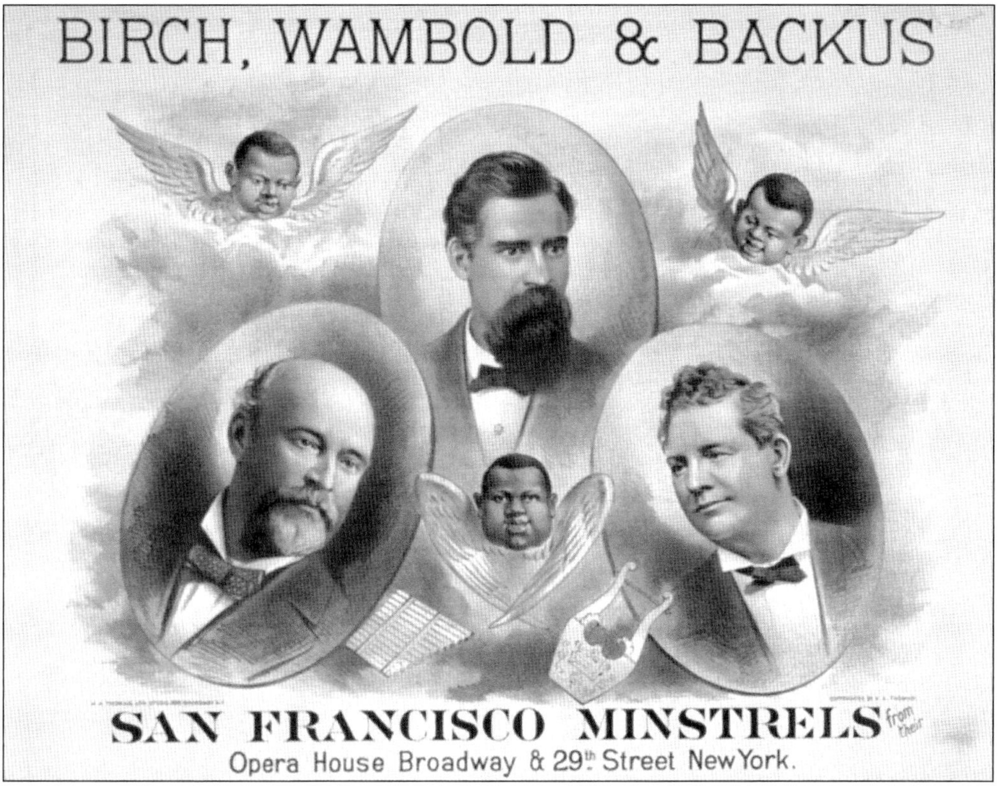

BIRCH, WAMBOLD & BACKUS

SAN FRANCISCO MINSTRELS from their

Opera House Broadway & 29th Street New York.

CHARLES BACKUS. Backus organized Backus' Original Minstrels in 1854 and played San Francisco with great success. Blackface caricature performances were immensely popular in mother lode towns. Performing at Auburn's Empire Hotel in May 1854, these "justly celebrated songsters kept a crowded house in a roar of laughter," according to the *Placer Herald*. They were welcomed back in May and July of the following year. (LOC.)

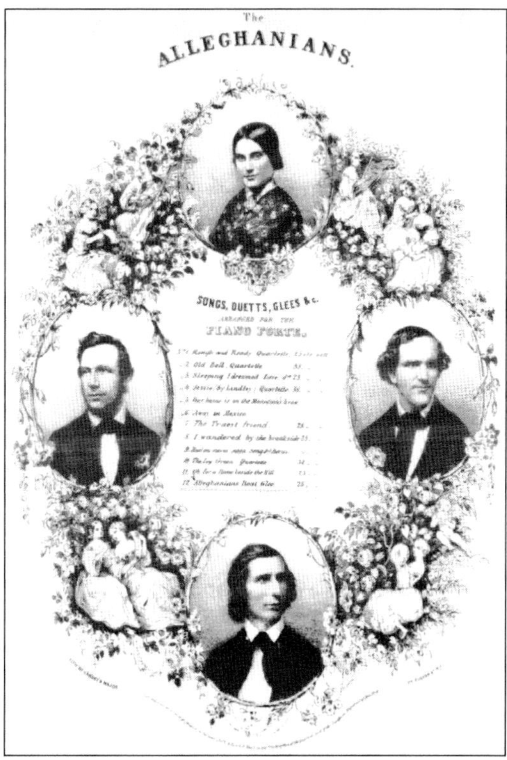

THE ALLEGHANIANS. James M. Bouland, Richard Dunning, William H. Oakley, and Miriam G. Goodenow belonged to one of the nation's most popular concert touring groups when they did a celebrated tour of Gold Rush towns in 1852. Known for sweet voices, close harmonies, and simple melodies, they played to overflowing audiences at Auburn's Mechanics Hall in October 1852. (LOC.)

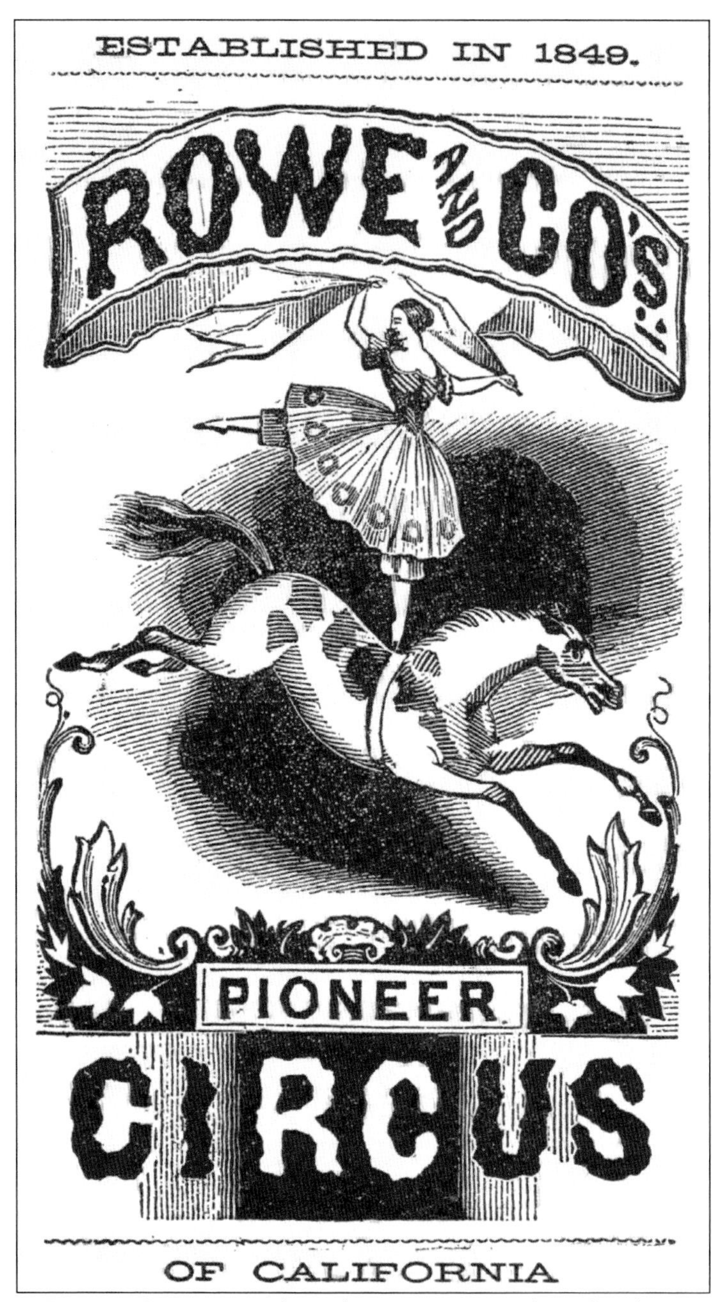

Rowe and Co.'s Pioneer Circus. Joseph Andrew Rowe was orphaned at the age of 8 and joined a circus company at the age of 10. A seasoned veteran by 1849, he brought his circus to San Francisco. Rowe and Co.'s Pioneer Circus performed in Auburn in April 1856. The circus featured mostly equestrian acts with acrobatic feats. Mary Ann Whittaker, the first female equestrian artist in America, was the highlight of the circus. She would leap from her speeding horse and over a 12-foot-high ribbon to land on her horse's back. The multitalented Rowe often did the wood engravings for his display advertisements, as shown in this example. Many different circus companies made regular appearances in Auburn. An empty lot on Sacramento Street was called "the circus lot" for many years. (AJS, *California's Pioneer Circus* book by Joseph Andrew Rowe.)

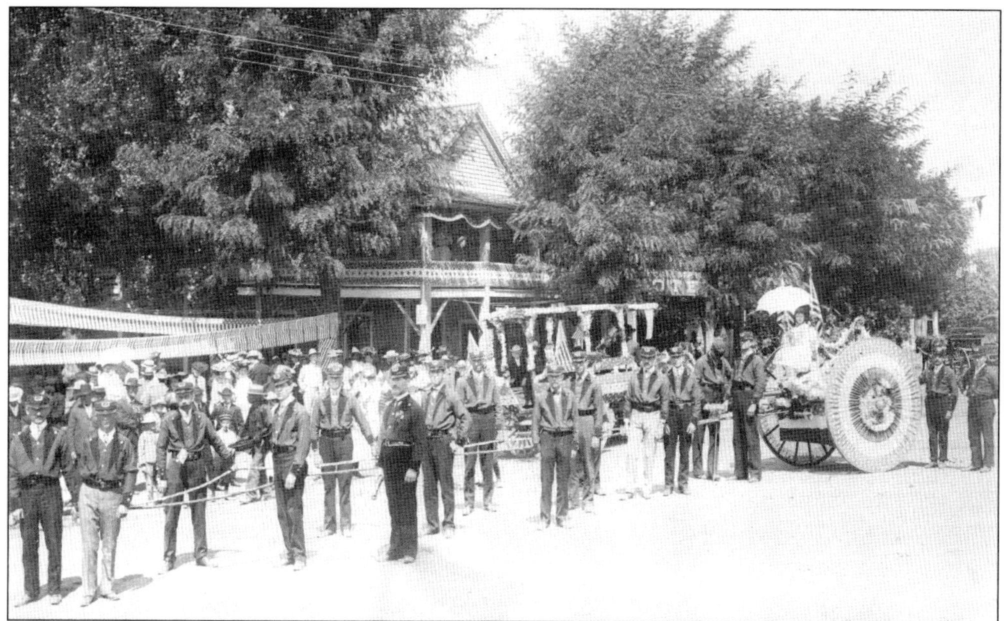

Fourth of July Celebration. Fourth of July celebrations have had a sporadic history in Auburn. The first, organized in 1850, was a gala day. Miners from both river and dry diggings gathered for a reading of the Declaration of Independence and the firing of a pine tree cannon, as well as to eat, drink, and sing songs. In other years, the celebrations were even more extravagant, but in some years, they were not held at all. (PCM.)

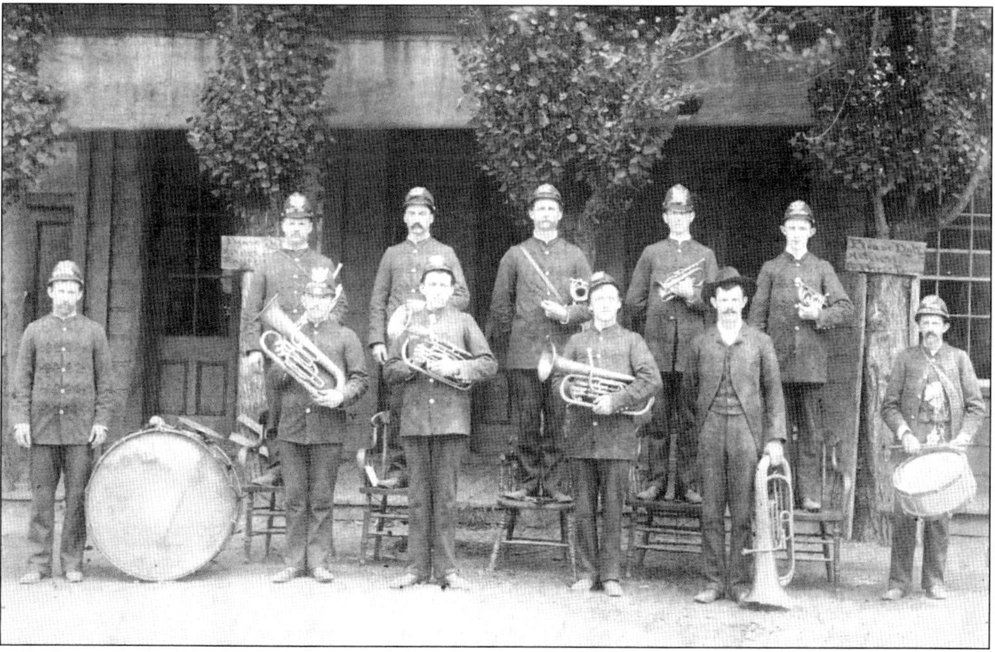

Auburn Brass Band. The Auburn Brass Band was first formed in 1858. The 1871 members organized a joint stock company to purchase the Armory Hall for $1,200 and renamed it the Music Hall. It was to be used free of charge, with the exception of expenses, for community affairs. The hall came down in 1892, but the band played on. (PCM.)

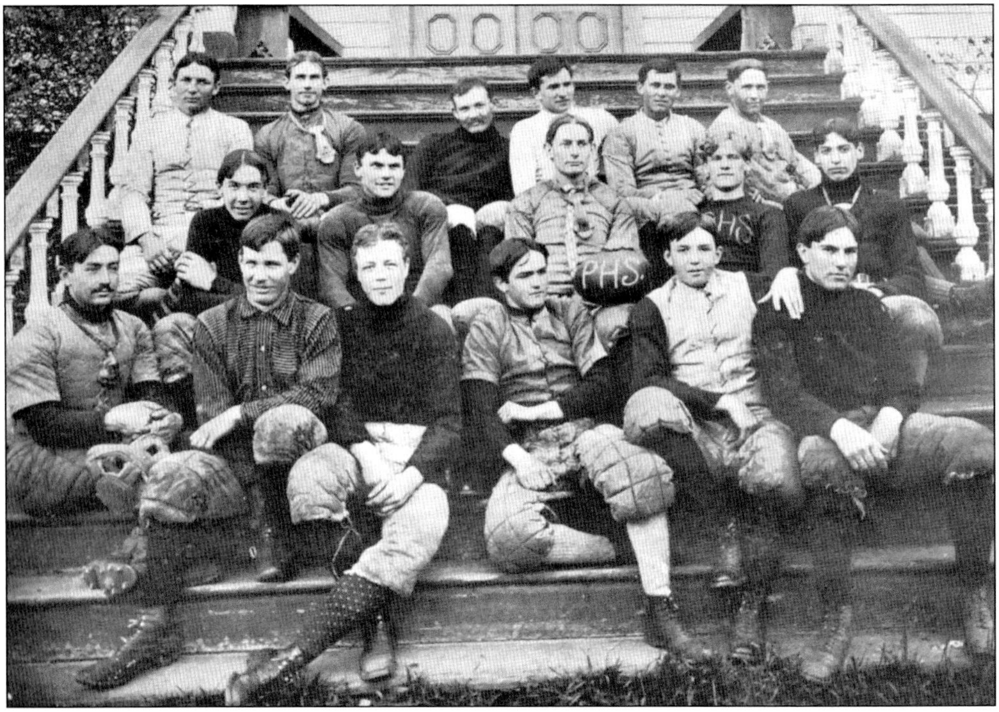

FOOTBALL. In 1874, football was quite the rage in Auburn. Few rules resulted in a mob-style game, and injuries to the fingers, eyes, and head were not uncommon. With such narrow streets, nearby windows were in constant jeopardy. A tamer version of the sport had developed by 1902, when this photograph was taken. In 1900, Ernie Birdsall was Placer High School's first football coach. (PCM.)

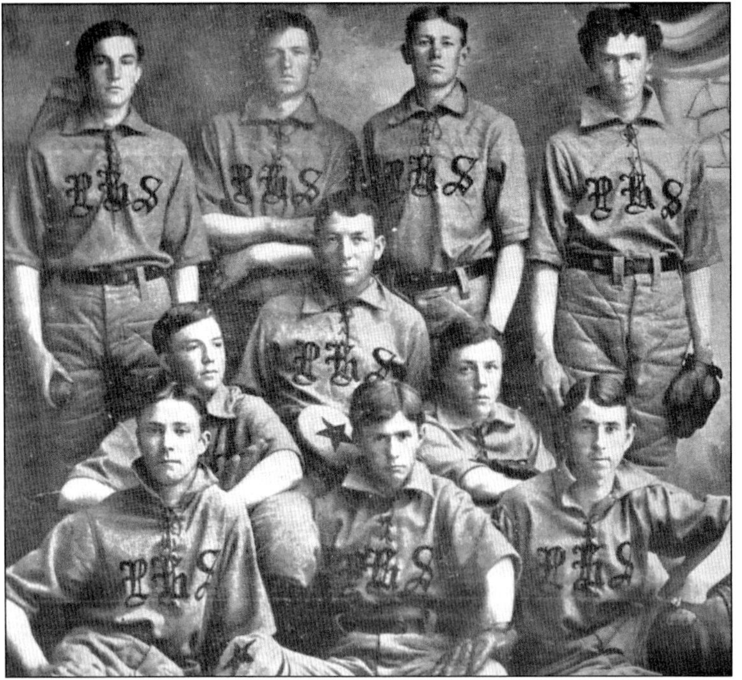

BASEBALL. The Placer High School baseball team is pictured here in 1903, but the sport's popularity had emerged many years before. In April 1871, the Mountaineer Baseball Club was formed with 16 members. In an 1874 match between the first and second nines (teams), the score was 53 to 34. The same year, Auburn won the county championship, and a year later, there was a first, second, third, and fourth nine. (PCM.)

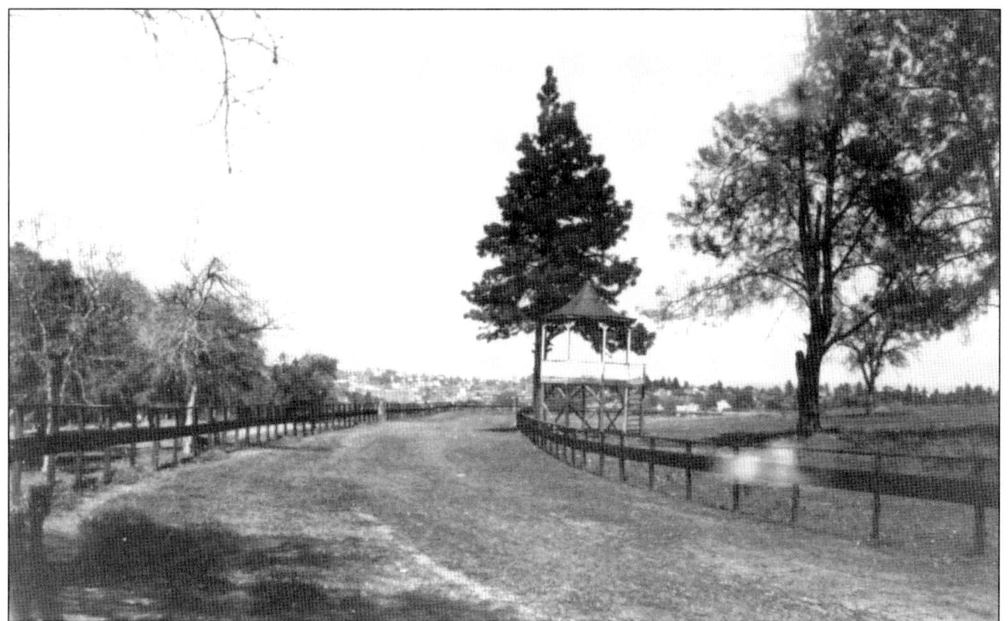

Racetrack. In 1871, under the leadership of J. Ives Fitch, Charles Crosby, Jacob Neff, and George Crisman, a racetrack, or trotting park, was laid out on land adjoining the south boundary of Auburn on present-day Racetrack Street. The area was used not only for equestrian events but also for baseball games, Fourth of July celebrations, fairs, the annual German picnic, and even a rodeo. (PCM.)

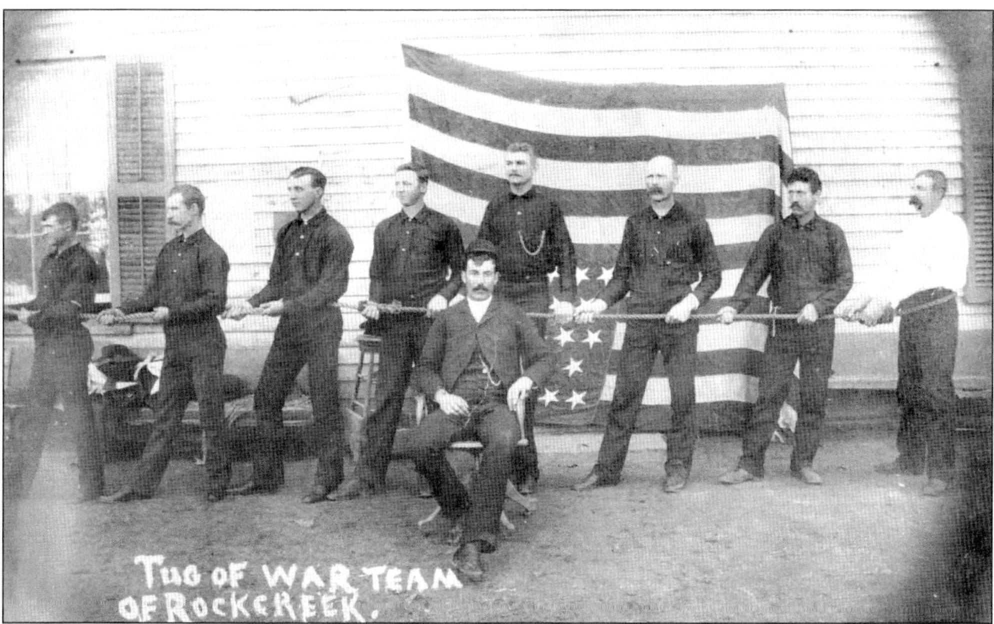

Tug-of-War. One of the largest audiences for this long-popular sport gathered for the fierce competition on the final day of a three-day tournament at the Auburn Opera House in 1892. Teams from Auburn, Sacramento, Rocklin, Newcastle, and Rock Creek competed. Auburn won the heavy team pull by half an inch after 50 minutes. Rock Creek easily won against Auburn's light team. Competing teams were invited back for a "return pull," another tug-of-war contest. (PCM.)

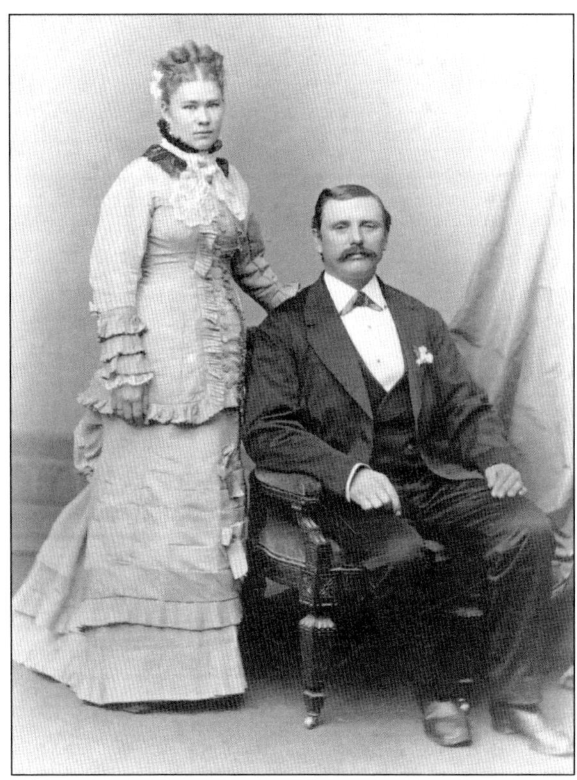

Special Occasions. Birthdays, anniversaries, and weddings were reason enough for social gatherings, but it was common for these celebrations to be held in conjunction with major holidays as well. Accompanied by good food and excellent wine, the toasting, dancing, and singing of such occasions would often last until daybreak. This is the wedding portrait of Anna Bernhard and Deadrick Barkhaus, who were married at her parents' house on December 27, 1881. (PCM.)

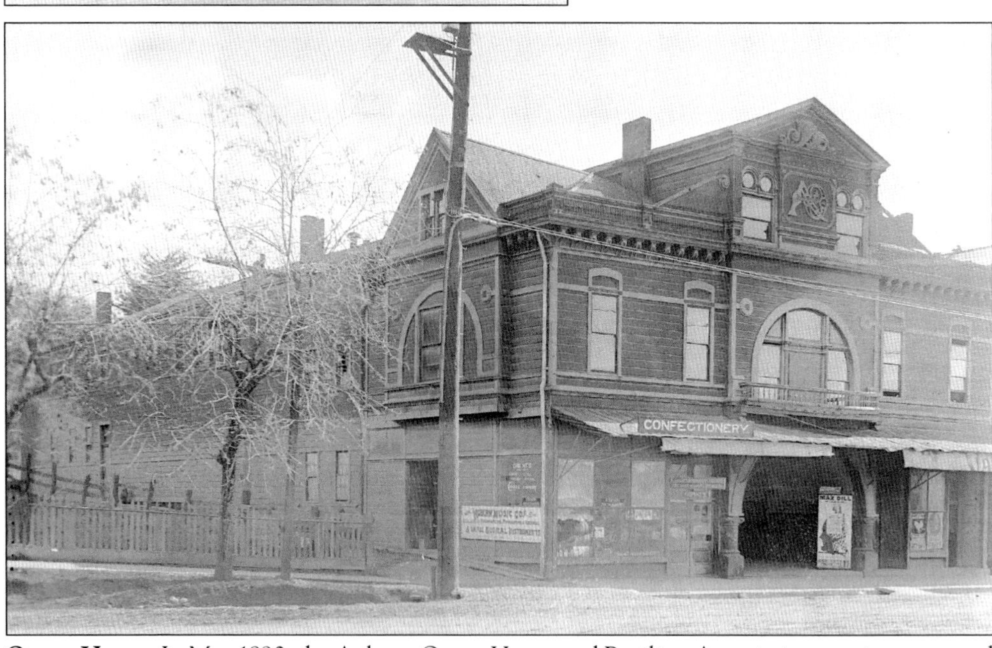

Opera House. In May 1890, the Auburn Opera House and Pavilion Association was incorporated with 62 community subscribers. Built in Central Square by Michael David Lininger, the opera house opened to much fanfare in November 1891. It was sold to Albert Kenison in 1894 and would remain the center of entertainment for many years. In 1924, Walter Jacobs bought the whole block. It gradually became less prominent and finally burned in 1957. (PCM.)

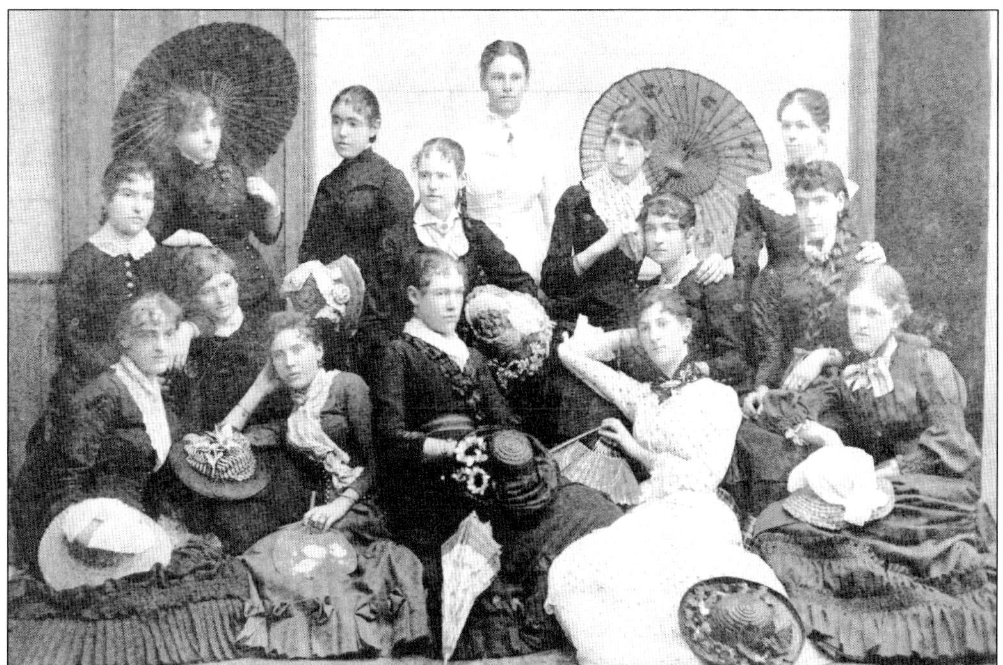

Young Ladies Social. This photograph was taken in the summer of 1882. Only one of the ladies, Jennie Walkup, is specifically identified; she is in the white dress in the first row. These young women were all about the same age and all lived quite close together in town. It was not unusual for them to sponsor fundraisers for their church by having a young ladies social. (JD.)

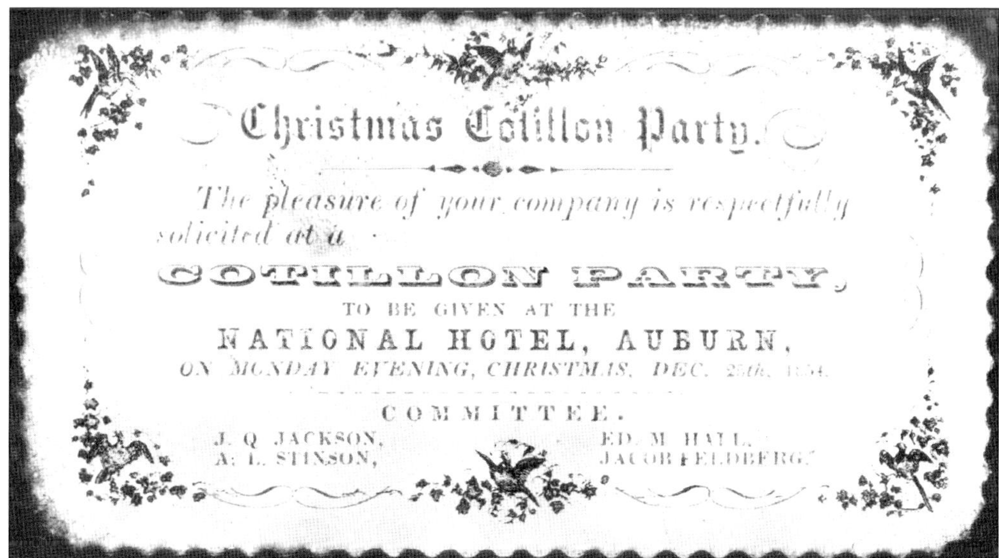

Christmas Cotillon Party.

The pleasure of your company is respectfully solicited at a

COTILLON PARTY,

TO BE GIVEN AT THE

NATIONAL HOTEL, AUBURN,

ON MONDAY EVENING, CHRISTMAS, DEC. 25th, [illegible]

COMMITTEE.

J. Q JACKSON, ED. M HALL,
A. L. STINSON, JACOB FELDBERG.

Dances. Auburn has had a long love affair with dance. According to John Boggs, there were only two women in attendance at a dance held in 1849. By early 1853, however, one dance had attracted 62 women and 100 men. Soon, there was a Negro Dance Hall, a Spanish Dance House, and Kintero's Dance Hall. In 1870, the Auburn Dancing Club was formed, with dance parties held every Tuesday night through the winter months. (PCM.)

SKATING RINK

—AT—

NEW ARMORY HALL,

PEDEN & LOBNER - - Proprietors.

Open as follows every day and evening.

Morning Session--For Men and Boys.
From 10 o'clock A. M. to 12 o'clock M. Admission Free, 25 cents for the use of skates.

Afternoon Session.
From 2 o'clock to 4 o'clock P. M. Admission Free, 25 cents for the use of skates,

Afternoon Session---For Ladies Exclusively.
From 4 o'clock to 6 o'clock, P. M. Admittance Free. Use of skates 25 cents.

Evening Session---For Gentlemen and Ladies.
From 7½ o'clock to 10 o'clock, P. M. Admission 25 cents. Use of skates 25 cents.

☞These Skat'ngs will be conducted with perfect order, and Ladies can come with perfect assurance that they will be paid every attention.

Auburn, May 6th, 1871.—tf.

ROLLER SKATING. The proprietors known only as Peden and Lobner opened Auburn's first skating rink at the Armory Hall in 1871. A layer of whiting (powered chalk) covered the floor, and the bad "rinkers" were noticed by their white spots. Bolstered by increasing popularity, John J. Smith opened a rink at his Auburn Hotel near the depot in 1884, followed by others, such as the rink at Recreation Park off Finley Avenue in 1906. (PCM.)

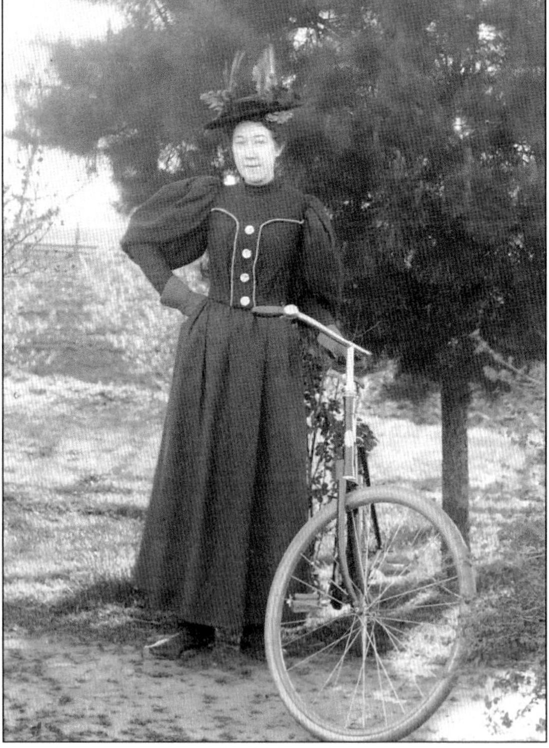

CYCLING. The bicycle craze peaked in America in the 1890s. Auburn had its own club, the Gateway Cycle Club. Cycling was intertwined with the women's suffrage movement; on a bicycle, a woman gained not only physical mobility but also freedom of movement in rejecting the restrictive clothing of the time. Susan B. Anthony said, "I think that bicycling has done more to emancipate women than anything else." (PCM.)

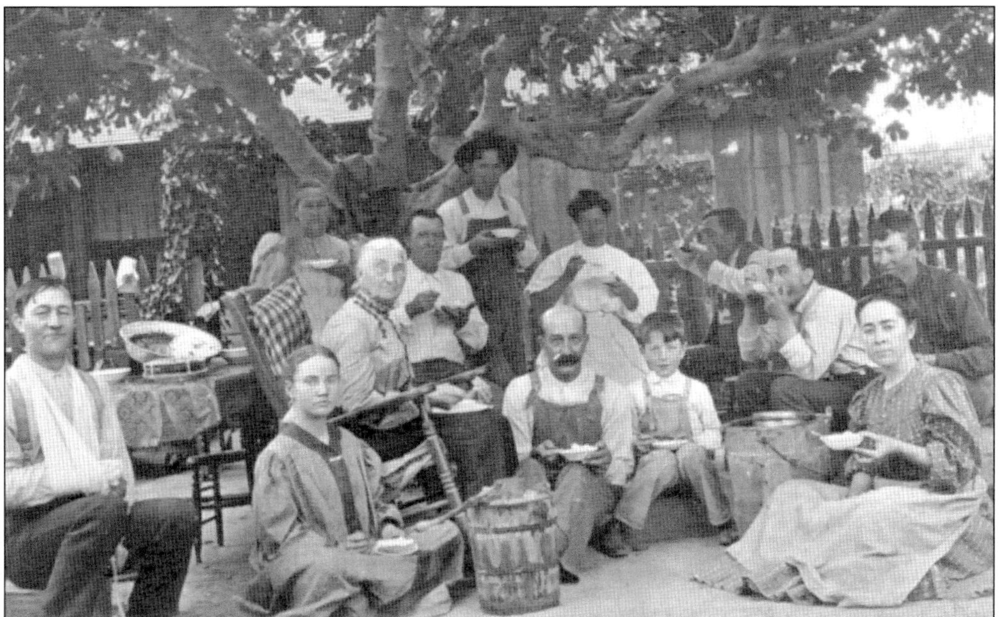

Ice Cream Social. Ice cream was available at the Gem Restaurant on Main Street as early as 1853 and at Miles Furniss's restaurant on Commercial Street in the 1860s. After 1870, the Ice Cream and Strawberry Festival became a regular fundraiser, especially for church and school groups, and was often combined with picnics and other entertainments. Homemade ice cream also gained popularity at this time. (PCM.)

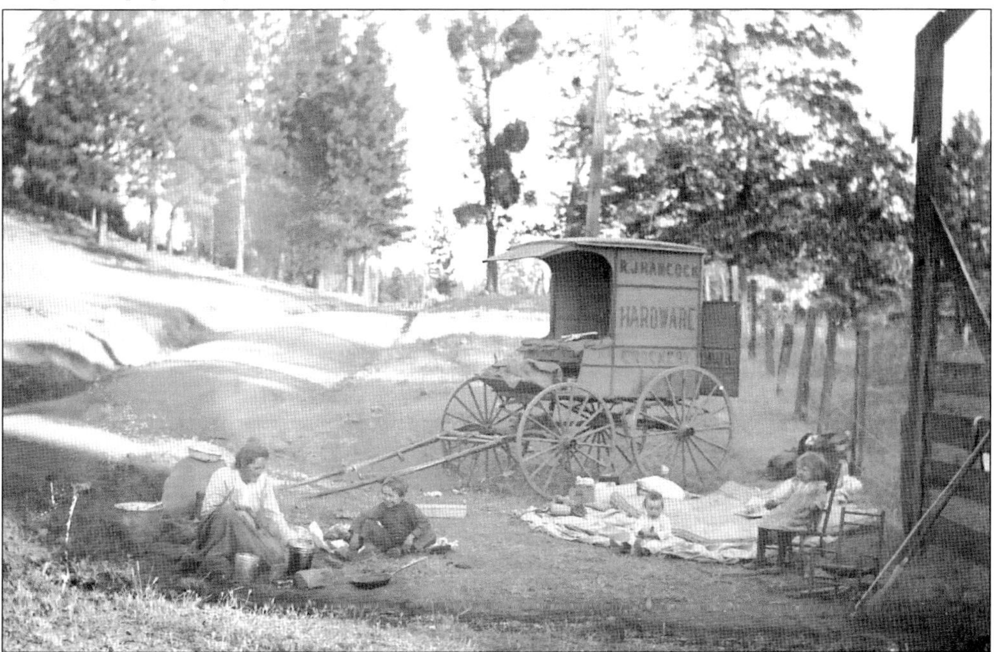

Picnics. Picnics were a common feature of social life in Auburn. In 1866, a large party went by train to Rocklin for a picnic and, on their return, had a dance at the Depot Hall. Picnickers might go out to Bloomer Ranch, the racetrack, Clipper Gap, or as close as Norcross's lot on Finley Lane. Annie Hancock is pictured here with her children at Lake Theodore in Clipper Gap. (HF.)